Novel Ideas

Novel Ideas

Contemporary Authors Share the Creative Process

SECOND EDITION

INTRODUCTION, INTERVIEWS, AND EXERCISES BY

Barbara Shoup and Margaret-Love Denman

The University of Georgia Press
Athens & London

Published in 2009 by
The University of Georgia Press
Athens, Georgia 30602
www.ugapress.org

Designed by Walton Harris
Set in 11/15 Adobe Garamond Pro
Printed and bound by Maple-Vail
The paper in this book meets the guidelines for
permanence and durability of the Committee on
Production Guidelines for Book Longevity of the
Council on Library Resources.

Printed in the United States of America

13 12 11 10 09 P 5 4 3 2 1

Library of Congress Cataloging-in-Publication Data

Novel ideas : contemporary authors share the creative
process / introduction, interviews, and exercises by
Barbara Shoup and Margaret-Love Denman. — 2nd ed.
     p.   cm.
Includes bibliographical references and index.
ISBN-13: 978-0-8203-3279-6 (pbk. : alk. paper)
ISBN-10: 0-8203-3279-8 (pbk. : alk. paper)
1. Fiction—Authorship. 2. Fiction—Technique.
3. Novelists, American—20th century—Interviews.
I. Shoup, Barbara. II. Denman, Margaret-Love.
PN3365.N63 2009
808.3—dc22   2008047844

British Library Cataloging-in-Publication Data available

Contents

Preface to the Second Edition

REREADING THE AUTHOR INTERVIEWS as we revised and updated this new edition of *Novel Ideas*, we kept getting sidetracked, jotting down bits of practical advice and inspiration that seemed to apply to our own novels-in-progress. The interviews are, without doubt, the most useful part of this book—both for the insights they bring to the writing process and for the way they make you feel that you want to get to work on your novel right now, and that you have some new information that makes this possible.

One accomplished novelist who found *Novel Ideas* helpful in a bad stretch wrote, "Every problem I was facing, and many I didn't know I faced, had been struggled through by one of the interviewed novelists. I have read passages to my husband, saying, 'This is it; I don't believe it.'" Another wrote, "You realize, reading these interviews, that the process of writing a novel is unique and individual, that even celebrated writers throw away many pages and tear their hair out, and that those who succeed are the ones who stay at the desk and keep doing the work." Aspiring novelists told us again and again that reading the interviews gave them the courage to begin and lots of help along the way.

This new edition includes what readers agreed were the best interviews from the first edition, as well as new interviews with Peter Cameron, Michael Cunningham, and S. J. Rozan. We've also added exercises to accompany the interviews, based directly upon writers' observations about the writing process and specific strategies they described for working through a novel. We've also redesigned the book to highlight the general exercises suggested throughout the first section, "Writing a Novel," making them readily accessible to the reader browsing for a way to solve some problem that his or her novel presents.

The spectrum of information in *Novel Ideas* was best described in our interview with Sheri Reynolds, who said, "In my classes, I teach about how writers make choices, and I try to get my students to examine why a story starts in one place rather than another, what the writer gains from this point of view rather than that one—why a writer may have chosen to mention Froot Loops rather than Cracklin' Oat Bran. And I know all these things are important. I know it. But when I'm writing, I am not considering these things—I was never, ever, ever even *considering* Cracklin' Oat Bran. Never. I don't know how to reconcile the part of writing that is technical and craft oriented with the part of writing that feels mystical. The technical part is what I teach, but the mystical part is what I love."

Our hope is that this new edition of *Novel Ideas* will help you find the balance of craft and magic you need to bring your novel into being.

Barbara Shoup
Margaret-Love Denman

Writing a Novel

Introduction

"The short story is a piece of work. The novel is a way of life."
— TONI CADE BAMBARA

THE GENESIS OF A NOVEL is a strange and wonderful thing. It can begin as early as one's childhood, in images or overheard conversations never quite understood. Toni Morrison's novel *Sula* began this way. All her life, she had carried with her the memory of a woman whose eyes were never completely open, whose brown skin had a lovely, dusky matte. There was something purple about her, Morrison said. Maybe she wore purple or maybe it was a quality of the air surrounding her. And her name, Hannah Peace, was spoken as one word, "Hannapeace," by the women of the town. Morrison remembered that it was spoken with a kind of awe. "As if Hannah Peace was a woman they had forgiven."

It was the mysterious sense that this woman had been forgiven that Toni Morrison found intriguing and that led her to begin asking herself a series of questions. "Why did they forgive her? What is there to be forgiven among women? What are the laws of women's friendships? What could *never* be forgiven?" In time, the memories and questions coalesced, and she realized what the novel would be about. Before she wrote the first words, Toni Morrison knew she wanted to explore the nature of friendship among women, particularly among black women. Understanding this, she made up Sula Peace and Nel, and made them friends. She made up a world for them, the Bottom, and peopled it with characters like Jude and Plum and Shadrack, Ajax and the Dewies. She created Sula's grandmother Eva, and the long-remembered childhood image found its place in Sula's mother, Hannah Peace. Then she set it all in motion. She let the characters play out their weaknesses, their fears. She let them find their strengths, the truths of their lives, and in so doing created the novel *Sula*, so real it seems to breathe.

The genesis of a novel might be the author's interest in political issues, as in the work of Joan Didion, J. M. Coetzee, and Brian Moore. It might be in the exploration of intense personal experience, such as Tim O'Brien's novels about the Vietnam War, or a technical challenge of interest to the author—Jane Smiley set out to mimic an ecosystem in the structure of *Moo*.

A novel's genesis might be in a place, real or imagined: Tony Hillerman's Joe Leaphorn and Jim Chee novels were inspired by his desire to write about the southwestern landscape. As a child, C. S. Lewis drew cartoons of an imaginary world that eventually became Narnia. It might be in another work of art—a concerto, a painting, a novel. Valerie Martin's *Mary Reilly* began with a scene in *The Strange Case of Dr. Jekyll and Mr. Hyde* in which the scullery maid was weeping. "I thought, what is she crying about?" Martin said. "She must know something."

A novel's genesis might be in a persistent voice you hear inside your head, or a single image. William Faulkner had a picture in his mind of a "little girl's muddy drawers," which became the germinal scene for *The Sound and the Fury*.

Sheri Reynolds's *The Rapture of Canaan* began with a dream. "I dreamed about this baby with praying hands," Reynolds said, "except his hands weren't really praying. They were seamed together at the heart line. I woke up just enamored with these hands. For days, the image stayed with me, and I thought, 'Who is this baby?' And then I thought, 'Who would this baby be important to?' And then I thought, 'Who is this child's mother?' And then I had the kernel of my book."

A novel might begin completely on its own, surprising its author, as Lewis Nordan's *Wolf Whistle* did. "On a TV show in Atlanta, I was asked what was I working on now," he said. "And I heard someone answer—me, it turned out—'I'm writing a book about the murder of Emmett Till.' That was the first moment I had ever imagined that such a book would be my next project."

No matter what triggers a novel, actually beginning is an act of faith. Eventually—often after many false starts—ideas, feelings, observations, images, and memories gather around a center as if magnetized, and the writer catches a glimpse of the novel he wants it to become.

Writing that novel feels essentially like this: You have seen or felt or dreamed something that you can't name, but that you know you can't live without. You set off on a journey to find it. There is no map; no one has ever been to this place. You barely know the people you are traveling with—your characters—but you know that they are the only people who know the way. You watch them, listen to them. You follow along, putting down the words to mark the path they make. It is a long journey, with many wrong turns and surprises. Every day, or as often as you can, you go to the world of the novel. Months pass. Sometimes years.

Your journey through this world becomes an alternate reality. The people you "see" there every day are as real and confounding as your own family. You live with these characters, worry about them at unlikely moments. You are amazed, sometimes, at the way all kinds of things work their way into the story: Newspaper stories you read, stories friends and family tell in passing, memories, ideas that delight you. The occasional glimpse of something beautiful, funny, or sad that you cannot forget. A passion for some person, place, or thing that you feel compelled to preserve—or that, perhaps, your life in the real world will not accommodate.

Sometimes you have to stop and do research; sometimes you have to stop and get a clear picture of what's actually on the page, as opposed to what's in your head. Sometimes, like a recalcitrant child, the book just stops, and you have to trick and tease it into moving forward.

As the end nears, possibilities narrow, as in real life. This is partly comforting, partly appalling. The novel won't be all you hoped it would be, but you keep on anyway. To abandon it now would be unthinkable, like walking away from your own imperfect life.

And finally it is done. For a few days, you feel wonderful, free. You attend to business, clean your house, rake your yard, change the oil in your car, read, watch movies—actually pay attention when someone is talking to you. Then you begin to miss where the novel took you, the people in it, what it was. You feel anxious. There's nothing to organize your life around. What are you going to *do*? Have you written every single thing you know?

Yes, if you were doing it right.

But pretty soon you know some new things. You look at the book again, and you see that what you thought the book was the day you finished it and what it actually is don't quite match up. So you go at it again. And again, if you must. Until it is as close as possible to what you wanted it to be.

Novel Ideas is a guide to help you through the novel you want to write. It is not a how-to book: as you'll see when you read the authors' discussions of their writing processes, there is no formula for writing a novel. Each book is unique in its needs, limitations, and possibilities; only by living with it, struggling with it, will you finally discover how to make it come alive on the page.

Novel Ideas is meant to be a source of information, advice, and reassurance in your own efforts to make this happen. Like a teacher at your shoulder, it will provide insight into the complex process by which a novel is created, the relationship between novelist and novel, and a glimpse of the way everyday life expands to accommodate the alternate reality of the book inside your head.

The Book in the Mind

"A book begins as a private excitement of the mind."
— E. L. DOCTOROW

"ALL WRITING IS AUTOBIOGRAPHY OF THE IMAGINATION," Susan
Fromberg Schaeffer says. "Part of what goes on in writing is [an] inter-
weaving of yourself and the subject." Thus, every novel you write will be
autobiographical, because it will grow out of your own experience of the
world. There are many ways fiction may be autobiographical:

- It may be directly autobiographical, giving the form and
  focus of a novel to a real experience or set of experiences.
- It may be indirectly autobiographical, using a real experience to spin a completely new story.
- It may find its genesis in your obsession with the experience of someone else, someone you know or someone
  you've only read or heard about. Such a novel is obliquely
  autobiographical: you recognize someone else's story as
  akin to the life issues you struggle to resolve for yourself.

In fact, these issues and your need to find a way to come to terms with
them are probably what made you want to write a novel in the first place.
Rooted in the most intense, often most painful, experiences in your life,
they are your material, the most fundamental elements of every story you
will ever write.

Each writer's material is unique, utterly his own. It carries the authority
of experience and shimmers with the yearning to understand and come to
terms with that experience. It is dangerous stuff. To find and use it, you
have to plumb the depths of your soul. As Dorothy Allison says, "The best
fiction comes from the place where the terror hides, the edge of our worst

stuff. I believe, absolutely, that if you do not break out in that sweat of fear when you write, then you have not gone far enough."

Chances are, you already know what your material is. You just have to find the courage to face it. If you don't know, or if you think your life has been too boring or small to have yielded anything interesting enough to write about, consider Flannery O'Connor's observation: "Anybody who has survived his childhood has enough information about life to last him the rest of his days. If you can't make something out of a little experience, you probably won't be able to make it out of a lot." For example, Jill McCorkle's *July 7th* tells the story of one day in the life of a small town in North Carolina.

No matter who you are or what your life has been, you have material. To find it, Theodore Weesner suggests, "Identify things that hurt, that caused pain enough to make you change how you perceive the world. When did it hurt? What made it hurt? Who were the people involved? It can be a modest hurt; it can be a big hurt. A very personal hurt, private, secret. Once you can do that, you can begin to try to create a story through characters and action."

In search of your own material, pump up your courage and consider these questions:

- What broke your heart?
- What broke, or nearly broke, your spirit?
- What scares you to death?
- What hurts you more than anything?
- What makes you so happy you can hardly bear it?
- What are your secrets?
- Was there some ideal time in your life to which you long to return?
- What is still so painful that you cannot let go of it?
- What enrages you?
- What never fails to make you cry?
- What do you wish had never happened to you or someone you love?
- What deeply offends your sense of justice?

- What about your own life do you feel that you will never understand?

Delving even deeper, make a list of the times in your life when change occurred, times you think of in terms of before and after. Your list might include a move, a divorce, a death, an accident, an illness, a love affair, the birth of a child. Anything that seems significant to you, anything that in your mind marks some kind of ending and beginning in your life. There are always visual images surrounding these kinds of experiences, usually involving tension of some kind. These images are your "stuff": the wellspring of raw material that will yield up stories for the rest of your days.

Spend some time freewriting about these things. Let your memory range back to the defining moments in your life. Look intensely at now. Pay attention to what floats up again and again, the way seemingly disparate experiences combine themselves. Look for patterns. Notice single moments, crystal clear in your memory, resonating down through time.

Novels are full of absolutely real moments from writers' lives. Moments that change them, make them who they are, and then, years later, appear as if by magic to underpin the lives of characters crafted from their imaginations. Such a moment was used by A. Manette Ansay in her novel *Vinegar Hill*. As a child, she stepped on the carcass of a dog that was submerged in a lake. "It looked like a beautiful dog until it hit the surface and just broke away. Just dissolved and off it slid," she explains. "It was a moment that stayed with me because it was the moment I first realized that my parents didn't know everything. For a long time I was really angry with my mother. I said, 'Why did you let me step on it?' . . . She was my mom . . . I just assumed she knew everything. It was what Virginia Woolf would have called 'a moment of being.' A moment which defines you."

Memories are not always used this directly:

- To reshape real experiences for fiction, you may combine memories, break them up to use bits and pieces throughout the novel, or take one small kernel of memory and spin it into a completely imagined world.

- Sometimes your memories are unreliable in some way and writing them into a novel leads you to a truth that will surprise both your reader and yourself.
- Sometimes memory does no more than simmer beneath the surface of your work. Though a specific memory never actually shows up in the text, it informs your understanding of the fictional world you're creating.

To help her students discover their material, Patricia Hampl asks them to write an autobiography in five minutes, then read it and write five minutes more about what they were surprised to have left out of it. In a third five-minute session, they explore what they are glad they omitted.

Grace Paley suggests, "Write what you *don't* know about what you know." See what floats up. Don't judge what you write, don't worry whether what you write is good or bad or too revealing. Just write. See what you say. Then write everything all over again. Does it change? Do you?

Your material is based on what shaped your worldview, but it is not static. It changes as you change. It grows as you grow. The novel taking shape in your mind and on the page will reflect aspects of your life that, for whatever reasons, come to the front of your consciousness. The very process of writing a novel will change you. If it is a good novel, it will force you to break through some wall of not-knowing and teach you what you need to know to resolve something inside yourself. Which doesn't mean that your material goes away. Rather, it transforms, becomes compelling in a different way. A novel fueled by anger and the desire for revenge may be followed by a novel born of forgiveness, or one that explores, in a new context, a different point of view.

Regardless of the degree of consciousness with which you confront your own life, that life alone isn't enough to make a novel. To it you must add the world outside your head, the real, usable details of the world you live in, the things you see, hear, and feel as you go about your day-to-day life. These impressions come from many sources:

- They may be things you observe directly.
- They may be things told to you by someone else.

- They may be bits of information, jokes, stories, quotes, snippets of overheard conversation—anything that you intuitively recognize as useful, yours.

What do you notice? What detail, large or small, rivets your attention? What do you remember? What is it impossible for you to forget? You notice what you notice because of who you are; details that are compelling to you are always related to your material in some way precisely *because* they are compelling to you.

The source of the real, usable details of your fiction may be as dramatic as your witnessing a murder, or as ordinary as watching a funeral procession pass, noticing among the mourners a man in a shiny, black Mercedes Benz talking on his cell phone. Who is he talking to, you wonder? What's so important that it can't wait until the funeral is over?

In fact, it often seems to novelists that the world purposefully offers up details that they need. In a pivotal scene in Robb Forman Dew's *The Time of Her Life*, a huge potted plant crashes down onto the table in the restaurant where two characters are lunching. The scene was born of a similar experience she had while writing the book. "You really think everything is revolving around your book," she says. "Everything seems to be happening for a reason. What can be more seductive than that?"

These real-world details may come your way in the writing process, as Dew's did, or they may lie dormant in the back of your mind for years, like Toni Morrison's memory of Hannah Peace. Like your memories, they may enter a novel whole, or you may use fragments of them, combine them with other details, spin them to create something new. Sometimes you know instantly where a detail belongs; more often, details gather inside your head, waiting for the right moment to appear in the novel you're working on—or maybe, years from now, in a novel you haven't yet imagined.

Eventually, a moment of combustion occurs, some inkling of shape and direction. What you know, what you've experienced, observed, and pondered, merges and transforms in such a way that you can imagine a novel into which a certain set of details might figure.

Lee Smith knew she wanted to write about religious ecstasy, but a novel idea didn't occur to her until she interviewed a snake handler. "We were in a McDonald's in a mall, eating Chicken McNuggets," she says. "It was hard to believe I had just seen her lifting up a double handful of copperheads. 'Why do you do this?' I asked her. 'It's so dangerous. You could be killed.' 'Well I'll tell you,' she answered, with a sweet, open smile. 'I do this out of an intense desire for holiness. And I'll tell you something else, too—when you've had the serpent in your hand, the whole world kind of takes on an edge for you.' At that moment, I knew I had to write the novel which became *Saving Grace*."

Your moment of combustion may come as Smith's did, as a direct result of an experience related to the ideas and images circling in your mind, or maybe when you're standing in the shower one morning, everything you know about your novel so far will fall into a pattern. For no apparent reason, you'll suddenly sense a beginning, middle, and end. Someplace to go. One true sentence may emerge from freewriting and carry you into a scene that, when you follow it, becomes a story. In the conscious acts of thinking, plotting, outlining, combustion might occur. Sometimes a strong character brings shape to a novel. You follow him through a series of scenes until he stops, suddenly, as if to say, "Now, you decide. Write. 'Utter me into the visible.'"

And you do, somehow, finding shape and meaning in his story. Sometimes you make a mistake, go in some wrong direction and have to start all over again. But that's revision, another topic. For now, it is enough to know that once the moment occurs, writers work differently toward finding the right structure and movement for each novel. Each book reveals itself differently, both in its beginning and in the way the novelist works through it to the final draft.

Combustion must occur again and again in the long process of making a novel come alive. Your ability to make this happen is directly related to your ability to dream. Your imagination is no more than this: Your ability to ask, "What if?" And to keep on asking it until the right idea presents itself and you can go on. Perhaps the novelist's greatest gift is the combination of delight and tenacity in asking this question, in staying engaged with her novel long enough to bring it fully from the mind to the page.

If it seems even remotely possible, just jump in. Start writing. There are many ways to get started:

- You might begin on page one and go as far as you can until you can't continue without further research.
- You might write the last scene and consider what it reveals about the novel as a whole.
- You might write any random scene you see in your mind's eye, trusting that, in time, you'll discover its meaning and find its right place in the narrative.
- You might write a series of scenes loosely tied together by the presence of a character or set of characters, or the fact that all the scenes happen in a single place or within a particular period of time. What binds them together will become obvious as you write.

Remember: a novel is revealed in the process of writing it. Thinking, dreaming, mapping will not get a novel started. Writing gets a novel started.

And remember that whatever you write now is a rough draft. You're trying to get the novel to reveal itself to you. You can go back later and polish the writing to perfection.

Maybe you're not ready to jump in yet. Maybe you feel that what you know — what you have immediate access to intellectually and in your mind's eye — hasn't brought you to a starting point. But beware! Deciding to delay the beginning for the sake of discovering more can be very seductive. Spending hours and hours cloistered in some brightly lit corner of a library collecting details and insights in a notebook can make you feel as if you're getting on with the book. You may be — such additional work may be necessary. But you also may be simply putting off the inevitable plunge.

To help find the way into your novel, take an inventory of what you know so far. Make a list of all the characters that you think inhabit this world you hope to create. Write what you know about them and what you still need to know.

Should you discover, for example, that one of these folks is a casket salesman — perhaps the man talking on his cell phone in the funeral procession — and you know nothing about the casket business, you may need to spend an afternoon or two exploring this profession, either through book research, on-site visits, or interviews. What is it like to call on a succession of funeral homes, lauding the merits of copper casket liners over aluminum ones? What language does he use with clients and coworkers, talking shop? How was he trained for the job — a casket workshop? How did he get into this line of work in the first place? Surely, no little boy in a baseball cap declares at age eight, "I want to be a casket salesman when I grow up!"

Learning the answers to these questions will help you better understand your characters, but research alone won't create a character. Nor will it make the time and place of your novel seem real. In truth, too much research can get in the way of the story. John Fowles, in an interview, once noted that he almost scuttled *The French Lieutenant's Woman* for that reason. His fascination with the time and the milieu in which the story took place became so great that he nearly lost the narrative.

So, if it seems necessary, if it gives you confidence, do your inventory and any additional work you need to do. Then jump in — *anywhere.*

Like Nike says, "Just Do It."

The Elements of Fiction

"Only those things are beautiful which are inspired
by madness and written by reason."
— ANDRÉ GIDE

OCCASIONALLY, AN INEXPERIENCED WRITER writes a brilliant first novel
through some combination of instinct and dumb luck. Maybe he comes
from a family of yarn spinners, with memories of family gatherings where
one of his elders held the rest of the family in thrall, and one of these remembered stories becomes his first novel. Perhaps he was a child who lived
in books. *Harriet the Spy*, *The Boxcar Children*, and *Encyclopedia Brown*
were more real to him than the kids down the street, and somehow a first
novel was born in response to these stories that sustained him. Perhaps he
has had some experience or a vision so vivid and focused that he is able to
sit down and pour it directly into a book.

If you believe in the muse, you might conclude that she is responsible.
Maybe she is. But you would do well not to depend on her. She's elusive
at best. A. Manette Ansay thinks she's downright dangerous: "My recom-
mendation is, if you ever see a muse, blow it away. Get rid of it. Poison it,
gun it down. All right, now you don't have to wait for the muse. Now you
can just start writing."

How or why a first novel comes into the world so easily is a mystery. If
you're lucky enough to pull a first novel out of the upper layer of your consciousness, thank whatever higher power you believe in for the gift — but
don't expect it to happen a second time. Novel writing is a craft — like
weaving or carpentry. To be successful at it in the long run, you must
master the tools of the trade and understand its rules and conventions.

Of course, the great writer invents new ways of using language, breaks
the rules, and goes against the conventions of the novel when they don't
suit her vision. You can do whatever you can get away with, the saying

goes. But the truth is, you can't get away with much. Innovations made by a novelist with a command of the language and a solid understanding of the way fiction works are far more likely to succeed than those attempted in ignorance. A novel's story, the characters who live in it, and their world may spring full-blown into your mind. Or you may create them as you go, by plan and process. Regardless of how your novel develops, you will come closest to matching your vision with words on the page if you learn all you can about the craft of fiction, how fiction works.

John Gardner, in *On Becoming a Novelist*, describes a good novel as a "vivid and continuous dream . . . captured in language so that other human beings, whenever they feel like it, may open his book and dream that dream again." A wrong note in dialogue, carelessness with logistics, contradictions in character, grammatical errors—any gaffe, small or large, that brings the reader out of the dream and makes him remember, even for an instant, that the world he has been absorbed in is not real—spoils to some degree the novel's effect.

Character, voice, dialogue, scene, plot, world, and time—through mastery of these elements of fiction, the novelist draws the reader into the fictive dream and holds him, from the first line of the novel to the last.

We don't suggest that you master all the elements of fiction one-by-one before beginning the novel you want to write; we doubt that's even possible. Plot grows from character; character moves the plot. You can't write a strong scene without creating a believable world, one whose vitality is dependent on the characters who live there and that's full of clues about what's happening in the story. Once you begin, every element will come into play and you'll have to juggle them all into place.

So if you feel ready to write, write! Learn craft on a need-to-know basis, and as you revise.

SCENE

Take a moment to imagine this scene. You're on an airplane, a few hours into a long flight, and you exit the world of the novel you've been reading to stretch your legs. As you walk up the aisle of the aircraft, you notice how many of your fellow passengers are absorbed in novels—many different novels, each one a completely different world.

The claustrophobic atmosphere of a long airplane flight is a perfect place to picture the average reader and consider why she reads novels, why all of us read novels for pleasure: because a good story makes the real world fall away.

You may be compelled to write a novel to share your philosophy of life, or to teach the reader something. Maybe you want to use your novel to change the world, to inspire readers to do something about domestic abuse, the hole in the ozone layer, or world hunger. Maybe you want to demonstrate your ability to write beautiful, descriptive prose, or prove how intelligent and witty you are. Indeed, your finished novel may accomplish all of these things. If it does, you may be justifiably proud. But when readers talk about the books they love, their highest praise is most often, "It was a great story!" Regardless of your personal motivations for writing a novel, remember that to make the reader care about it, you must embed your ideas, knowledge, and visions in a *story*.

This is no simple task. Think of a five-year-old child recounting the story of his day. "And then we fed the gerbil, and then Mrs. Harvey read us the story about the moon, and then there was a fight on the playground . . ." Adorable, perhaps, if it's *your* child, but if it's the tot from next-door? You're checking your watch before he gets to recess.

Writing a good story is more than simply recounting a series of events. You must make your readers feel as if the story is happening right before their eyes. Watching the characters act, listening to them talk, observing their surroundings, readers should come to their own conclusions about what's happening and begin to care about and even to try to predict the outcome of events. You accomplish this by moving your characters through a series of scenes.

A good novel, like a film, presents evidence through a series of scenes and lets readers come to their own conclusions about what the characters do and say. A scene can be small, quiet: the casket salesman driving a Mercedes in the funeral procession, talking into his cell phone. A scene can be teeming with people, loaded with complications and possibilities.

In fact, as you read this, you are living a little scene. You are dressed in a certain way, stretched out on a couch, a fire crackling in the fireplace. Or maybe you're sitting upright in one of those uncomfortable airport chairs, waiting for a flight to Zimbabwe.

To write the scene you find yourself in while reading this book, you would consider all the visual details that identify the place and time. You'd sniff, identifying the mix of odors present. You'd listen; maybe there's just the sound of your own breathing, the whisper of pages turning. Maybe there's the clatter of dishes being washed in the kitchen, the muffled laugh track of a TV sitcom in another room. Or, if you're in the airport, the scream of jets taking off, kids crying, the *beep-beep* of a golf cart carrying elderly passengers along the concourse. What is the temperature of the room you're in? Where does the light come from? What is illuminated? What falls into shadow?

Now consider which details best convey the mood of the place and your own mood in it. If the place is calming, what specific things contribute to that sense of calm — the color of the walls, the furniture, the sounds you hear, photographs, objects of art, personal objects, a view through the window? When you've decided what details you want to work with, render the scene simply. Focus on painting resonant word pictures with strong nouns and verbs, avoiding adverbs and adjectives that guide the reader's thinking.

It helps to imagine how you would film the scene. What would you show first? Where would the camera move after that first image? How would you introduce new elements that deepen the effect of the scene? Thinking as a camera, you're more likely to create a strong scene that presents evidence, not judgment, leaving it to your reader to decide what the evidence means, how it supports or alters what she knows about the story so far.

To help you flesh out this (or any) scene, consider these questions.

WHO: List who is present in the scene. Observe how these participants look. What are they wearing, what is their body language? What are they saying? What catches your eye? Who is *not* there? Why not?

WHERE: Indicate the setting. Write a physical description of the setting. What is the significance of the setting? Are there objects significant to the scene?

WHEN: Place the scene in time. Give the specific date if you can. Write a weather report for the day. Is the weather significant? How? Is there anything significant happening just outside the scene that affects how it plays out? Is there anything happening in the world at large that is important to the scene? What other times come into play in terms of references, memories? How are they significant to *now*?

WHAT: Describe what happens in the scene—give a little plot summary. How much time passes from the beginning of the scene to the end of it? What does each character bring to the scene that may affect its outcome? What mood does each character bring? What unrelated problem or joy? What history with the others involved?

WHY: Why are these people together in this scene? What issues are involved? Where's the tension and/or conflict in it? What's at stake? If there's dialogue, what are they talking about? Individually, what does each character want the outcome of the scene to be? Is there a difference between what they say they want and what they really want? Are they aware of the difference? Remembering that good stories deal with the yearnings of people, consider who in this cast of characters wants the most and is willing to go the farthest to get it.

To help you grasp the concept of how scene works, watch the first twenty minutes or so of a movie, jotting down what you know and how you know it as the scenes unfold. Then watch again (and again and again), paying close attention to the way images convey information about character and situation to the viewer. Focus on one small moment in the movie and try to transcribe it, allowing yourself to write only what the camera could record. "Witness," which tells the story of a young Amish woman and her son, caught up in the murder of an undercover narcotics agent, and a hardened Philadelphia detective who becomes their savior, is an excellent film to use for this exercise, but any good film will do.

The study of film is so useful to writers that novelist Thomas Mallon suggested creating a film treatment as a way of establishing a series of scenes to tell a novel's story. In fact, it's helpful generally to consider what happens in your novel in terms of what a camera could register, especially if your stories tend to focus on the inner lives of your characters. Of course, not every crucial moment in a novel can be rendered in scene. Every good novel has necessary passages of exposition and wonderful moments when the reader is given access to the characters' inner lives. As your novel unfolds, you must consider everything you know that's happened to your characters, and decide which events in their lives should be narrated or processed internally and which should be rendered in scenes. Then you must discover how best to order this mix of scenes and narration to tell your story.

That man in the Mercedes, for example. What life experiences brought him to the day of the funeral, the moment when the cell phone rang and he picked it up? Run the reel of his whole life in your mind and pluck out the scenes that mirror this moment or somehow prepare him for it. Do you see him in high school, desperately waiting for the phone to ring? Do you see his father get up from the dinner table to answer the phone and attend to a client's business? Do you see him as a child at the funeral of a beloved grandparent, unable to cry? Or sitting mute and powerless in a stalled car while a meeting that could change the course of his career is starting without him?

Now, turning to the novel you want to write, consider everything you know about it. Freewrite about what's gathered in your head so far: memories, insights, ideas. Examine things you've collected in a binder or thrown into a file folder: newspaper clippings, articles, photographs. Read the notes you've written in a notebook or on scraps of paper. New bits of information about the novel may occur to you in the process of looking over what you've gathered. Write those down, too.

Without analyzing, jot down a list of scenes that might appear in your novel. It doesn't have to be a comprehensive list. You're not obligated to *use* the scenes that come to mind. Just let things float up and see what appears.

When you feel you've achieved the full benefit of considering the possibilities, it is time to decide which of these memories, details, scenes, and ideas belong in the novel taking shape in your head. Which of the characters you've imagined seem necessary? Where do they live? What are they doing? Examine the scenes you've imagined so far, considering the following:

- Which scenes reveal character?
- Which scenes move the story forward?
- Which scenes create tension?
- Which scenes evoke emotion?
- Which scenes seem to be related to one another?
- Which behaviors, images, themes, and issues recur, creating patterns?
- Which scenes make you, the writer, curious, make you ask, "What if?"
- Which scenes suggest new possibilities for the novel?

If you are lucky, this process will cause the scenes to fall into place, revealing a workable structure for your novel. More likely, you'll feel like you have a pile of puzzle pieces and only a vague idea of what the finished puzzle will look like, not to mention the knowledge that you don't yet have all the pieces. Writing a novel differs from putting together a puzzle in that the novelist decides where the known pieces go. Then he creates shapes to fill the empty spaces as he goes along. There are limitless possibilities. Any ten writers given the same set of pieces would come up with ten different pictures!

You can order the scenes and events of your novel any way you want to, any way that makes sense to you. But remember that the choices you make in this phase will greatly determine the focus and effect of your story. The picture that emerges must be as clear as a finished puzzle would be.

Identifying and ordering what you know about your novel is the first step toward making that picture appear. Now you must work toward one of those moments of combustion described earlier, asking "What if?" until these known things begin to shift, split, combine, and trigger new insights that will help you shape the plot of your story.

PLOT

What exactly *is* plot? Dorothy Allison answers the question this way: "Something happens. Something real." Wally Lamb says, "If you boil it down to the lowest common denominator, you're telling a story about what a character wants—and what the character wants on a conscious level may be different than what the character really wants. To oversimplify, plot is the character getting from point A to point Z in pursuit of what he or she wants. But if it's a more complex story, there is the character's pursuit of what he thinks he wants and the eventual discovery of what he really wants or needs. That's what plot is for me." Larry Brown believed "that if you create interesting enough characters, characters who are real enough, then whatever happens to them is the plot."

Plot moves the story forward and makes the reader want to turn the pages. It is fueled by questions. There is one overriding question that addresses the theme of the novel, and a series of smaller questions that move the novel along beneath its arc. In her novel *Hummingbird House*, Patricia Henley explores the overriding question, "What happens to women and children when there's a war?" Smaller, more specific questions hold the reader's interest page by page: Where is Maggie? Why is Sunny so mysterious about her work? Will Kate and Dixie sleep together? These smaller questions and their answers constitute the subplots of a novel. They grow organically from the issue at the heart of the novel, each one a story in its own right, with a beginning, middle, and end. At the end of a good novel, the reader understands why the story had to be told. She feels satisfied that the smaller events, or subplots, of the novel played themselves out in a believable manner and, in so doing, addressed and answered the large, thematic question the novel posed.

A plot may be based on exterior circumstances, the fates of its characters completely dependent on a series of events, as in a detective novel; a plot's engines may be interior, moving the characters toward some emotional insight, as in the novels of Virginia Woolf. Most likely, the plot you create will fall somewhere in between these two extremes.

How you go about creating that plot is another question. Some writers work out the plot of the story before they begin to write, creating an elaborate outline that they will flesh out during the actual writing process. Small surprises are likely to occur along the way, but essentially, they know the story before they begin. For most novelists, however, plot and character are interchangeable. They don't know what the plot will be until the characters begin to reveal themselves. "I never have a plot," says mystery writer S. J. Rozan. "What I do is start with an idea—an emotional or thematic center for the book and a world that it's set in." Characters, plot, and structure appear and develop as the idea complicates itself.

Once you discover and develop the plot, it is important to make sure that you follow through on every element you introduce. For example, you wouldn't let the man in the Mercedes reconnect with an old friend at the graveside ceremony, hint at some significant shared experience in the past, and then let that friend completely disappear from the novel. Similarly, if there are subplots, each one must be a complete story, with a beginning, middle, and resolution.

Novel plots differ wildly and each writer plots in his own way, but every strong plot has the following characteristics:

- Things happen and those things are significant.
- Events have causes and effects, creating a web of tension.
- The choices made by characters play out, driving the novel toward its resolution.
- A series of small questions are posed and resolved, paced to hold the reader's interest and designed to deepen continually his understanding of the thematic question the novel poses.
- The writer follows through on each element she introduces; all subplots are fully developed and resolved.

In real life the people we love, hate, fear, and worry about most elicit our strongest emotions, and so it is in fiction. Events are of little interest unless we care about the people involved. The best plot in the world becomes boring if it is recounted in a bland voice and enacted by characters who have no stake in its outcome.

In a sense, you have to grab your reader by the lapels and say, "I must tell you this story, or I will die!" To say that telling your story is a matter of life or death may be overstating its importance to you, but you do have to care about the story, to feel compelled to tell it by something deep inside. You're not writing it because it's an interesting idea—though it may be. You're not writing it because you think it's marketable—though it may be. You're writing it because there's something you can't forget, something you have to understand. Your story must evoke in you a sense of wonder, a voice that whispers to the reader behind the words, "Can you *believe* this?" You must also be a little scared of the story on some level. Writing it has to cost you something. At the very least, there must be the possibility that, writing it, you might discover something you don't want to know.

This doesn't mean that the subject matter of your story has to be as important or dramatic as, say, war. But it has to be as important as war to *you*. Even comic novels—good ones—confront issues that matter. Small, domestic dramas can bristle with tension. What makes a novel compelling is the sense, as you're reading, that it is absolutely real.

POINT OF VIEW

Point of view—how you choose to tell your story, through whose eyes the story is seen—is one of the most important decisions you will make about your novel, crucial to creating the desired effect on the page. If you're lucky, the point of view will be obvious to you from the start, part of your original conception of the novel, and you won't have to make a conscious choice. Most writers, however, have to experiment with points of view and voices before finding the ones that best suit the novels they want to write.

While there is no formula for choosing a point of view, some writers come to their own personal formula through practice. Lewis Nordan chooses the point of view that makes his job easiest. Madeleine L'Engle said that she listened to the voices in her head and granted point of view to "the one who won't leave me alone."

Using a single character's point of view to tell the story gives a novel focus and a clean arc. Secondary characters and subplots are introduced to deepen the main character's story and move the plot forward, but the novel belongs to the main character. This makes it easier for the writer to assess how the novel is working and make decisions about what belongs in it.

In novels that use multiple points of view, several interconnected stories unwind, each of equal importance in addressing the novel's overriding question. In concept, this is similar to ensemble acting. For example, there's no single star in any of the award-winning films "Grand Canyon," "The Big Chill," or "Crash." Instead, there are several main characters, each driving one of the interconnected stories. Each story has its own plot, the arc and outcome of which contribute to the viewer's understanding of the big picture.

A first-person narrator draws a reader into a story in a very personal way. If the voice is strong, it feels as if you're right there, listening to a real person tell his story. But it's important to remember that a first-person narrator is always an unreliable narrator to some degree. He tells the story based on what he knows, consciously or subconsciously choosing what to tell and what to leave out. Other characters must speak and act in ways that bring perspective to what the narrator says, expanding the reader's understanding.

Working in the third person creates a more detached view of the story, offering the writer a variety of options for presenting and/or commenting on the action and the inner lives of the characters. But be aware that it involves more than simply deciding to use *he* or *she* instead of *I*, *we*, or *you*. There are three different ways of writing from the third-person point of view: close third, objective third, and omniscient third. Each has its own requirements.

Close third is most like first person in that the narrator is inside the main character's head. He knows what the character thinks and feels; he knows what the character knows, sees what the character sees. No more.

The narrator in objective third person is like a camera positioned on the main character's shoulder. He sees and hears what the character sees and hears, but is not privy to the character's thoughts and feelings, which the reader must infer from action, dialogue, and details.

The omniscient third-person narrator knows everything about everyone in the story. She can enter the thoughts of any character, and even comment on the action. Impersonal and very difficult to sustain, this point of view is rarely used by contemporary novelists.

Of course, there are exceptions to every rule, but generally, once you establish a point of view, you should use it consistently throughout the novel.

Telling a story in the present tense gives it a sense of immediacy, making the reader feel as if the events of the novel are unfolding *right now*. Telling it in the past tense gives the story a more reflective feel. The events are finished, and there's a sense that they must be told to be fully understood.

When you hit upon the right point of view for your novel, the following common-sense considerations may help you assess and refine it:

- Realistically, can you get into the head of the point-of-view character you've chosen?
- Can your point-of-view character be in all the necessary places at the right times to recount what's needed to make the story clear to the reader?
- Is your point-of-view character the "moved" character? Even if the action of the novel does not focus on her, is she the one most affected by it?
- Is the point of view of one person sufficient to reveal the complexity of the story?
- If you discover that multiple points of view will best serve your story, how will you balance them so that the reader will go willingly and without confusion from one to the next?

Once you find the point of view, sustaining it throughout your novel will present a major challenge. "Point of view runs me nuts," Flannery O'Connor wrote to a young writer. "If you violate the point of view you destroy the sense of reality and louse yourself up generally."

CHARACTER

Maybe you want to write a novel about the effects of violence on American youth. Noble idea—but not necessarily good fiction. The best plot in the world, the most passionate feelings about ideas or issues are worth little without characters who make the story spring to life. Discussing her novel about the civil rights era, Sena Jeter Naslund says, "The only way I know to make a statement about violence is to create characters whose lives the reader treasures. And then to sacrifice them."

Learning to create characters whose lives readers treasure, characters who seem like flesh and blood, characters who are interesting, lively, and complex enough to sustain a novel, is your most crucial task.

As in real life, people in a novel appear in a variety of ways. A character may appear, full-blown, and instantly engage you. You may catch a glimpse of a character in your mind's eye, then see him again, and again—only realizing over time that he is a person worth developing a relationship with. You may think, "I need a certain kind of person," and then create him. Sometimes a character from a short story or an abandoned novel re-appears in the novel you're working on. Maybe a person you know in the real world steps into the world of your novel. Maybe a character is some version of yourself.

Regardless of how your characters first appear, you will come to know them much as you have come to know the people in your real life. Consider the way you came to know someone for whom you have strong feelings. Maybe you saw him first from afar. What caught your interest? Something he was wearing? The way he moved? Something he did or said? Whatever it was, it made you come to some conclusion about him. He's funny. He's handsome. He seems like such a happy person. Or maybe you thought, "He's a jerk." Then, some time later, you saw him again. Maybe he did something that underpinned your first impression; maybe he did something that contradicted it—or added something new. "He's funny *and* kind," you thought, or, "He's funny, but mean." Eventually, you met him, and in that first exchange you learned more. From then on, each time you were together, observed him when he was unaware, or heard someone else make an observation about him, your sense of him became clearer and clearer—rather like holding a Polaroid photo in your hand and watching the image emerge. Years have passed. You know him better than anyone else in your whole life, but he still has the capacity to surprise you.

Characters in a novel surprise us, just as real people do. What a character does in a scene grows out of who she is; that same action may contradict our prior understanding of her and cause our sense of who she is to change. Controlling this paradoxical element in the relationship between character and incident is necessary to make lively characters who are capable of surprising the reader in a believable way.

A character's capacity to surprise is where the elements of plot and character merge in a novel. Getting to know a character is a matter of learning what his fixed actions are, his particular way of being in the world. But while this kind of constancy is an excellent way to show the reader what your character is like, it is not enough to sustain a novel. "I think about all my characters until I know what each one would be doing on any given day of their lives," Doris Betts says, "then I write the story about the day when something *different* happens."

It's when a character's fixed actions change for some reason that a novel gathers tension and begins to move. Take that man in the Mercedes. Every morning he drives out of his gated community, stops at Starbucks for a latte, hits the freeway, and picks up his cell phone. He loves driving his Mercedes, doing deals on the phone. He loves the rush he gets when people in crummy cars glance over at him, envious. He does business anytime, anywhere. It would never occur to him to turn the phone off while he's on the way to the cemetery. When it rings, he picks it up. Maybe nothing comes of it. He makes a deal, hangs up, goes to the gravesite, then on through his day. But what if, distracted by the conversation he's having, he doesn't notice the car that comes into the intersection, disregarding the funeral procession, and he gets broadsided? He's hurt badly enough to be taken to the hospital in an ambulance, where, shaken by the experience, he contemplates those fixed actions that have put making deals and making money at the center of his life. This cosmic wake-up call is moving action.

What sets the action moving doesn't have to be as dramatic as a car accident. Let's run the scenario again. Arranging a time to meet later, the client our man is talking to on the cell phone says, "So where are you right now?" "On my way to the cemetery," he answers. "I figure the service will take maybe twenty minutes—" The client laughs. "So much for quiet contemplation of the life of the deceased! Do you ever *not* work?" And suddenly, surprising himself, the man in the Mercedes feels ashamed. It's a new feeling for him. From it comes new thought: "Is this the kind of person I want to be?" If the answer is no, the novel will move.

So a character has to surprise a reader now and then for the reader to remain engaged in his life. The tricky thing is that he has to surprise *you*, the writer, as well. Almost any successful novelist can describe a moment when she set a character in motion and that character did something she'd had no idea the character would do. Dorothy Allison perceived Delia's granddaddy in *Cavedweller* as an evil man, but he surprised her midway through the second draft of the book when he appeared with flowers for the window of Delia's beauty shop. Sometimes such a surprise takes the book in a direction you hadn't planned for it to go. This can result in a breakthrough that takes you closer to the core of your story, as it did for Allison, who suddenly understood Delia's silence about her childhood. It may also ruin your day, as did the death of one of Lewis Nordan's characters. "When Hydro died in *Sharpshooter*, I was so shocked I had to take the rest of the day off," he says. "My wife had to comfort me. I came down the stairs from my office, ashen. She said, 'Honey, what happened? What's the matter?' I said, 'Hydro died.' She said, 'Oh, no. Oh god, no, Honey.'"

Occasionally a surprise will send you way off track, skewing the story, compromising or even destroying its credibility. "Real characters are alive," E. M. Forster wrote in *Aspects of the Novel*. "They arrive when evoked, but full of the spirit of mutiny . . . often engaged in treason against the main scheme of the book. They run away, they 'get out of hand': they are creations inside a creation, and often inharmonious towards it; if they are given complete freedom, they kick the book to pieces, and if they are kept too sternly in check, they revenge themselves by dying and destroy it by intestinal decay."

When one of your characters decides to alter the course of your novel, you must assess his behavior objectively, bringing to bear your understanding of human nature and of craft in deciding whether what he did suits the book you want to write. It's up to you. "You decide, you choose, you are responsible," Richard Ford says. "That's what authorship means."

First and foremost, a novelist is curious about people. He is constantly observant, noting the behavior of the people he lives with, works with, dines with, travels with on the subway or stands in line with to see a movie on Saturday night. He wonders why people do what they do, running this scenario or that idea through his mind in an attempt to understand it. Novelists listen, too; indeed, most novelists are inveterate eavesdroppers. They are known to gossip, as well—a habit that Jane Smiley defends. "What gossip does is enable people to assimilate events around them and to create an emotional and moral fabric out of their daily lives," she says. "Gossip is what we use to find the balance between the moral precepts and the particular cases. That, to me, is what novels are for."

If curiosity about the human condition and constant observation of the way people act and speak are crucial traits of the novelist, so is love—the kind of unconditional love that people of faith believe God has for all humanity. Such a god creates each soul, sets it in motion, and monitors its journey through life, watching, hoping. An effective novelist creates characters in the same way. He knows them as God knows each soul he has created. He hopes for their salvation, even though sometimes he's virtually certain it's impossible.

The peculiar detachment necessary for such observation is something that many novelists seem to have been born with. They are the children standing outside the circle, watching the others at play, the adults who gravitate to the edge of a party. Lee Smith says, "I believe fiction by its very nature is about alienation, about being 'different.' If a character feels perfectly at home in her world, then there's no conflict, so there's no possibility for fiction."

The worst reason for creating a character is hatred or anger: the intention to use a character to hurt a real person or to get revenge. It will almost certainly keep you from rendering a complex character that the reader will care about. But creating a character as a way of helping you *understand* the hatred and anger you feel toward its prototype may have a very different effect. Writing honestly from such a character's point of view may reveal a greater complexity than you had imagined, and reveal insights that create interesting tensions in your novel and a sense of resolution in your real life.

Creating a character for revenge won't work, and creating a character or set of characters to make a point won't work either. If you want to teach, write a nonfiction book. If you want to promote some religious or political belief, write a persuasive essay. Your only agenda with characters should be to put what seem like real people on the page. To accomplish this, you must let go of your preconceived notions about people in general, and your characters in particular. Failing to do so will result in cardboard characters, capable only of fixed action. Neither villains nor paragons of virtue have much capacity to surprise.

A character based *solely* on yourself presents a different problem: you know yourself too well. A strong character is created through a process of discovery; you put him in a situation and begin to write, not quite sure what will happen. His personality and belief system develop as you move him through the novel. But if the character is *you*, there is much less to discover. Worse, he is less malleable than a character you invent. Even if you're willing to innovate—to add experiences to your character's past that are different from your own, or allow him to behave in a way you never would—your alter ego is likely to become as recalcitrant and wooden as you do when someone tries to force you to behave in a way that doesn't feel right to you.

Paradoxically, you also know too little about yourself to turn yourself into fiction: you are limited to your own idea of who you are. It is impossible to know how you appear to other people, what they think of you, or the true effect you have on their lives. Forster explained that the special gift of the novel is that the writer can talk *about* his characters as well as *through* them. He lets us listen when they talk to themselves. But real people don't talk to themselves truthfully, he says; we can't, because our secret joys and miseries proceed from causes we can't quite explain. A novelist must command the secret life of a character in a way he cannot command his own secret life. Thus, he is bound to fail in any attempt to put himself on the page.

The same is true of trying to put people from your real life into a book. When Robb Forman Dew finished her first novel, *Dale Loves Sophie to Death*, she called her mother and said, "I want you to know before you read this that you're not Polly" and she answered, "Well, of course I'm not. You only know me as your mother." Dew was stunned, but realized that her mother was right.

Like Dew, you probably know too much and too little to translate real people into fictional characters. And it may cause real difficulties, even bring an end to lifelong relationships, to try. Faulkner said, "If a writer has to rob his mother, he will not hesitate. The 'Ode on a Grecian Urn' is worth any number of old ladies." Your feelings about this statement are probably a good indicator of the degree to which you are willing to risk hurting the people you care about by appropriating their lives for fiction.

Of course, some novelists have crafted wonderful characters of themselves and of people in their real lives. Dorothy Allison's *Bastard Out of Carolina* is peopled with a number of characters straight out of her childhood. Alex, in Theodore Weesner's *The Car Thief*, is the author's young self. Sheri Reynolds says, "My characters are all me, of course, some aspect of myself that I explode into someone new. I put my vulnerability and mean-heartedness into my characters to make it more tolerable in myself. I put my fear into my characters, and also my secret pride and hard-jawed determination. They are my best selves, my others, my shadows, my sisters."

So if you are the star of the novel you are burning to write and you really can't imagine telling it any other way, go for it! Who knows? Maybe you'll be added to the list of novelists who have succeeded in fictionalizing their own lives. But if you get halfway though and the novel freezes up on you, segue. Find the heart of your story—the grief, joy, or confusion that compelled you to write it—and give it a new face. You'll have to do this eventually, in any case. Only so much of any life is worthy of fiction, and it's unlikely you'll get more than a few directly autobiographical novels out of yours. When you begin to spin the facts of your life into stories that make little or no use of your literal personal experience, you will have become a novelist in the truest sense.

Whether they're based on real people or purely invented, there are three basic kinds of characters in a novel: the main character or characters, upon whose life or lives the action of the book centers; secondary characters, who underpin the main characters' lives and provide opportunities for moving action; and minor characters, who appear in passing, providing occasional information and creating small tensions that contribute to the overall effect. The need to create main characters who reflect the complexity of the human condition is obvious, but secondary characters must be drawn with the same complexity if the novel's going to feel like real life. Even the minor characters who play only cameo roles must be authentic, their fixed actions rendered like the deft sketches of a master draftsman.

Secondary characters must serve the overarching question of the novel. You may know who these characters will be at the outset, or they may emerge, in the writing process, as the story needs them. Sometimes they trigger the moving action of a novel, but sometimes they hijack a book, sending it into a new, more interesting direction. If the novel goes cold, you may need to create a secondary character to shake things up a bit. Similarly, you may create a secondary character to solve some problem you discover in revision.

Though secondary characters are there to serve the main character's story, each one must have an arc of her own within the novel; essentially, she is the main character in one of the novel's subplots. For the novel to work, each secondary character's story must illuminate the focus, move the plot, and come to a satisfying resolution. Her story must be so entwined with the main character's story that the whole novel would collapse if you removed her.

Perhaps the greatest achievement in creating a set of characters is for the reader to reach the end of the novel and feel simultaneously satisfied with its resolution and convinced that its characters are still out there somewhere, living the rest of their lives. Readers who fall in love with the characters in a novel often hope for a sequel; but more often than not, the writer doesn't have a clue about what happened to them when the book ended, beyond some general thought that their lives either did or did not turn out okay—and doesn't really care. He's ready to move on to new material and create new characters with whom to explore it.

Occasionally, though, new material may be served by a familiar character or set of characters. Upon completing *Dale Loves Sophie to Death*, Robb Forman Dew knew that the Howells' child Toby would die, and some years later she successfully explored the aftermath of his death in the family in *Fortunate Lives*. Richard Ford remained interested in the life of Fred Bascombe from *The Sportswriter*, but he approached writing *Independence Day* with some trepidation. "A sequel is often just a retelling of the first book, or a better working out of a book that was ill worked out originally," he says. "I spent a year preparing to write it to be sure that I really did have a book that was whole."

Series writers like Tony Hillerman and S. J. Rozan base their careers on recurring characters that they get to know as well as members of their families. A series character might be a writer's alter ego, allowing the writer to live both in the real world and in the more focused, more exciting world of books. Such characters may be alter egos for readers, as well, who see them as better, smarter, stronger, more adventurous versions of themselves. But the writer must take care. If the character becomes *too* good, too smart, too strong, too adventurous, he becomes a cardboard figure, predictable and unreal. The key to creating a successful series character is in finding the balance between the character's larger-than-life qualities and the qualities that make him seem human. Perhaps Aristotle had such a character in mind when he said, "A true hero is someone better than we are, yet like us."

Each book in a series must stand alone, the character completely understandable in the context of the story playing out in it. At the same time, each book must be built on and build upon all the books that came before. Often secondary characters, like Robert B. Parker's Hawk, and James Lee Burke's Clete Purcell, cycle through the series, adding depth and complexity to their worlds. Some series characters, like Sue Grafton's Kinsey Millhone, live forever at a certain age in a certain era; others, like Hillerman's Joe Leaphorn, change and grow over time. In the latter case, plots must be constructed to reflect and enhance this growth. Talking about Leaphorn, Tony Hillerman says, "My story ideas have to be affected by the passage of time. Leaphorn is retired, bored, lonely. His memories are important in plotting—the book on which I now am working is pegged to his memory of an unsatisfactory solution of a crime committed years ago."

S. J. Rozan gives equal time in her series to private eyes Bill Smith and Lydia Chin, alternating between Bill's and Lydia's points of view from book to book. She created Smith first, a classic private eye; then she created Chin, a Chinese-American woman, in opposition to him. "Obviously, she had to be a she since he was a he," she says. "She had to be small because he was big; young because he was middle-aged. And if she was someone from a completely different culture, then *everything* would be called into question." How does she know if a story idea better suits one of the other? "It's always clear," she says. "The stories come out of their worlds, which are really different.

Crucial to creating any fictional character is the writer's ability to *be* that character—live inside his skin, think his thoughts, and see the world through his eyes. Finding your way inside a character's skin is a playful process.

Our man in the Mercedes, for example—see him in your mind's eye. Listen to him. Where does he live? How does he live? What is his daily routine? Consider the smallest details of his existence. What happened in his past? How does it show itself in his present life? Who are the important people in his life? How does he relate to them? Consider his dreams. Imagine him in a scene, then set the scene in motion, and see what he does, what he says. Freewrite dialogue in which he talks to people—his wife or girlfriend, mother, boss, the cashier at Starbucks, the maître d' at an expensive restaurant. Write dialogue in which people talk about him behind his back.

Questions and considerations that will help you flesh out a character include:

- What are the contradictions in his life? If your character is meticulous and fussy, what is the one way he behaves that is, in some way, reckless or out of control? If he is rotten and mean, what one person is he a sucker for?
- What are his secrets? If your character is a decent person, what is the one thing he does or knows that he is ashamed of or embarrassed by? If he's not a good person, consider what kindness he might (secretly?) render. What might make him cry?
- Explore the small details of his existence. What is his favorite color, his favorite music? What kind of furniture is in his bedroom? What is his cat's name? If he went to the

post office to buy a stamp, which design would he choose? What kind of underwear does he buy? What's in his wallet, on his bedside table?

- What is he afraid of? Are his fears emotional or physical? How do they affect his behavior?
- What does he want more than anything? Does he believe there is any possibility at all that he will get it? Does he try?
- What does he remember from his childhood? What *doesn't* he remember?
- Add "But" to some things you know about him and see what pops into your mind. He has blond surfer hair, but _____. He loves to travel, but _____. He grew up in a nice suburban neighborhood, but _____. He drives a Mercedes, but _____.
- Describe your character so that he would be recognizable to someone picking him up at the airport.

Go deeper. Freewrite the answers to these questions in your character's voice:

- What do you look like?
- How old are you? How do you feel about being the age you are now?
- How do you spend most of your days?
- What do most people think about you?
- What are (were) your parents like? What do you love/dislike most about them?
- What makes you happy?
- What or whom do you hate most in the world? Why?
- How did you get into this story in the first place?
- Describe your state of mind when the story begins.

DIALOGUE AND VOICE

As you get to know your character better, his voice will emerge, deepen, and become more and more idiosyncratic. It will be there in dialogue, of course: the way he consciously or intuitively chooses certain kinds of subjects, sentence rhythms, and words that reflect his personality, upbringing, education, and experience. But "voice" is more than the way a character sounds when he talks. It is his inner voice, as well: the thinking voice with which he processes his experience. Whether written in first or third person, this inner voice makes the reader privy to what a character thinks, what he notices, what he believes, what he knows.

Good dialogue is people talking about things that interest them. There is a delicious feel to it, an intimacy. Speaking, a character tells a secret, tells the truth as she sees it, or perhaps dissembles. "That makes sense," the reader thinks. Or, "Wait a second . . . she's lying!"

Good dialogue reflects a character's background, his degree of education, his interests, his values. It reveals feelings in broad and subtle ways. It helps define the relationships he has with other characters in the novel. The man in the Mercedes speaks one way to a client, another to his girlfriend, another to his mother. Like people in real life, characters use language in a variety of ways, depending on the situation they're in and who they're talking to. The way they speak has to make sense to the reader—a character probably wouldn't curse in front of his mother and talk like a choirboy at the gym. In real life, conversation is often pointless, a dialogue of assent. "Hi, how are you?" "I'm fine. How are you?" "Pretty good. How's your mom?" Dialogue in fiction is distilled, the essence of conversation, or, in Amy Bloom's words, "conversation's greatest hits." Strong dialogue contributes to the novel's web of tension; it moves the story forward.

It should not be a form of narrative exposition in disguise. Such "soap opera" dialogue sounds like this: "Have you heard about Cherise?" "Do you mean the Cherise who works at Acme Casket Company and was having an affair with Greg, the salesman who drives a Mercedes, until he dumped her for that blond woman he met at a funeral?" Allow your readers the pleasure of collecting information about the story by way of rich sensory clues rather than through stiff, clunky dialogue that carries no tension and serves no purpose but to tell readers what the author wants them to know.

When you need to use dialogue tags to let the reader know who is speaking, a simple "he said" or "she said" is almost always sufficient. Avoid melodramatic tags like "he hissed" or "she shrieked" and the use of adverbs like "he said furiously" or "she screamed violently" to bolster the effect. Instead, let the quality of the dialogue—the choice of words, the rhythms in which they are spoken—carry the information the reader needs to know. Give evidence of emotion in the characters' actions, as well.

Dialogue rarely occurs in a vacuum. People are usually doing something as they speak—washing dishes, driving, painting their fingernails, fishing, changing a baby. They pace, gesture, fidget, bite their lips, chew gum, sip coffee. What characters do, how they move while they speak or listen, is important evidence to the reader as she puzzles out what's going on, what to think about a scene. This is particularly important to remember if a character is making a long speech. Pace the speech with action. Let the reader watch him stalk around the room, twist the telephone cord around his fingers, look in the mirror, brush a piece of lint from his wife's shoulder.

Characters give the reader evidence about themselves through dialogue; what characters say in dialogue also informs the writer's perception of them during the composition process. Listen to what your characters say. What phrases do they use repeatedly? How do they register surprise, annoyance, disgust, delight? If, moving a character through a scene, you thought he'd say, "Oh, my goodness, what a surprise to see you!" and instead he says, "Hot damn, you old son of a bitch! What brings you back?" you may want to reconsider what you think you know about him!

A character's inner voice clarifies and deepens what he says and does on the page; capturing it is crucial to creating a person a reader will care about. The inner voice brings understanding to acts that are outwardly reprehensible, and insight to acts that seem virtuous but may in fact be manipulative or even evil in their intent. Forster again, on the fundamental difference between people in daily life and people in books: "In daily life we never understand each other, neither complete clairvoyance nor complete confessional exists. We know each other only approximately, by external signs." Some people may display more external signs than others, but on some level they're still choosing the external signs they display. People in a novel can be understood only to the extent to which the novelist wants the reader to understand them.

You won't, of course, put every single thing you know about your characters in your novel. Hemingway compared what a writer knows about a story to the mass of ice that supports the visible tip of an iceberg. The tip is the story; the mass beneath it is everything the writer left out, but had to know in order to tell the story. It is an apt analogy for character as well. You will use only some of what you know about your character; the rest lies beneath, supporting her visible presence on the page.

So once again, you are faced with the process of selection. But in the case of character, it almost always works best to let selecting what belongs in the novel happen naturally as you move a character through the scenes. What he does, says, and thinks will inform you, directing the conscious choices you'll need to make in shaping and polishing the rough scenes toward completion.

WORLD

You've got a story, a cast of characters, and at least some glimmerings of plot. Now you must create the world in which the actions and events of your novel will take place. Whether it is a small town in Kansas, a medieval village in France, or an unknown planet in outer space, the world of your novel must be tailor-made for the story you want to tell. Tony Hillerman's love of "that huge, high, dry, mountain-rimmed landscape and the immense sky which looks over it" made him choose to set his first novel on the Navajo Reservation. "It is open, empty country, and the great storm clouds which rise above its mountain ranges remind me of the glory of God," he says. "But this landscape is also important because the stuff I write often requires empty places, ruined cliff dwellings, isolation, the kind of isolated people who notice things."

Whatever its nature, its trappings, its appeal to *you*, the world of your novel must draw the reader into it. "Come," an unseen voice whispers. "This place is fascinating. The things happening here will make you gasp, will offer you solace, will reveal something you need to know." Specific, telling details are the building blocks you'll use to create this world. Houses will most likely be in it, for example. But what kind of houses? Ranch houses, Tudor houses, bungalows? Adobe houses? Shotgun houses?

Brownstones? Or maybe your character lives in an apartment. A fifth-floor walk-up or a penthouse? Are the walls thin, letting in the sounds of neighbors arguing or making love?

What kinds of cars are parked outside? What do the yards look like? What newspaper is tossed onto the driveway or left on the stoop in the morning? Peering through dormer windows, bay windows, leaded glass windows, cracked or broken windows, what do you see?

What is the weather in your characters' world? How might it impinge on the action of the novel? How does it shape the characters' sense of who they are?

The particularity of places and objects in a fictive world makes that world come alive. "Adobe house," for example, carries with it a certain set of images and sensibilities for almost any reader. Brown, box-like, of the earth. A southwestern landscape, cactus and hard blue sky. "Brownstone," on the other hand, calls up the image of a city. People passing on the sidewalk, traffic going by.

Because these images are so powerful, the details you use must be accurate—you can't put mountains in a landscape where mountains don't exist. A wrong detail is like a wrong note in music, jarring and unpleasant. It brings the reader out of the vivid, continuous dream. In addition to being accurate, details must inform and underpin the action of a novel. Don't set a scene in Paris just because you visited Paris and want to use all the details you collected there; set it there only because something important is revealed by your characters being in that place.

If you set your novel in a familiar world, you can rely on memory and your powers of observation to choose the kind of details that will ground the reader in it. Look at that familiar world anew, as Theodore Weesner did, walking the streets of Portsmouth, New Hampshire, to chart his characters' movements through *The True Detective*. If you set your book in an unfamiliar place, research is essential. Nothing is better than on-site research, of course. Touring the city you want to write about, notebook and camera in hand, is the best way to capture its atmosphere. But if on-site research is impossible, head for the bookstore or the library. Read travel books, novels, histories. Look at photographs. Pore over maps. Watch movies. Talk to people who've lived in or visited the world of your novel.

Historical fiction presents a particular kind of challenge. Not only do you have to render the place correctly, you have to be accurate about the physical details of the time. Researching *Mary Reilly*, which is set in Victorian England, Valerie Martin studied the diary of a scullery maid and read interviews with working people and street children of the time. She did library research on Victorian customs, language, and clothing, and read novels that were set in that era. She toured period homes in London to help her imagine Mary's surroundings; in one, she found a list of house-maid's duties that gave her the specific information she needed to find a shape for Mary's days. Mary's struggles with the coal bucket, how she did the laundry, the particular kind of nightdress she wore—these and other carefully rendered details ground the reader in her world.

If you want to write a science fiction or fantasy novel, you have to create a whole new world. You can't research it—it doesn't exist! Perhaps you're thinking, "No big deal. It's my world; it can be whatever I want it to be." But if you hope to draw a reader into that world and hold him there, you must make him believe in it. Whether the world of your novel is a distant galaxy or a dark glen at the center of a magic forest, there must be logic behind its creation. Things can't just happen out of the blue. They must be explainable and believable, governed by a structure you design.

The general setting of your novel—the city, town, or planet where your story plays out—is just one aspect of the novel's world. Imagine a series of concentric circles, the innermost circle being the smallest, most private place a character inhabits—a bedroom, perhaps. Move outward from that place, into the other rooms of his house, then beyond the house into the garage, the yard, the street, the neighborhood, his work place, the places where he spends his leisure time. Each one of these circles is a little world in its own right and must be rendered authentically. Each little world contributes to the larger world's effect.

Just as important as well-chosen, authentic details is the way you use those details to deepen the reader's understanding of your characters. Our man in the Mercedes lives for a little while in the same world as the other mourners in the funeral procession. But each person in the procession notices different things on the way to the cemetery. Perhaps the man in the Mercedes notes For Sale signs in front of mansions he'd like to own, while a woman in the car behind him notices houses painted in interesting colors. Her child notices which houses have play equipment in their yards. The deceased's wife sees the apartment house they lived in when they were young, and looks away, narrowing her focus to the cracked leather of the limousine seat.

The tone you want to achieve, the way you want your world to feel, directs the use of detail as well. Try describing the same place through the eyes of a character who is alternately afraid, ecstatic, nostalgic, bitter, curious. Each time, the landscape will shift, presenting different aspects to the reader.

The density of visual and auditory details shapes the world, as well. You might use a pileup of detail to capture a city like New Orleans, whereas you'd use details sparingly to create a Shaker community. Even the rhythms of language contribute to this effect. New Orleans is lush, damp, dangerous. There'd be jazz in the sentences you'd use to capture it on the page, whereas simple, solid sentences would better describe the Shaker life.

Consider the rhythms of the world in your novel. Write a short descriptive passage, choosing words and structures that reflect and underpin the way the setting feels.

Making a world, the writer lays down place in broad strokes. Then, like a painter laying on glazes, he deepens the effect with the details that make the *particular* world in which her characters live.

STRUCTURE AND TIME

The structure of every novel is greatly dependent upon the way events are framed in time. In fact, finally discovering the right time frame, a novelist often feels as if the tumblers of her locked novel have clicked into place, opening a door and allowing her to view her novel's architecture. Once this happens, she must figure out how to move the reader through that time and space smoothly.

"The events in our lives happen in sequence in time," Eudora Welty wrote, "but in their significance to ourselves they find their own order, a timetable not necessarily—perhaps not possibly—chronological. The time as we know it objectively is often the chronology that stories and novels follow: it is the continuous thread of revelation."

Unlike real time, fictional time can be expanded, compressed, manipulated—even put into slow motion if that's what suits the needs of a story. To help yourself understand how this works, consider a day in your own life. If you try to record every single thing that happens from the time the alarm wakes you in the morning until you drift off to sleep near midnight, you will quickly get bogged down with boring, inconsequential details. You woke, you got up, you brushed your teeth, you ate Cheerios for breakfast. Who cares? Keep going anyway, until you have a page or two, then look at what you have and highlight what happened that was *significant* in some way. Maybe you wrote, "Mother called." If she calls a lot and never says anything of consequence, you'll skip this. But what if it's the first time she's called you in a year? Will it be the first thing you mention if you're asked how your day was? Will it fall somewhere in the middle? Will it be the *only* thing you tell? Will you go back in time and describe your relationship?

Back to our man on the cell phone. In a list of what happened to him that day, is the fact that he was talking on his cell phone on the way to a funeral significant? Probably not, if it's a funeral he's attending as an outward show of respect to a client's family. But what if he's a guy who came of age in the sixties and this is his college roommate's funeral? He's driving to the cemetery, remembering what it was like to be nineteen and full of passion, determined to make the world a better place. And his cell phone rings. "It's come to this," he thinks. "Pogo was right: 'We have met the enemy and he is us.'" The phone call is a significant moment in his day. He might even choose it as a significant moment in his whole life.

To see the big picture of your novel, list the scenes and events you have decided on in chronological order, then ask yourself:

- What is the range of time between the first and last scene? Years? Months? Days? Hours?
- Are there gaps in time between the significant moments of the novel?

- Do you notice a cluster of important events that occur at or near the same time?
- Which scenes mark transitions in the character's story?
- Are there moments that demand full rendering, others that might simply be reported?
- Is there any one scene that best evokes the theme of the novel? Where does it fall in time?
- If you could spotlight one thing in this whole series of events, what would it be?

Exploring these and other questions will help you find the "now" of your novel and decide how to handle the various levels of time that will come into play as the main character moves through it. "Start as near to the end as possible," advised writer Vesle Fenstermaker. Avoid long introductory "information dumps" that describe and explain events leading up to the heart of the story. Generally, the less time a novel covers in present time, the better. A shorter time frame requires fewer decisions to make, fewer transitions to effect. The larger the time frame, the more diffuse its impact. A shorter time frame is more likely to result in the essence of real life on the page.

In most cases, the structure of a book, how it moves through time, is dictated by the evolution of the story. Most likely, the structure of your novel will be revealed to you through a process of trial and error, in moments of combustion that bring insight after long periods of frustration or despair.

Still, knowing the conventions of structure and observing how other writers improvise to create unique structures for their novels will help.

Of course, the easiest way to tell a story is in simple chronological order. The shorter the time frame, the simpler the plot, the easier it is to tell a story in this direct manner. Yet if told chronologically, novels that cover many years can have the same plodding feel as that five-year-old's account of her day. *And then, and then, and then*. To hold the reader's interest, you must cast a web of tension over the whole stretch of time, raising and answering questions as you move through the events of the novel.

Theodore Weesner's *The True Detective*, which covered the several days following an abduction of child, was told chronologically, in multiple points of view. "To sustain the overall story, I had to connect moments that allowed for the development of the story and for the progression in time," he says. "Each character had to have a narrative line unfolding that was interesting on its own. I'd think about the mother, for example. What is her story and how do I make it arch in the novel? What is Matt's story? What is the detective's story? How can I interweave them so that there's always progression of their individual story as well as the overall story?"

Most novelists use a chronological structure, using flashback to inform the action in present time—perhaps because this structure most mirrors real life. "What person in the world goes through life in a straight line?" Gail Godwin asked an interviewer. "I'm sure as you drove up this driveway, you were not totally in the present moment: you were all over your life, maybe in your dreams as well. I think that most people, whether aware of it or not, are never in one place or time. We have this idea of linear time imposed on us. That's why we have such trouble with concepts like eternity, heaven and hell, and all that. If you start looking at it, it's all here and now."

Using flashbacks effectively is the key to making this time structure work on the page. A flashback may be as short as a sentence or as long as a whole chapter or section. A past event is most easily revealed through straight narrative all at once, but you can also feed it to the reader bit by bit, using memory, dialogue, letters, diaries, and news articles. The skillful use of flashback greatly enhances a novel's effect. Just remember that every time you move from the now of the novel, you risk jarring the reader out of the fictive dream. If you decide to handle time in your book this way, consider the following as you work flashbacks into the text:

- Each flashback must be necessary, carrying information that informs the action in present time.
- You must make transitions that move the reader smoothly from one time to another. Sometimes you can indicate the move to a different time by a different verb tense. Sometimes separating one time from another by white space or a chapter break is enough.

- Take care not to make the flashbacks so long that they deflect the forward movement of the story.
- Avoid flashbacks within flashbacks. To avoid creating confusion for the reader, keep the various levels of time straight in your own mind and keep them in good balance on the page.

If you discover that the novel you want to write deals equally with two or more distinct periods of time, you may structure it to reflect this by alternating sections. Maybe each section will be of comparable length, moving the reader through the separate times in a steady pattern. Maybe you will begin the novel in the present, introducing the past a little at a time, lengthening the flashbacks gradually until each time is getting equal space. Regardless of how you present these different times, you must do it in such a way that the reader goes from time one to the other willingly, but with lingering questions that will make him equally willingly return to the time where he started.

Another way to structure two distinct periods is to create a frame. You may begin the story in present time, jump to the crux of the story in the past, then circle back to the present with the sense that there has been some resolution.

Ha Jin's novel *Waiting* begins about two-thirds of the way through the actual chronology of events covered by the novel with the sentence, "Every summer, Lin Kong returned to Goose Village to divorce his wife, Shuyu." Ha tells the story of that summer, then backtracks to the beginning of the marriage, retracing it from beginning to end. "The idea of how to start a story helped me construct *Waiting*," he says. "Chekhov advised young writers to break their stories in half, throw away the first half and start with the second half. The advice implies that a story should start as closely as possible to the center of the drama."

Perhaps none of these time frames suits the novel you have in mind. "Forget that appalling narrative business of the realist: getting from lunch to dinner," Virginia Woolf declared—and breaking every rule by which novels had been judged in the past, wrote *Mrs. Dalloway*, one of the greatest novels of the twentieth century. The truth is, some of the best, most original novels ever written move through time in a way that is uniquely their own. Michael Cunningham tips his hat to Woolf in his Pulitzer Prize–winning *The Hours*, which tracks twenty-four hours in a fictional Woolf's life, alternating those chapters with twenty-four-hour periods in the lives of two other women, each living in a different era.

Penelope Lively's *Moon Tiger*, winner of England's prestigious Booker Prize, moves back and forth between present and past, flashbacks opening into flashbacks as its main character lies in a hospital bed reliving her life. The narrator of Alice McDermott's *That Night* presents a single, violent incident in the first pages of the novel, then moves backward and forward in time to tell all that happened before and after it, sometimes taking the reader through four or five layers of time in a single page.

Once you settle on how to move your story through time, you can divide the text into chapters or sections in any way you see fit. Time may be the governing factor, but it could as easily be place or character. Again, there are no rules. Look for the natural stopping places and consider the reader's attention span. Do your best to move her through the architecture of the novel as comfortably as you move her through the various scenes.

Seeing It Through

"A true novelist is one who doesn't quit."
— JOHN GARDNER

DESCRIBING THE PARTICULAR CHALLENGES of writing a novel, Patricia Henley says, "My life as a short story writer went like this: I would write a draft in maybe a week or ten days, let it sit maybe for a week or ten days, revise it for a couple of weeks. In a month or six weeks, I would have a story. Maybe I would go back to it in another month or so, but I could have a sense of completion and take some time off. Live my life. Writing a novel requires so much more letting go of the rest of your life."

This alternate reality, your novel, is a constant, powerful presence in your real life: delicious, seductive, maddening. Suddenly, in the middle of dinner or a game of Frisbee, your characters come alive in your head; they say or do something that you must write down *immediately* or risk forgetting it. Then you sit down to a full day of writing and they go completely cold on you, leaving you blank, panicked, incapable of working, and unfit company for family or friends. Months and months pass. Years. And you are still trying to utter these characters into the visible.

Seeing a novel through requires massive amounts of intellectual, emotional, and physical energy. "There is a peasant in every novelist," F. Scott Fitzgerald said, perhaps commenting on the sheer drudgery of the form. Michael Chabon thinks it's "like a war: always begun in the highest enthusiasm, with full confidence of right, and of the certainty of it all being over by Christmas. Two years later you're in the trenches and the mud, with defeat a real possibility, doubting everything, in particular the wisdom of the commanding general."

Some writers work steadily, when they can. Other writers work in spurts—maybe because they work best that way, maybe because that's the only schedule their busy lives allow. There are novelists who write their books in white heat, in total isolation.

Each novelist must find the time, place, and energy to write her novel. It's up to you to discover the way to write yours. Perhaps, like Dorothy Allison, you work best at night. By all means, write all night if you can! But if you make your living at a nine-to-five job, you may have to do your writing in the evening hours. Or you could get up at four in the morning and work a few hours before the day's demands are upon you.

But be realistic. Even if you don't have to make a living, you surely have responsibilities and relationships to tend. Which obligations in your life are nonnegotiable? Which might be renegotiated or even let go? Do you have time slots you can give to the novel? How much time do you spend watching television, for example? The most simple solution to finding time to write a novel may be to *turn it off* and spend those hours inside your own head.

Once you find time to write your novel, do your best to develop a healthy relationship with it. "Every good book, every bad book, and all the great books, too, were all written a little at a time," Richard Bausch wisely says. "A day's work, over and over for a period of months or years."

What is reasonable to expect from a day's work? This depends on the way you write. Some people write quickly, pile up the pages—twenty or even thirty pages a day. Other writers are happy to get two or three good pages in a day; ten would feel like a small miracle to them. Remember: no formula! Figure out what a good day is for *you*. Write as regularly as you possibly can. The longer you stay away from your novel, the harder it will be to get back into it again.

Strict schedules and production goals work well for some writers, but they cause others to freeze up. Again, you must look at yourself, your life, and this particular day's work. If the novel goes cold on you, it serves no purpose to sit at your desk for seven hours just because you said you would. Wash the dishes, take a run, do some gardening, help out at the soup kitchen, go fishing: you're not really abandoning your novel, you're putting a layer of activity on top of it. Perhaps, rod and reel in hand, the waves lapping at the edges of your fishing boat, the conversation between your main character and her mother will resolve itself in your head and suddenly you'll know, beyond doubt, what the conflict is really about.

Finding a community of writers to support you in the long process of birthing a novel can be a huge help. If you are lucky enough to have a writers' center in your town, join it. Pick and choose among its programs with an eye to connecting with writers with whom you are compatible. Attending writers' conferences is another way to connect with fellow writers. Attend readings and lectures related to books and writing, frequent bookstores and cafes where writers hang out, tack a notice to the bulletin board in your local grocery store. Some writers look to the Internet for kindred spirits.

If you can't find a writers' support group, start one. The purpose of the group may be to critique manuscripts, or it may be a regular time you set aside for shoptalk. Nobody knows better what it's like to live inside a book than another novelist, working to achieve his own vision.

The technical and emotional problems that you might face between the conception of a novel and the moment you type "The End"—and really mean it—are countless and infinitely varied. Here are some problems you might encounter in the writing process and suggestions for dealing with them.

You don't know how to begin.

Legend has it that E. L. Doctorow sat for forty-five minutes one day and no thought came. So he typed "the wall," because that's what he was looking at, then "the room," then "the house," then "1902." Then he wrote *Ragtime.* Perhaps this is true; perhaps . . . embroidered. It is certainly true, however, that you will get nowhere if you do nothing but sit and stare at the blank page. So, like Doctorow, just start typing. Write anything and call it a beginning. Remember that the first sentence of a published novel is very rarely the first sentence the author wrote. Consider the way scaffolding is constructed to allow workers access to a building-in-progress, then torn down when the building is finished. Write scaffolding. Pull it away when the novel can stand on its own.

You haven't done any of the exercises in this book or any other work to develop your idea. You just want to start writing.

Go for it! Use the exercises to help you shake things loose when you get stuck along the way.

You started, but the book feels cold when you sit down to write. It seems to take forever to get to the point where you're seeing the scenes, hearing your characters talk.

It would probably be impossible to find a novelist who did not have this problem, at least once in a while. In fact, why not write this quote from Hemingway on an index card and keep it on your desk for such moments? "I would stand and look out over the roofs of Paris and think, 'Do not worry. You have always written and you will write now. All you have to do is write one true sentence. Write the truest sentence that you know.' So finally I would write that one true sentence, and then go on from there."

Many writers develop strategies for getting to that "one true sentence" as quickly as possible. Hemingway stopped when his work was going well, when he knew what would happen next, so that when he sat down to work the next day he knew where and how to begin. Eudora Welty left a page in her typewriter with an unfinished sentence on it. A. Manette Ansay poses a technical question at the end of every writing session as a way of easing herself into the next day's work.

Finally, things are cooking. Your characters are living out a scene inside your head and all you have to do is watch them and write. But then, suddenly, you realize that you're missing some crucial bit of information. Do you tag that spot somehow and keep going? Do you stop writing and do the research?

The nature of what's missing best dictates the solution to the problem. If you can keep going without doing the research, *keep going*. Fix it later. If the missing information is crucial in defining the outcome for the scene, you'd better head for the library or segue to the Internet.

You don't know what's going to happen next, but you're pretty sure about something in the middle. Or maybe you know what the end will be.

Don't stew over that unknown thing. Write the scene you can imagine. With luck, something will happen in it that will give you the key to the stuck place.

You know what's going to happen next, but you can't make a transition to it.

Leave space for now, write what happens next, and go back to the transition later. Or look at the last paragraph and see if you can carry a word, an idea, or an image forward to the next section. Consider a simple transition like, "Two weeks later . . ." or "Back in Waco . . ." Or just leave a white space between one section and the next. Sometimes that gives a reader all the transition she needs. Or leave a space for now, write the next scene, and go back to the transition later.

You know what's going to happen next, but you just can't seem to write the scene.

Flesh out your answers to the questions in "The Elements of Fiction" to clarify the crucial elements in it: who, what, when, where, why. Freewriting responses to the questions may trigger an idea or sentence that will give you entry to the scene. If that happens, abandon the exercise and write the scene.

If you get to the end of the worksheet and still feel you can't start, try writing a brief narrative describing what happens in the scene. Consider the narrative a first draft and work to bring it alive with description, characterization, and dialogue.

If you still can't make it work, maybe the material doesn't actually require a full-blown scene, and a narrative passage is all you will need to move the novel along.

You have no idea what will happen next. Period.

Write "What if?" Freewrite an answer. Write "What if?" again. And again and again and again. Consider the most absurd possibilities. If freewriting doesn't work, give your analytical mind a shot at the problem. Make a list of scenes, study the progression of them. List all the places your character could go from this juncture, and consider what might happen in any one of them. If you're still getting nowhere, try reading all you've written so far to see if an idea for continuing floats up. Or give the manuscript to a good reader to whom what should happen next might seem obvious. Still stumped? Take a walk, go to the gym, cook a fabulous meal. Let your subconscious work toward one of those moments of combustion that will get you going again.

Days have passed and you still don't know what happens next. Do you have writer's block?

Maybe, though no two writers agree on exactly what writer's block *is*.

There is the kind of writer's block just described: "I'm stuck. I've reached a wall and I don't have a clue about how to get beyond it." But at another time, you might feel overwhelmed by so many images, so much knowledge about your characters, that you can't determine what is most important and find a clear path. Or you might see the path, see the characters moving through scenes in your mind's eye—and for some unknown reason be unable to conjure them to the page. You might feel absolutely empty, with no ideas at all, or none that seem worth writing about.

Writer's block is just another problem to solve. The problem may be simple or complex; it may take moments or years to solve. Objective analysis might give you direction; feedback from a good reader might allow you to see possibilities you hadn't seen before. Freewriting might yield the "one true sentence" to carry you back into the flow of the novel. Try anything, everything. *Keep* trying. If you're stubborn enough, you'll break the block and be able to go on.

You can write; that's not a problem. Your characters are alive on the page, going off on all kinds of interesting tangents—but you have no idea where the novel is going.

You may not need to know exactly where the novel's going at this point. It might be perfectly fine to let the book take its own course and sort it all out in the revision process. But if the focus of the novel feels unclear to you, proceeding this way may be a waste of your time.

In either case, you'd probably benefit from taking a break from writing to clarify what the novel is about. Complete this sentence: "This is a story about what happens when . . ." This will help you establish and/or clarify the focus. Then consider each tangent in terms of how it deepens the reader's understanding of the characters and the situation. Cut those that don't apply or are repetitive. Before returning to the novel, you might try brainstorming ideas for scenes that might help move the novel toward resolution.

Just remember, there's no guarantee that a focus fix at this point in the process will be final. It's not uncommon for a novel to shift focus as it evolves. You may complete the first draft (or the second or the third) and find that the novel is telling you it really wants to be about something else. It might be right. So pay attention.

Somewhere along the line, the book took a turn, and you suddenly find yourself writing a completely different story.

It could be that all you wrote before the moment the story turned was a kind of scaffolding, that somehow, in the drafting process, you arrived at the true heart of the story. If this is the case, after cutting the material, rejoice, rethink, refocus, and proceed.

On the other hand, you may have followed the characters into a blind alley. If that's the case, you'll have to go backward to the place where the book went wrong and start the discovery process again, moving your characters toward the resolution of your original idea. This will almost surely feel discouraging, but take heart in knowing that you are not alone. Books get away from writers all the time. "They all got away from me," John Yount says, "every single one of them, and they had to be rescued constantly from error and wrongheadedness, even thrown away or burned and begun again from the very first line."

You hate your novel. The very idea of it seems stupid to you at this point. When you read over what you've written so far, it seems crushingly boring. You think, "Maybe I should just quit."

All novelists feel discouraged about their novels-in-process from time to time. Chances are, this explains the doubts you're having about your own book. On the other hand, maybe it really *is* boring. If the feeling persists, you'd better take a close look at everything about the book and, perhaps with the help of a good reader, figure out why. Is the plot too predictable? Too dense, leaving no room for the characters' emotional development? Or is there no plot at all, just endless emotional musing? Are the characters too predictable? Are you allowing yourself to stay open to possibilities for their development? Are you shying away from material that would bring much-needed tension to the interaction among them? Is the time frame of the novel too long? Could you collapse it for better tension on the page? If your assessment shows that there's something fundamentally wrong with the book, your work time is probably better spent in rethinking the novel than it is in forging onward with it.

But what's the point, really — when I'm so clearly lacking in talent?

Well, maybe. Depending on what you think talent is. Conventional wisdom insists that it's some inborn "word gene" that makes it easy to write. But writing isn't easy for anyone. And while there may be a word gene that contributes to a talented writer's accomplishments, those writers have their own idea about what real talent is. It's curiosity, according to Theodore Weesner. Perseverance, according to Wally Lamb. Compulsion, according to Thomas Mann.

"Talent is, with luck, one of the two out of three required elements for success, both artistic and material, as a writer, over which the writer has absolutely no control, and for which he or she can take no credit at all," Michael Chabon says. "The third absolutely required element, and the only one the writer can both ensure and take pride in, is discipline."

Chabon continues, "My view of talent is like that of the catcher Crash Davis in *Bull Durham*, when he's lecturing Nuke LaLoosh on the importance of discipline in pitching: 'God reached down and turned your right arm into a thunderbolt. It has nothing to do with you.' Literary talent is an accident of birth, like the ability to spot four-leaf clovers, and about as meaningful in the absence of hard work."

So decide what you think talent is before you browbeat yourself about not having it. Remember why you wanted to write a novel in the first place, and what Flaubert had to say on the topic: "Talent is a long patience, and originality an effort of will and of intense observation."

Revision

"The best part of all, the absolutely delicious part,
is finishing it and then doing it over again."
— TONI MORRISON

THERE IS NOTHING BETTER than the feeling you get when you write the last words of a novel. "Finished," you think — "at last!" Maybe the book really is finished; more than likely, it's not. In any case, avoid the impulse to start looking for a publisher immediately. Set the manuscript aside for awhile, concentrate on other things, and come back to it when you're ready and able to look at it with a cold eye.

When you think you're capable of doing that, sit down and read the novel from beginning to end, jotting notes as you go. What's there? What's not there? Since it's your novel — in a sense, made of you — it's impossible to completely separate the novel you managed to get on the page from the novel you meant and hoped to write. And on the second, third . . . tenth draft of a novel, the ghosts of scenes, characters, and ideas you've abandoned complicate this problem.

This is where the real work of novel writing begins, where you begin to see what the novel actually can be. "You have to be very patient and realize that there are so many things you don't know, that you can only find out by writing the book," Patricia Henley says. "And then you have to rewrite it, sometimes many, many, many times."

Ultimately, you must do the hard work of revision yourself. Some novelists believe this so strongly that they won't let anyone look at their work until they declare it finished and ready for publication. But a good reader — or readers — may be able to shorten the revision process, particularly by helping you discover the problems you need to address. "I never have an editor, and I don't discuss what I'm working on with *anybody* — not my publisher, not my agent," Isabel Allende says. "When I think I have a final draft, I send a copy to my mother in Chile. She knows that I'm writing, but even she hasn't the slightest idea what it's about. Then she takes a plane—and a red pencil—and comes to visit me. We·spend the next month locked in a room, fighting."

If your mother is too inclined to praise, you might choose a member of your writing group or a professional editor, who will bring his knowledge of craft to reading your novel. You might give it to someone who just loves books for a reader's perspective—or find a serious book club willing to read and discuss it.

Whoever you give it to, it is important to listen carefully to any criticism you are given and make an objective assessment of it. Did the reader understand what you were attempting with the novel? Do her criticisms seem to suggest changes in your fundamental idea of what the novel is? Is it possible that some preconceived notions of life and/or literature are interfering with her ability to give you useful criticism?

Sometimes you can't answer these questions immediately. A reader's comments may seem all wrong the first time you read them—they may even infuriate you. But it's possible that, as time goes by, you will begin to see some merit in them.

Good revision demands ruthless objectivity. You must be open to all possibilities, willing to do whatever is necessary to bring the finished novel closer to the ideal. You must be patient. You might revise your novel successfully the first time around, but it might take many revisions. If you are fortunate enough to sell your novel, it is likely that you will find yourself revising it again under an editor's direction.

At the most difficult times, remember that revision is a natural part of writing a novel. It gives the book its polish, makes it feel seamless, real. If you believe this is true, it helps. It helps even more if you can learn to enjoy revision, to regard the novel as a puzzle to solve. In any case, approaching revision is easier if you can create a set of questions to answer, and identify specific problems to address.

Novelists approach revision differently, of course. One writer might revise as he goes along, sentence by sentence, page by page, or chapter by chapter. Another may hurry through the first draft, then assess what he has and go at it again—and again and again.

Different novels may require different approaches to revision. A writer used to revising as she goes along may capture a voice so strong that she feels compelled to write without judgment until the story is told. A writer accustomed to hurrying through the first draft may get halfway through and realize something is fundamentally wrong with what he's done so far—to go on would be a waste of time. He must go back and revise before he can move forward. Regardless of when in the process you approach revision, it is good to be able to diagnose the problems you'll need to address as you work toward bringing the written novel closer to your vision.

LANGUAGE: CLARITY AND STYLE

With luck, revision will be a matter of going back through the manuscript and tending to language issues, solving problems of clarity and style. Is it clear to the reader exactly what's happening in a scene? Does the dialogue clearly convey the characters' thoughts and feelings? Does the description create a clear picture in mind's eye? Do the transitions make a clear path from one part of the story to the next?

To achieve this kind of clarity, the novelist must work at the sentence level, considering syntax, punctuation, and vocabulary until each sentence in the novel says exactly what she means for it to say and connects smoothly and logically to the sentence before and after it.

Style poses a different set of questions about language. Are the tone and voice of the novel appropriate for the story it tells? If so, is the novel's tone sustained throughout, or are there places where the choice of words, syntax, and rhythm of sentences create wrong notes that will jar the reader, spoiling the overall effect? Does your dialogue capture the cadence of real people speaking—*your* people, each one with a lifetime of experiences that have brought him to this moment? Does the world you describe reflect and underpin the lives of the characters you've invented in it?

Solving style problems requires an intuitive approach. The novelist must ask, "Does this sound right?" She must accept that there's no definitive answer to the question, and trust her ear and instinct—and perhaps the advice of a good reader—to know when the problem is solved.

CUTTING AND EXPANDING

Some novelists easily write a voluminous first draft. Assuming that a novel written like this is structurally sound and there's just too much of it, revising will involve cutting scenes, description, and narrative passages that aren't necessary to move the novel forward, either because they are outside the book's focus or because they repeat something the reader already knows. If you work this way, you must learn to look at your draft with an objective eye so that you can identify what the novel can use. You must develop the courage and discipline that will allow you to cut the rest—even good writing, writing you love—in the service of the story. As Faulkner said, "You must learn to kill off your darlings."

If your first draft is no more than the bare bones of your story, your challenge will be to figure out what's missing, then reopen your mind to creative possibilities as you work back through the book from beginning to end, layering in additional scenes, details, dialogue, and narrative to deepen the effect. Sometimes a novelist who works this way skims over things that need to be researched, leaving them to be laid into subsequent drafts. So he must attend to research during the revision process as well.

These opposite types of revision are not mutually exclusive. Even if your major revision task is cutting, some of the scenes you retain may not yet be fully rendered, and crucial characters may not be fully developed; on the other hand, a spare first draft may include unnecessary scenes, characters, or narrative.

CHARACTERIZATION

Sometimes, revising, you realize that a character doesn't quite make it to the page in the first draft. Perhaps his behavior doesn't make sense, based on what readers know about him. To solve this problem, you'll have to delve deeper into your character's life to discover past experiences that shaped the action of the novel. When you know him better, you can work back through the book, adding telling details, flashbacks, and/or scenes that will bring the character more fully alive on the page.

A character whose behavior contradicts the principles of human psychology poses a more difficult problem. For example, child abuse and alcoholism exhibit themselves in patterns of behavior that affect the individual development and family dynamics of fictional characters in the same way they affect real people's lives. If you have created a psychologically inaccurate character, it is usually for one or both of the following reasons: ignorance about some aspect of the character's life or some personal prejudice that prevents you from considering the character objectively.

You can overcome ignorance through research. Your character's point of view may be affected by cultural traditions you are unfamiliar with, or perhaps her behavior is affected by a psychological disorder that manifests itself in specific patterns of behavior. Books, movies, interviews, and observation will help you to discover what's wrong with the thoughts and behaviors you have attributed to her. Don't stop with a little bit of information: try to understand the full range of behavior and effect so that, rethinking your character, you'll come up with a solution that is believable because it suits her personality and situation.

Novelists with an agenda, political or personal, are most often the ones whose prejudices keep them from creating characters with a strong psychological base. A sure indication of this problem is a character that is all good or all evil. Unfortunately, such writers rarely discover this problem in their own work, and usually aren't happy when a reader or reviewer points it out to them. So, to the best of your ability, be honest with yourself. Remember Faulkner's advice: "Watch people, never judge. Watch what they do without intolerance. Learn." Curiosity is the best antidote to prejudice. If you realize that prejudice is influencing your novel, do whatever you must do to put yourself in your character's shoes. Try to see the world as she sees it, based on her life experiences. Learn to see all humankind in its maddening, glorious complexity.

But beware: the insights you gain doing this kind of character work may change *you* so much that rethinking your novel may result in a story you never imagined you would write.

FOCUS AND STRUCTURE

Almost every novel you write will surprise you in some way, making it necessary to reconsider the book's focus and structure. Perhaps putting a main character in action on the page revealed something that changed the direction of the novel; or a minor character became important to the book in a way you didn't imagine at the outset. Maybe a scene expanded or contracted, taking on more or less significance than you had anticipated. Or people and places you never imagined at the outset suddenly appeared.

The surprises that occur during the writing process are one of the great pleasures of writing novels, but you must learn to look at them objectively. When a new character or idea appears, tempting you to go off in some new direction, ask yourself if this change in direction enhances the focus of the novel or obscures it. If you believe the change enhances focus, you must identify where that new character or idea entered the novel, then go back to the beginning and work up to that place, underpinning the new element in such a way that its presence throughout the whole novel feels natural. The finished novel should feel seamless. The reader should have no reason to guess that the addition wasn't a part of your original plan.

Sena Jeter Naslund understood from the beginning of *Ahab's Wife* that her novel would have a three-pronged structure. The three marriages of Una Spenser that were implied in the book's first sentence: "Captain Ahab was neither my first husband nor my last." When asked if she knew that Ishmael would be the third husband from the outset, she says, "No. It came to me as I went along." An early draft did not include the scene in which Una catches Ishmael's eye in the ship's passageway. Naslund inserted it in revision, to underpin the novel's outcome.

Talking about finding the structure of his novels, Peter Cameron observes, "It seems to me that to get an idea I have to conceive [the architecture] of a book more ambitiously than it turns out to be. Then in process it gets simplified and scaled down."

Repairing a flaw in structure is probably the most challenging kind of revision you will face, for it will require you to consider your work on the most fundamental level. Essentially, structure is the way a story is told. It usually involves reconsidering the novel's point of view and/or its time frame. If structural flaws are extreme, it may be necessary to reconceive the book completely.

If you have structural problems, it is helpful to sort out your revision tasks in terms of those that are "local" and those that are "global." Local revision involves work at the sentence and scene levels, checking off tasks one by one. Global revision requires consideration of the entire novel.

Our man in the Mercedes, for example—the casket salesman. He just doesn't seem right to you. So you track his movement through the novel to see if you can discover why. Revising locally, you look for places where you can deepen the effect of characterization by deleting details that seem wrong and/or adding new details.

Looking globally, you search for patterns. For example, you might notice that every time the cell phone rings, he turns off the CD player blasting in his car before he answers it. Tracking dialogue throughout the draft, you notice how many references he makes to rock stars. And for heaven's sake, there's a copy of *Rolling Stone* in the back seat. The job you chose for him is all wrong, you realize. This guy's actually a frustrated lead guitarist who sold out to become a concert promoter. Now the Mercedes, the expensive suits, the bitterness begin to make sense to you. Things fall into place and you go back to the start, working locally, scene by scene, to bring this new version of the man to the page.

The more you read and study novels, the more you learn about the craft of fiction and how novels work, the easier it will be for you to see the flaws in your own work and figure out how to correct them. Sometimes you'll find the solution to a problem lies within the work itself. Describing this phenomenon, Eudora Welty wrote, "It's strange how in revision you find some little unconsidered thing which is so essential that you not only keep it in but give it preeminence when you revise. Sometimes in the dead of night, it will come to me. 'Well, that's what I should do, that's what I'm working toward!' It was there all the time."

STRATEGIES FOR REVISION

First, Read!

Before you do anything, sit down and read your manuscript. Then free-write answers to these questions—and any others that float up as you read. You might ask a good reader to do the same, then compare your responses.

The Shape and Focus of the Novel

- Which character do you think the novel is mostly about?
- What about that character's situation is interesting enough to sustain a novel?
- What is the central problem or tension in the story? Is there enough tension?
- Based on the beginning, what issues do you think the reader will expect the novel to address?
- What is the time frame of the novel? (How many hours, days, months . . . will pass from the beginning of the novel to the end of it?)
- How important is the past to the novel? How do past events inform and affect the action in present time?
- Are there other ways you think this story could be told? Do you sense any conflict between what the novel wants to be and the author wants it to be?
- Does this novel remind you of any particular published novel? What might be learned by comparing the two?

How the Novel Works

- Does it have a strong beginning?
- Does it move through time smoothly, or are you sometimes confused? Pinpoint the places that confuse you.
- Is there a good balance between past and present?
- Are there jarring gaps that require stronger transitions?
- Is there information that doesn't belong and/or that seems out of place?
- Are the characters believable? Does anything they do seem contradictory to the information we have about them?
- Are there places that drag, places where you find yourself disconnected and skimming? Where? Why?
- Is there more than one point of view represented? Whose? Why? Does the story spend significantly more time in one point of view than the other(s)?
- In what way does the end circle back to resolve the issues introduced in the beginning?

"This Is a Story about What Happens When . . ."

Atlantic Monthly editor Michael Curtis offered this "trick" for seeing your story clearly. Finish the sentence "This is a story about what happens when . . ." using as much specific detail as you can. The finished sentence doesn't have to be beautiful; it just has to say clearly what the story is about. For example: This is a story about what happens when a casket salesman involved in a life-threatening automobile accident while talking to a client on the way to a funeral reassesses his priorities and finds a new life.

Finishing the sentence tells you what the story is about, gives you the arc of your story, and provides a standard against which to judge characters, scenes, ideas, and plot twists in your efforts to make sure that every single thing in the novel belongs there. Anything in the draft you're considering that doesn't bring clarity, depth, and complexity to the novel's focus should be abandoned.

The Left Brain, No-Fail Novel "Outline"

Especially if it's clear that your revision strategy will require a global approach, try this exercise, which, paradoxically, allows you to see the whole novel by focusing your mind on each small part.

Go through your manuscript page by page, typing or writing a brief (preferably one-line) description of what happens on each page, skipping a line between chapters. It's okay if this description is in a kind of shorthand that only you will understand.

This will take a long time, probably several work sessions. You may be tempted to quit because it feels pointless and so anal-retentive that you think it can't possibly have anything to do with the creative process. But keep going. Weirdly, keeping your left brain busy somehow allows the renegade right brain to range all over the place, triggering all kinds of useful ideas and observations once you get into the flow. So keep a notepad nearby to jot them down.

When you get to the end of the manuscript, before you consciously consider what insights you've gained, freewrite. Trust your right brain to tell you what you know. Let it surprise you.

Now consider what floated up as you wrote the "outline" and what you learned from freewriting as you make a list of things you want to look at closely. For example: character, description, the balance of scene and narrative, dialogue, transitions.

Isolate one item on your list and go through your "outline," highlighting each place this element appears on the page. Work through everything on your list, using a different color for each element.

You may track a character through the book, highlighting every place that character is present, mentioned, or even thought of. Insights and ideas often occur in this process, as they did when you went through the manuscript page by page. Jot them down, of course. But the greatest insights will most likely come when you finish the highlighting, spread the pages on the floor, and literally *see* the path of the character through the novel. Are there whole chapters or sections where the character is not there at all? If so, is his absence appropriate or do you need to find ways to weave him more tightly into the novel? What might those ways be? Scene? Narrative? Flashback?

Perhaps it occurs to you, looking at one character, that it would be helpful to see his relationship with another character more clearly. In this case, highlight the second character with a different color. Where do both colors appear on the same page? What happens between the characters on those pages? How does the accumulation of moments define—or fail to define—the relationship?

You can highlight for anything. If you notice a lot of narrative passages, highlight for both narrative and scene to see if they are in good balance. If your novel moves back and forth in time, highlight each level of time with a different color to help you see if one time dominates. If it has multiple points of view, highlight each. Is each character given equal space? Should each be given equal space? Is each different point of view necessary?

Perhaps tension concerns you. Consider the various elements in the novel that contribute to the overall tension, and highlight for each one. For example, if one of the novel's tensions lies in a character's fear that his girlfriend is pregnant, highlight every place in the book where pregnancy or anything relating to it comes into play. What do your discoveries about this and other tensions in the novel suggest in terms of heightening the tension throughout?

Where are the tense moments in the novel? Where, exactly, does the story torque? Are there enough torques, are they paced effectively, do they work? What do they suggest in terms of heightening the tension throughout?

When you've finished highlighting, spread the outline pages on the floor end to end. Viewed this way, the outline looks rather like a tapestry, the various elements threading their way through it. Let your eye take in the effect. Do the colors seem in proper balance? Are there any chapters that are significantly shorter or longer than the rest?

Now consider the elements you highlighted, one by one. Use your eye, your analytical skill, your intuition, and all you know about the craft of fiction to create a list of specific observations, questions, and tasks to consider during revision.

Index Cards

You can use 4 by 6 or 5 by 8 index cards to make a shortened version of the outline, using one card for each chapter. Summarize the "plot" of the chapter. If highlighting seems useful, highlight. Then write the answers to these questions (and/or any others that come to mind). Who's present? How many scenes are in the chapter? What's the balance of scene and narrative? How much time does the chapter cover in the "now" of the novel? How many levels of time are added by flashbacks? What's introduced? What's left hanging? What's resolved? What's at stake in the chapter? Where are the moments of tension? Where does the chapter torque? Jot down your observations as you go.

You can also use index cards to help you decide on the sequence of scenes, using one card for each scene. Write a summary of the scene. Answer the who/what/when/where/why questions for each, jotting down observations about character, time, and place as you go. Then play with the scenes. Organize them in a variety of ways to help you discover the best order for them to appear in the novel. Maybe some of them don't need to appear at all.

If you are using multiple points of view in your novel, you may modify either of the above exercises by using a different color index card for each point of view. This will help you establish the best sequence and balance of points of view in the book.

Charts

Charts help you see the relationship of one element of your novel to another. Making a chart may be as simple as listing a character's actions and thoughts in a scene or chapter, then writing the emotions they accompany next to them. Do the emotions make sense, based on a particular action? Do reactions fit the actions or thoughts that triggered them? Does the emotional movement of the chapter make sense, based on the series of thoughts and actions? You might create a grid, writing chapter names and numbers down the left side and the names of your characters across the top, and then putting an X in a character's box if she is present in a chapter. This will show you who's in a chapter — and who's not. A more extensive grid might include boxes in which to write what happens in the chapter, how the plot is moved, and what each character is doing on- or offstage.

Talking about his novel *Leap Year*, which has multiple points of view, Peter Cameron says, "There were so many characters and so much action I needed to keep track of it in some way. So I kept this notebook — a musical notebook with staffs. There was one staff for each character, so I could track in a linear way what they were doing. For every week there's a page with everybody on it. It was a way of visually looking at the book, mapping it out in a way I've never done with another book."

You might chart time by year, month, day, or even hour, depending on the structure of your novel. You might chart the elements of your plot to see how the story moves, where it torques. You might make a chart that lists each problem in your novel and the specific tasks you will undertake to solve it.

Each novel is different. Create any kind of chart that makes sense to you in your attempt to assess and solve your novel's problems.

Maps

You might make a map of your novel's setting to help you better understand how to move your characters through the physical reality of your novel. What you map will depend on what you need to know. Perhaps you need to see a whole town; perhaps only a neighborhood, or a farm with its land and outbuildings. Perhaps you need to see the floor plan of a house where some crucial action takes place. Or just one room: where the windows and doors are, how the furniture is arranged within.

Timelines and Calendars

Timelines can be useful in considering a novel's logistics or clarifying its backstory. A timeline might cover only the years, months, weeks, or days in the present time of your novel, or you might use it to consider the whole span of time that comes into play in the novel. Simply list in chronological order the years, months, weeks, or days you want to consider, then write down what happens in each one that is significant to the novel. Perhaps you'll notice patterns and possibilities. Maybe you'll see empty spaces or logistical gaffes. Considering a novel's backstory, you might track the significant events of several characters on the same timeline to make sure that references made in the text of the novel are possible and make emotional sense. Such an exercise might also suggest adjustments to the backstory that will tighten the narrative and allow the characters' pasts to merge in new and significant ways.

You might also use an actual calendar that encompasses the whole timeframe of the novel and write down the scenes that occur on each day as the book proceeds. This will help you see the novel's movement through time, often revealing insights about pace. Are things happening too slowly? Too quickly? Are there gaps in the action that need to be filled in somehow? Is there a time span in which most of the important action is clustered? If so, what does this tell you about what the time frame of the book should be?

Freewriting and Research

Freewriting and research are strategies best used to solve problems in a novel, one by one. Freewriting, letting your subconscious mind consider a problem, is often the easiest and best way to find a solution to it. Let your characters talk to you and reveal themselves.

Write "What if _____?" and see what you say. Keep going, even when what you write seems pointless or even absurd. Such absurdities often follow what's predictable and make a bridge to some thought that is completely new. And while we're on the subject of the subconscious: pay attention to your dreams. The images they evoke and the odd connections they make may reflect your unconscious mind at work and, when considered, offer insight or even a coded solution to some problem that is driving you crazy.

Research has obvious advantages: you search for something you need to know, and find it. Thus, you are able to solve a certain kind of problem in your novel. But research can be serendipitous as well. In the process of learning what you need to know, you find things you'd never have thought to look for. Such discoveries may trigger solutions to problems you weren't trying to solve through that research, or reveal problems you didn't know you had. Often, the little surprises of research offer new possibilities for plot, character, scene and/or backstory.

As in many aspects of life, necessity is the mother of invention. Novelists stumped by their novels come up with all kinds of tricks and techniques for looking at what's there and figuring out what to do about it. "Once I printed all the pages of a manuscript-in-progress and taped them to the wall in order, and I did a revision that way, scribbling on the walls," Sheri Reynolds says. There are countless ways to look at a novel, each one likely to reveal some small or large aspect of it that could be improved.

In fact, you could revise forever—and some novelists do! In their drive for perfection, they forget the most basic truth of the creative process: perfection is not possible. The novel you see in your mind's eye, the shape you sense inside yourself, must be translated to words; but words are a second language to the heart. Ultimately, they fail us. The trick to good revision is not only accepting that this is true, but regarding the challenge of making the gap between the novel inside you and the one in the world as small as it can be.

There's no rule, no formula to tell you when a novel is finished, yet declaring your novel finished is one of the most important decisions you will make. You must be patient enough to keep on through the most difficult times, determined to bring the novel to its full potential. You must also resist the impulse toward perfection, and learn to recognize the moment when revision begins to make the novel worse instead of better. As Toni Morrison says, "All art is knowing when to stop."

The Interviews

Dorothy Allison

Dorothy Allison is the author of two novels, a collection of stories, a collection of essays, and a memoir. Born in Greenville, South Carolina, she received a BA from Florida Presbyterian College (now Eckerd College) and an MA from New School for Social Research. The poverty, incest, and abuse that Allison experienced as a child figure heavily in her first novel, *Bastard out of Carolina*, which was nominated for the National Book Award. Other honors include Lambda Literary Awards for Best Small Press Book and Best Lesbian Book. Allison is a popular workshop teacher and lecturer. She lives in California with her partner and their son.

Trash, 1988 (stories); *Bastard Out of Carolina*, 1992; *Cavedweller*, 1998

How do you approach and sustain work on your novels?

I've watched my whole life recircle, alter significantly. I think that part of it's having a kid. Some of writing is so deliciously self-indulgent: you just live in your bathrobe or your pajamas for days. I work long binge sessions — in a state of misery and sweat, rocking back and forth and wringing my hands, or in exultation. Most of my life, even though I lived with other people, I had my own private space and nobody would go in there. Then I went and had a child. We were living up in Sonoma County and my compromise was to go out to a little building on our property to write. But that didn't really work.

When you're finishing a novel, you've got all these balls up in the air, and to get them up in the air, keep everything in your head is an intense emotional job. If it is interrupted, you can lose a book. I learned that the hard way: by losing a couple. After some terrific bouts with my own psyche, I developed the practice of going to stay with other people when I was finishing, or I would check into a motel. But I keep feeling I'm doing it wrong. I continually try to be reasonable, to work at reasonable hours while Wolf's in school, but it doesn't work that way. I work in the middle of the night the best and I work binges.

There's nothing reasonable about the process. It's a completely unreasonable process. It makes me feel like I'm guilty, like I'm sinning against being a good mama—and it's a big issue for me to be a good mama. When we were about to make Wolf, I went and read everything I could find about what it was like to be a writer and have a kid, because I could set the gay and lesbian movement back a thousand years by raising a fucked-up child. Or not being able to write when I have a kid, because I'm a feminist and I'm arguing that you can do that. Then for years I tried to pretend, "Oh, no problem." But it's a terrible problem! I've lost whole books, and acknowledging that is difficult.

When you say you lost whole books, what do you mean? Describe that.

Well, there's the sneaky way and there's the God-help-me-it's-gone way. The sneaky way is that you don't know it's gone until it's gone. You have to get enough of it done when the tide is up inside to be able to do the long work of living in the novel. If you don't get enough of it down, you will lose it, or it will become something else. Then you lose what you were originally going to do and you have to make peace with what you wind up with.

Isn't there always that gap between what you hope and envision a novel will be and what the novel actually is?

Yes. That's a given. But having it *shift*! I started working on *Cavedweller* when I was still working on *Bastard*. I started it with Cissy, the young girl. I started with this incredibly angry, resentful, God-help-me-I-don't-want-to-be-in-the-South kind of little girl. I was pretty clear that I wanted to write about sisters who really have every reason to hate each other and who make a kind of accommodation. I started it before I had Wolf, and I wrote it mean, really mean. I knew that her mother was a drunk, that she'd been a rock-and-roller and was just a terrible mother. I knew she was going to be trying to be a good mother; that was going to be what the story was about. I wanted the background of this woman to be someone who really hated herself and couldn't forgive herself. But she was minor, except for the violence.

Then I had this kid. Instead of writing about this girl, I was being a mom. There was a year in which I couldn't work at all, and I lost the book. I just lost it. And when I went back to it, I wasn't Cissy anymore. I was Delia. I was dealing with all my guilt. Was I going to be a good mama? Probably not. There's no genetic tendency toward good motherhood here. There's no social construction. I'm going to have to do this by hand. Then I started writing Delia, writing out of being this woman who was so ashamed of herself that she is basically willing to wall herself alive to do something different. And it's a different book. It's not a bad book, but totally different.

What do you think the first book would have been like? How might it have been better?

Now I can tell you I don't know if it would have been better. But it *would* have been different. It would've been entirely Cissy's book. Then I wrote all the Delia stuff, and I lost *that* book, because I had to run out and earn some money quick. I had six or seven months that I could not get to the manuscript at all, and when I went back I wasn't either one of them. So instead of writing a Delia book or a Cissy book, it was much more interesting to me to be moving among these four females.

What was it like to go from the really focused first-person point of view in Bastard *to multiple points of view in* Cavedweller?

The other thing that happened, which is also very hard to talk about: you become an enormous success. This is very dangerous for writers. Everybody treats you like you're God on earth for about a minute and a half. And the other thing that happened to me—do you know the concept of the dancing dog? It ain't that the dog dances good, it's that the dog dances at all. So here comes this lesbian, working-class piece of shit, and she writes a novel that comes in second for the National Book Award. I'd go around and I'd do these interviews and I'm a feminist and I'm a lesbian mom. I have a new baby and they're all treating me like, "God must have lit on your shoulder, whispered in your ear." Meanwhile, they're treating me like this dog. "Oh, you're kind of just a freak of nature, ain't you?" So then I go back to *Cavedweller*, which, originally, had been written in first person, in Cissy's voice. Then I had shifted to Delia in third person. I thought, "They think I'm a dancing dog. I've got to prove something." So I wrote the whole damn book in third person and went into multiple narrators so that I could prove that I could do it. Which is a damn poor way to construct a novel.

Unless it works.

Yeah. But it took me two years longer than it should've, though I learned more doing it than I would've learned, maybe, doing the other thing. But instead of the story telling me how it's supposed to be written, which, theoretically, is how it's supposed to happen, the world made me write it the way I wrote it. It's embarrassing. Why is it not a first-person narrative? Well, because I had to prove I could write a third-person narrative. I had to prove I could shift point of view. I had to prove I could do these different characters and make you believe they were different.

And then, part of it was also having a boy. This tender little baby boy. I'm a mean woman when I write. I write terrible things. But I had this tender-hearted, tender-skinned little boy, who, in the course of my writing this novel, went from an infant to four. I learned what kids were, which I'd never known. In my mind, the way the book would always go was that I would take Delia back, I would raise Cissy in Cairo. I would raise this little girl that was growing up to be a lesbian, but had never heard the word. I wanted to get that down and show what that was like. And I wanted to write this woman who was bargaining for redemption, bargaining with every ounce, and doing a damn good job. I was going to kill one of the girls, because I believe that you can't bargain for redemption. I killed all three of them, but it wouldn't work. Every time I would try to kill one of the girls, it was cold on the page. It felt cold. I think it was Wolf. I think, because of him, I couldn't kill one of Delia's girls. So there you go. The narrative would've been stronger if I could've murdered one of them. If you look at the construction of novels—climaxes and crises and how characters change—the simplest and most straightforward way would have been to do that. What I finally had to accept was that I couldn't do it. Then I thought, "There are very damn few books that show you what it's really like to raise children and set them loose in the world." In fact, at the end of the book, she loses all of them.

Your characters are clearly very real to you. How do they first appear to you? How does a novel begin?

Somebody starts talking in my head. That's always what it is for me.

There are these visual images. I see somebody, see something. But for it to really start, somebody has to start talking. And for it to really work, several people have to start talking. If they start arguing, we're going to no clothes and no showers for a few days.

Once the characters start talking, how does the story gather and form?

The original stuff with Cissy was drunk on glory. I had this teenage girl, who never felt right in the world. Then she went down in a hole in the ground and felt like she had found her place.

So her interest in caving, the cave scenes came first.

Yes. I had this weird experience at the Delaware Water Gap when I was, like, twenty. I went with a girlfriend. We drove up through the Delaware Water Gap and we had to stop. I got out of the car and I felt something weird. Really weird. I've gone back there many times. Every time I go back, I feel like I've been there before. Something happens. That's what I wrote for Cissy; but for her it was, "I've come home." Then she started talking. She hated her mama. She felt her mama was entirely responsible for everything that had happened. She hated the South. She hated these small-minded, evil people that treated her like dirt. She felt like she was an alien, like she'd been dropped on this planet. She had to have been. She couldn't possibly have been born to this crazy mother and these crazy people that she despised. She was an obnoxious teenage girl. An adolescent girl who's beginning to be fully in her body in that way that happens to you when, suddenly, you have to stay up all night and jerk off. You have to dream dreams. The whole world has opened up and you're magical and terrified. That voice was really strong. So I wrote all that stuff.

How do you come to plot? What is *plot, by your definition?*

Something happens. Something real.

Do your characters unveil the plot for you?

I see the person and what happens is implicit in the person. You see Bone. You know the way she's dressed, so you know she's poor. And you know the way she looks at you, so you know she's suspicious and careful.

Was it Bone's voice that started Bastard?

Oh God, it took a long time to get Bone's voice right.

How did you go about doing that?

I kept writing it over and over. I'd pare it down. It kept being too wise.

It took me years to figure out what was bad about it, and then it took me years to figure out how to make her. You had to fall in love with her. You had to fall in love with her *immediately*, so she had to be this really strong but brittle and completely wrong-headed little girl. And she had to be a little girl. I did, like, thirty-eight drafts. I counted at one point. The first half of them were all just too smart. She knew too much, and to make the story work she had to not quite know.

But the reader had to know.

It was a tricky thing to make that work. I kept throwing stuff out and paring it down. I had to let her be wrong on the page, passionately wrong on the page. When she hates herself, you've got to absolutely believe that. At the same time, the reader's got to know that she's absolutely wrong. She's not evil, she's not a monster. This son of a bitch is fucking up this child, and this mother that she adores is failing her completely. You've got to believe that Bone genuinely loves them and genuinely feels herself guilty and responsible. It required paring down and paring down. I had to eliminate every explanation—and that's the hard part. You keep wanting to explain.

How long did it take you to write that book?

To really write it, it took about three years. But it took me a decade to figure out *how* to write it. And I went a little crazy writing it. That was the other problem. You know, I'm always teaching and I'm always saying, "You've got to work up a sweat, you've got to go where your fear is." But the thing that I leave out is that you will go crazy when you do this.

Is that because so much of what you're working with is autobiographical? Or would it be like that anyway?

People can't tell the difference. There's a wonderful Doctorow quote. As soon as I saw it, I put it up on the wall because it's completely true. He said, "Writing erases memory." You take autobiographical material and begin to work it into story, the story becomes what you remember. You lose your real memory. It's why I did *Two or Three Things I Know for Sure*, to try to figure out—"Now, wait a minute, did this really happen?" It took me a long while to sort it all out. In the writing, in the making of a character, if you use real incidents, your autobiographical reality becomes unreal and the story becomes stronger. Eventually, the real is gone. You can't say anymore what did and did not happen. It's very embarrassing. And tenuous. Especially when you're talking about sexual abuse, which is always defensive and problematic in this culture. I have finessed it on many occasions, because I don't want to have to tell all that stuff.

Near the end of Cavedweller, *Dede tries to get Delia to talk about her life. She says, "We don't talk," and Delia responds, "We're not the type." So often writers are people who come from families that don't or can't talk to each other.*

It makes a good writer. There's a wonderful science fiction story I read when I was a teenager about making geniuses. It's about this horrific family. There's this little boy who's four or five. All the cupboards are locked and they're always yelling at him. They won't explain anything. But what they are making is a child who is desperate to know, and curious as hell. It's all deliberate. By the end of the story, you realize that these parents are literally constructing a kid who will puzzle out things and who will grow up and make them rich. It was a terrible, wonderful story, and I kept thinking, "That's it!" I was raised in this hellhole, but it made me this person who wants to understand and explain and create a reason to love and live. Well, this is how you do it.

It has interesting implications about talent. What do you think talent is?

I don't know. I really, genuinely don't know. I do know when I see it, and I know that it's a tragedy. You get these young people who want so badly to write. They're desperate and they're hungry and they're willing to work. You can work with them and work with them and eventually, maybe, they'll begin to have something. Then a kid will walk in. Doesn't care, won't work, but they've just got it. They've got voice and they've got a story to tell. There's no justice in it. But even that doesn't mean they'll be writers. Sometimes they can't shape it, they can't cut it down, they can't step back and work it.

So what is talent? I don't know. Talent is magic. Talent is the ability to make words sing on the page. But to actually have something of worth, you have to have both talent and perseverance. You have to have the ability to step back, get a little distance from the narrative, especially if you're aiming your narrative as an act of revenge or toward the acquisition of justice—about which I have very complicated feelings. I've had students who were so gifted that they'll never be writers. It's too damn easy. And then I've had students who've had just a little bit of talent, but who would work their butts off and keep rewriting and rewriting and take me seriously when I say thirty, forty drafts.

So in a sense, hunger is a kind of talent also.

Yes, and to see it as work. To be willing to go back and do it over and over. Also, there is an ear. My partner can play any brass instrument; it's genetic. In fact, the whole family — they're all musicians, opera singers, composers. That's what they do. That's the thing that comes down. Wolf, at three, picked up a trumpet and started playing it. *There's* talent; it's innate. But I've watched Alix develop her embouchure. It is entirely about the muscles in your mouth and lips and being willing to go on even though it hurts. I've seen her bleed to get better and better. I've watched her reacquire the embouchure. She played clarinet and all these instruments when she was in high school, and then didn't do it for twenty years. Then she went back. At first she could go for three minutes, then she could go for six minutes. Now she can go do concerts and play for two or three hours. But she has to keep working it. Writing is exactly the same. You can come in with talent, but then you have to develop your embouchure. It's purely about seeing it as an instrument that you use. The more you use it, the better you get. It's a muscle of the mind. You have to develop it, and you *can* fuck it up.

What happens when perseverance fails you? Is there such a thing as writer's block? Have you ever experienced it?

I finally had writer's block. I finally have to admit that I had writer's block. I find this completely humiliating. I used to think, it's all those middle-class, self-indulgent sons of bitches who get writer's block. They get to walk around all morose and pitiful and ask for help. I was completely contentious. I was also afraid of it. So I always constructed my life so that I was working on more than one manuscript. That's why I started *Cavedweller* in the middle of *Bastard.* That's why I started *She Who* in the middle of *Cavedweller.* I thought, "This is the safety and grace. I'll never have writer's block. If this one goes cold, I'll shift to this one."

What I didn't understand was that — at least for me — writer's block is about completely losing confidence in your ability to do it all. And that's something that just hit me with *Cavedweller*. Eventually I just stopped the book. I said, "I'm not doing this anymore. I'm done." And I published the book. Now I can read it and see that I should have cut another 20 percent, tightened it up, redone the end, and it would be a much better book. But at the time, all I felt was, "This book is not as good as it should be and I can't fix it." And it just destroyed me. Then I had to take the book around. The book looked a lot worse to my eyes than I look at it now and see it is. It was just devastating. I stopped being able to work at all.

Do you think that it was partly because Bastard Out of Carolina *was so incredibly successful? That's a mixed blessing.*

A very mixed blessing. I expected that *Cavedweller* would get a lot more criticism because *Bastard* had been so successful. I tried to be ready. Now I've decided it's a good book and it does a lot of the stuff I wanted it to do. I should've gone through another pass and, perhaps, I should've found another editor to work with, but I didn't. The hard thing is—I think Jeanette Winterson said, "Art is not bulletproof." But I've always been trying to find a bulletproof posture. I don't like to hurt. I'm looking for a place to get safe; and like any hurting person would, I tried to construct a kind of safe territory for myself. But safe doesn't happen. You have to go through the process. You have to go through the second book; you have to go through it. I tried desperately to avoid it. And I tried desperately to avoid writer's block.

But clear to me, God had something in mind that I should learn, and I'm learning. I always thought that because I could do all the drafts that I had to do to get *Bastard* right, and all the drafts that I did to get *Cavedweller* into the form that I published it in, I had stamina. But it's like the bar is always rising. The stamina you need now is always more than you had before, and it's different. So now I'm getting to the point where I'm writing this story that begins—and I don't know anything. I don't even know what I'm doing. I'm using that as an exercise to get past being afraid, and it's starting to open up again. I always set myself tasks that are almost impossible.

Like what?

"Let's design a narrative in which there are four strong female voices that will clash all the way through the book. Let's not do anything predictable. Let's make the fundamentalist, crazy one the most interesting, loving character in the book." Now I'm writing a book about a young woman who is destroyed and has to be remade. It's about violence and surviving violence. It's about being crippled. And not being magical.

When you can work, what kind of feedback helps you keep going?

I need a voice I can trust to tell me where I've gone wrong. I count on a good editor to help me eliminate the fat and the overwriting and make a mean, powerful book. Editing is a talent, and there are damn few people that have this talent. I'm a good editor for other people, and I can do some for myself. But I need a voice that comes at it fresh and different.

Are there tricks or techniques that you use to help you look at a manuscript?

The best and only trick—and it *is* a trick—is to put the damn thing down for a year. It's partly why it takes me so long. My editors go nuts. They would like a book from me every other year, and they ain't gonna get it, because one of those years it's laying in a box while I'm thinking about something else so I can go back and it's a surprise. You read it fresh. That's the trick I know that absolutely works. I think for some of us, the time it has to be fallow differs. For some people, it can be a month or a couple of weeks. They're lucky. You have to get distance. You have to inhabit the character and then get distance to edit it. That's very hard, but I'm getting better at it through necessity.

Another trick is to shift voice, write the story from a different character in the story. I do that all the time. I go first to third person. That always works. Shift position.

Another one is, "What if?" What if it wasn't Bone's story, what if it was Anney's story? I do that. I wrote a whole lot of Anney, justifying her existence—explaining and arguing. None of that went into the book, but I had to do it to be able to write the book. And you go wrong sometimes. I got 109 pages that went out of *Bastard* completely. Bone was in juvenile hall with a little girl, Elsie, who tried to kill her mother. Elsie's black. In 1956 in South Carolina—'56–'57—was exactly the time when this could have happened. It was segregated until then. So I wrote all this and it was wonderful and extraordinary and gorgeous—and it's out of the book because it took over the book.

Will it be its own book someday?

It might. I expect it will. It's there, in a file. [In] *Cavedweller*, Delia—when she's cleaning houses on a crew—meets this guy, Thomas. Thomas is sixty pages, wonderful. But he's too strong. He took over *Cavedweller*. I had too many strong characters already. So he's in a file. What I find most problematic is that these are black characters. Elsie is black and Thomas is black. I usually set myself the task of, "Let's write black because you're a white girl. You're from the South and you really should look across this wall and try to do it." I always try and I always wind up cutting them out. I have to look closer at this soon.

I think I've got the same thing happening in *She Who*. It's about a young woman who's a golden girl. I see them all the time—these kids who are twenty-one, twenty-two. Their mamas loved them. They're pretty, they're smart, their teeth shine. They can do any damn thing. So I made myself a golden girl who speaks four languages. She's about to graduate from Stanford and is lovers with this young woman who adores her. They're happy. There's every reason in the world to be happy. Golden. They go to the movies in San Francisco, and they park in one of those garages where you have to pay the ticket, then put the ticket in to get out. They forget to pay for the parking ticket, so Casey goes to get the car and Amy goes to pay the ticket and is going to meet her at the checkout, where you have to slip the card in. Casey never comes, and as Amy's going upstairs to find her, [falls] off the top of the parking garage and lands in the street. She ain't golden anymore. She spends the next year in and out of coma, with surgeries. She's reconstructed and put back together and she wakes up and she can't talk. She's lost the memory of everything that's happened since she was hurt. She barely speaks English, much less four languages. And she don't remember Amy at all.

You venture into dangerous, violent worlds in your novels. Terrible things happen. People are sacrificed. How do you bear that?

That's not the hard part. The hard part is not to get drunk on it. To keep it very matter-of-fact and real. The problem is that most writing about violence is writing of excess. Too much detail, wrong detail. What you really need is to write down to it, keep it very low-key. Emotionally charged events need a very real, matter-of-fact language to communicate them. Otherwise you get drunk on the language of it. Most of the time — I teach a lot, so I see it — people write up to it. They think that the way to write it is to rise to it, but that's not how it works. If you see people in extremis in the emergency room, they are as matter-of-fact and basic as they can be because they're trying to survive the unsurvivable. And that's how you have to write it. You have to keep reining it in, which means you have to keep cutting, throwing out all the adverbs.

Also, you have to have people talk like they really talk. God, I get sick to death of reading people who believe that writing is different from speaking. Either they give everybody good grammar, which nobody uses, or they write unreal speech. It's very hard to get people to train themselves to write believable speech. The only way to do it is to read it out loud over and over until it sounds right. That's the only way I know to do it. I make my students tape themselves and listen, but they can't hear. It took me forever to figure out that it wasn't working because they literally couldn't hear it. You've got to have the ear, and then you've got to train the ear to make it finer. But you've got to have the ear to begin with.

Do you finish a draft before you rewrite and fine-tune?

Not always. I should write more before I start slicing, but I jump-start myself a lot of the time by revising. I get a draft, start cutting it back. It has to be mean on the page. You have to learn what that means for yourself.

So you cut as you go along and then take another pass at it, or maybe several.

The thing is, as you're going along you think, "This isn't quite right, but let's get enough of it down so that we can make it right." You have to trust the process enough to do that and then you come back and you fix what's not quite right. Sometimes, if you're lucky, you'll see the specifics of what's not quite right — too much information, or the wrong language. But it's an exercise. You have to find the way to show that to yourself, and then you have to figure out what the hell to do. Sometimes you just have to wait for the gift. You have to be patient and keep going back until it comes.

What if the gift never comes? What if you come to a place in a book when you know, absolutely, this isn't right at all. What kind of revision do you do then?

You put it in the box. Elsie is an interesting character. Some of her language is to die for. But it's not right. Something so fundamental is wrong that I can't fix it. When I can fix it, then it can be a book. But I haven't got the gift yet.

Is what's missing the right conflict?

No, I don't think so. I think it's something in the character. Something I don't see yet. Something I don't know, or haven't been given yet. Let's be very clear about what we mean by having a character: we can have somebody talking. We don't have a vague idea what they look like. We have a picture in our mind of the place where something is happening, and often what's happening is in that picture. My image of Bone was this little girl who looks kind of sturdy and strong and her hands are open and they're full of blood. If you look at her from a little distance, you can't see that it's blood on her hands. You just see this strong, stubborn-faced little girl. The picture was, in large part, the story. The story was why she is so strong. That's character. When the character isn't complete, you don't really see who she is.

That's the problem I've run into with Casey because I'm writing two different characters. I'm writing Casey before the accident, who, admittedly, I have some trouble with. I have trouble with the golden children. I'm jealous of them, and that's hard for me. I look at these kids and I think, let's break them. It's just my nature. I know that's why I break this girl. I'm trying to construct a new Casey, too, someone who's also golden, but a very different kind of golden. I'm trying to get to something I need for myself in the story, which is what we all do.

We write for ourselves, to find out something we need to know.

I wrote Bone to learn how to love a little girl who hated herself, and you know why. I was trying to figure out how to love myself and not be ashamed at my core. I wrote Delia to try to forgive myself for the sins in my own life. I wrote Amanda to try to love my sister, who got God and went bad with it. You write these characters for your stuff. You come to them for your stuff. I'm writing Casey because I spent a few months unable to walk, and I had to forgive God for putting me in a chair. I've got enough to be mad at God at already. He did not have to pull this shit. I had to be able to figure out how to be human if I was not going to be able to walk anymore. Then I managed to be able to walk again, and when I started walking again I was so angry. And angry is a big one for me. I have to write past being angry. I started Casey in the recovery unit with the pins in her hips trying to get out of a wheelchair.

In your memoir, Two or Three Things I Know for Sure, *and in several interviews and essays, you talk about having to start with outrage.*

It's a great place to begin, but you can't stay there. Writing through it is what makes it something of worth. Staying there is a dead end. Americans love revenge writing. Fully a third of American novels are written out of revenge. We confuse it with justice. I break fiction into two categories. There are the novels that stay there and the ones that go somewhere else. And I'm interested in the ones that go somewhere else. To stay in revenge, you become the one you want to destroy. Something else has to happen.

But your work directly addresses issues that we should all be angry about. It's political, but it doesn't feel that way. How do you accomplish that?

It's a different concept of politics. Grow up white trash in this culture, and you don't think simple about politics. Well, you *could,* but God help you. I want something more. I was raised on Toni Morrison. I was raised on writers who had every reason for revenge, for hatred, had every reason to make a reader suffer. But the books I love are the books that took me past that. *The Bluest Eye* saved my life. You read that book and you read a character who has every justifiable reason to damn God and her own soul, and who doesn't, who takes it somewhere else. You forget that the book is actually written in the voice of these two little girls who are watching Pecola and can see into her heart. They hate her and resent her and are ashamed of her for all these complicated reasons. And Toni Morrison takes you somewhere else, to compassion. Compassion is where I think I want to go. It's not always where I manage.

This seems related to what you said in "Believing in Literature." In that essay, you hold young gay and lesbian writers to a standard. You say, "Terrible things may have happened to you, but that's no excuse to write poorly."

For any oppressed class of people, whether it's working class, south-erners, lesbians, incest survivors, black children—whatever category you inhabit that is made to feel wrong in the world, writing is about justifica-tion, about explanation. And, yeah, there's a part of you that wants to slap them around. Them: those people that did not love you as you should be loved for just being human. You want to get their attention, you want to call their attention to an injustice. This is a great reason to write. Part of it is outrage, part of it is the desire for justice, part of it is the desire to make the world a different place.

The problem is, you have to think past what you want to do. You have to think past slapping them around; you have to think past just getting their attention. You have to think, what do you *genuinely* want? Who do you genuinely want to be when the book is done? I always think about my goal for a book in terms of what I want the reader to feel when they close the book. That was real simple with *Bastard*. I wanted you to be so angry that when you put the book down the impulse to get up and do something would be unstoppable. I constructed the entire book so that at the end that would be the feeling. I'm clear that, at the end, some people rise up from the book completely outraged at Anney; some people want to go hunt down Glen. I didn't care. I just didn't want anybody to look at any Bone ever again the same way. With *Cavedweller*, I wanted you to come around full circle. I wanted you to look at Delia and think, "Now what? You've earned your redemption, you've raised these kids. Now who the fuck are you?" I wanted that kind of open-mouthed, "Now what?"

The problem that I see with a lot of political writing is that it's designed at the end to provoke a slogan, to have a simple bumper sticker kind of idea—and I don't believe in bumper sticker ideas. I don't think they fix anything. I also don't believe in guilt as an ending feeling. It's not enough revenge for me. I'm serious about that. I want a hell of a lot more than for people to be ashamed of themselves. I want them to act. I don't think people act so well out of guilt. I think they act when you make them inhabit somebody and feel differently than they've ever felt before, and that's more complicated. I think, in fact, we have set ourselves a standard that is too small—especially as political writers. A lot of times, we want to do one thing. Okay, let's make them believe that lesbians have the right to exist. It's a damn small goal. Let's make them believe that class is a real issue. Okay, that's a small one, too. Large would be to see a human being that you have never really believed is human as human. That's large.

Your characters are complex, and there's a lot of grief in their lives. But you don't paint the world so that there's no hope.

There's always hope. When I first started to write stories about my family, they were bleak. I had to write through a lot of the bleakness to admit the fact that, in the midst of a lot of violence and horror, we had a pretty damn good time surviving. Our sense of joy in life is what gets left out of deliberately politically motivated working-class fiction. The tragedy is so unrelieved, but that's not how it really is. One minute you're being knocked into the wall, the next minute you're being comforted. Life is about this pacing of violence and loving affection. I wanted to see books that reflected what I knew, which is we're miserable and also, occasionally, deliriously happy.

Larry Brown

Larry Brown was the author of six novels and two collections of short stories. Born and raised in Oxford, Mississippi, he served in the U.S. Marines in the early 1970s. Upon his return, he worked as a firefighter and taught himself how to write fiction. In 1987, his soon-to-be editor, Shannon Ravenel, was reading *Mississippi Quarterly*, looking for stories to include in *New Stories from the South*, and came upon Brown's second published story, "Facing the Music." She included it in the anthology and in 1988 Algonquin Books of Chapel Hill published his first collection of short stories. Brown's honors include the Southern Book Critics Circle Award and the Lila Wallace–Reader's Digest Writer's Award. Gary Hawkins's documentary, *The Rough South of Larry Brown*, premiered at the Double Take Film Festival in Durham, North Carolina, in 2000. Brown lived in Oxford, Mississippi, with his wife and children until his death in 2004.

Facing the Music, 1988 (stories); *Dirty Work*, 1989; *Big Bad Love*, 1990 (stories); *Joe*, 1991; *Father and Son*, 1996; *Fay*, 2000, *The Rabbit Factory*, 2003; *A Miracle of Catfish*, 2007

Where does a book begin for you?

The way I get a story that's a keeper is when something comes in my head and won't leave. If it leaves, then I don't worry about it. But when I think up a character and I keep thinking about their situation, finally I get motivated enough to put down a few words and see where it goes. That's how I begin. I don't really have any kind of a theme and usually not much of a story. It's always a character and a situation. And there's always some trouble going on early. Let's take for example *Father and Son*, where the first page Glen is going home from three or four years in prison. You find out that his mother has died and he has an illegitimate child. And he hasn't seen the baby's mother in four years and he's going to see her for the first time. So he's coming home to a bunch of trouble. And I just proceed from there.

I don't know who any of the other major characters are going to be. People just pop up, and some of them turn out to be minor characters and some of them turn out to be major characters. That's why I never use an outline. I usually don't even have any notes. I usually just begin, and then the whole writing of the story of the novel is a process of discovery for me, day by day. Where it might take a reader only a few nights to read a book, it might have taken the writer years to write it. If a book is any good, it almost always took the writer years to write it. You make all these mistakes, and have to go back and fix them. It's just a big mess until you get about nine-tenths of the way through it. Then you look back and maybe figure out what the story is about. And you know what to go back and emphasize or cut out or strengthen. That's the way I go about crafting a novel.

How do you create plot?

I'm the kind of person who believes that character is more important than plot. I believe that if you create interesting enough characters, characters who are real enough, then whatever happens to them is the plot. When you think about it, *life* doesn't have a plot.

Brother Roy, the fallen preacher in Father and Son, *is really the only character in the book that Glen can relate to. How did he make his way into the novel?*

The lake they were fishing in is an actual impoundment out here at Tula where I was raised. Two of my high school friends, a brother and a sister, each has a big home on either side of it. They have big decks overlooking this twenty-seven-acre lake that's just full of bass — they will just hit anything you throw in. These people won't let anybody fish in it, but the guy that built it was a friend of my father's when they were little boys. So, I had the setting, but I really didn't have Brother Roy. I just knew I had to have somebody that Glen was going out there to meet. When he finally got out there, I said, well, here's a guy, and he's cooking chicken out there on the front porch and drinking beer and his name is Brother Roy. Glen used to go hear him preach when he was a little kid and he baptized him. They remained friends and he's a good guy. He doesn't preach anymore.

So Brother Roy makes Glen remember that there was a time in his life when things weren't falling apart.

Yeah, so he still likes this guy.

Glen finds a kind of redemption with the fallen preacher. In fact, many of your characters find redemption in the most unlikely places. Walter in Dirty Work, *for example. Where did that book come from?*

Dirty Work is based on some people that I actually knew when I was stationed at the marine barracks in Philadelphia in '71–'72. We had this NCO club behind our barracks, next to the mess hall where we ate. That's where I spent just about all my off-time because I didn't have a car when I was up there. Didn't have much to do. It was a huge navy base, but the marine contingent was very small—a couple hundred marines or so. We did guard duty and that kind of stuff. But there were all these boys who were attached to the naval hospital there. They had all lost limbs in Vietnam. They were all in wheelchairs.

There was one guy—and I've told this story before—he had lost both of his legs right here [directly below the hips] and he had a pair of artificial legs and he got around on crutches. Just to see him come in on his crutches, you couldn't tell he didn't have any legs. He'd get up on the barstool, order himself a beer; and he had his car fixed up with hand levers and he'd drive himself around where he wanted to. He had a girlfriend, lived a regular life. There was also another boy, who was about twenty-one then. Perfectly good-looking young man, wasn't disfigured the way Walter was, but he had been shot clean through the base of his skull by a sniper. They couldn't cure what was wrong with him because of the scar tissue, and he would just pass out every once in a while. They couldn't let him be on active duty, so he was on 100 percent disability. They would sit down and tell us stories about Vietnam. And that's where *Dirty Work* came from.

But you didn't write it until many years after that.

We built our house in '86 and we built it ourselves—me and some boys from the fire department. I knew I couldn't drive nails all day and write at night. So I just stopped. For six months. At that time, I had been writing for six years and had only published a few short stories. I had already written five novels, too, that were all unpublished and probably eighty or ninety short stories — most unpublished. But during that time I got an idea of a guy whose face was disfigured, who lived with his mother and wouldn't come out of his room. And that was all I had. This thing was just burning to be written inside me. But I couldn't sit down and write because I had to finish my house. We started in March and moved in in August when we finally laid the carpet. And the minute I had a table to put my typewriter on and a chair to sit in — the *minute* — I sat down and started writing *Dirty Work*, because it had festered in my head for six months and I had all this stuff thought up.

Of course, I began it the wrong way. In the third person, with Walter knowing this old man named Noah who had this sawmill and was convinced that the flood was coming and he was building this huge ark down in this hollow. He had a brother who was a sinning preacher who was doing wrong with one of his choir members — all this crazy stuff that eventually got thrown out. I got down to the gist at page 160, with him waking up and seeing this guy who didn't have any arms and legs and saying "Whoa, where in the hell am I at? How did I get here?"

I wrote that novel five times. Completely. I didn't show it to Shannon [my editor] until I had the third draft and she said, "The bad news is that your novel starts on page 160, Larry." And I said, "Well, bullshit! I'll just quit on it." And she said, "No, no, you can't quit on it." She convinced me. Algonquin had very little money, but they gave me what they had to keep working on it. Eventually I delivered two more drafts of it and wound out throwing out about six hundred pages. But I always do that. I always throw out — I threw out about twelve hundred pages with *Fay*. And it was all done on a typewriter!

I finally figured out the way to tell this story was two alternating first-person points of view. But it didn't help me any when I got down to the ending. Shannon couldn't help me any. She said, "I don't know how you're going to tell it. If there was any way for me to advise you, I would, but this is something you are going to have to figure out on your own." So I figured out that it had to come from a phone call from Walter's mother. And while she was telling it to him, it jogged his memory and he began to see it like a movie running in his head. You know, he was so crazy about movies.

What made you decide the alternating points of view were right? Your other novels are written in multiple points of view, too. Is there some kind of reasoning behind your choice to give the reader access to a number of points of view in a novel?

I just like to do it that way. To me, it's disconcerting to have multiple points of view within a chapter. I like to focus on one point of view for each chapter, even though I may have the same two characters in two successive chapters [or] scene next to scene. I may be in one's head for one chapter and the other's for the next. But I try to tell what the other one is thinking by what they say and what they do, even though you can't go into their head.

So, choosing point of view is not a conscious thing?

Yeah, for me it's just the simplest way to tell the story. And the most convincing—to get inside somebody's head and see what's going on from their point of view.

Where did you get the idea to give Braiden the fantasy about being an African chieftain that opens Dirty Work?

I just figured if he was so bored out of his mind that he had to do something with his imagination. So he would invent these trips—I called them trips—that he could go on. And he would be thinking, like, "If they hadn't captured my great-great-great-granddaddy and sold him into slavery three hundred years ago, I wouldn't be here in the first place. I'd be out impala hunting and I might be a king in my own country and have all these nubile young women."

The terrible aftereffect of war is a thread that runs through your work. In fact, you dedicated Dirty Work *to your daddy, who "knew what war did to men." Would you talk about why war is of such great interest to you?*

I was very lucky that I didn't have to go to Vietnam. I joined in 1970, joined the marines, just because the army was fixing to draft me in the next few weeks. When they had the lottery system, they drew my birthday out number one. I was already classified I-A. I'd already been to Memphis and had my physical when I was eighteen—that's how we used to buy beer, with our classification card. So I just went ahead and joined. And it just so happened that after I got in, the American public had gotten so fed up with how many boys were getting shredded every week—all these protests were going on. They'd killed those students at Kent State—all this stuff was going on and the troop strength started winding down. They began the peace negotiations and all that. So the marines' policy is they are the first in, and they are also the first out. When they start withdrawing troops, they withdraw the marines first. So nobody much out of my platoon got orders. Some did; there was still some ground fighting going on, but not near what it had been in '68 and '67. So I just lucked out, being born when I was.

In your wildest dreams as a little boy did you ever think you'd have the life you have now?

No, I thought I'd be a fireman once I got grown. Once I joined the fire department, I thought I'd be a fireman for thirty years.

What made you think that you could be a writer?

Well, I just loved to read all my life. My mother instilled early a love of reading in me. By the time I was five, she made sure we all had library books and one time when I was pretty small, she purchased a set of encyclopedias that had another little ten-book set of classic fiction and Greek mythology, Grimm's fairy tales, *Beowulf*. I read all that at an early age and developed a love for reading that has stayed with me for my whole life. Even when I was in the marines, whatever base I was on, I'd go to the library and get me some books. I don't know any writers for whom reading is not a passion.

I was twenty-nine years old and I was fixing to hit that thirty mark—wondering what I was going to do for the rest of my life. Was I going to stay where I was at? I mean, firefighting was a good, steady job—a job that was a noble profession. In the business of helping people. But I just think I wanted to do something more. I just reasoned: How does somebody learn to write? Do they go to college and do it? Or do they take a correspondence course? Or do they just sit down and start doing it? So I figured that they just sat down and started doing it. I sat down in October of 1980 and started writing a novel that would ultimately be rejected over and over until I finally saw that it was no good. I wrote four more that were unpublished and I burned one of them in my mother-in-law's back yard.

I gave up my firefighting job some years ago and I've been a full-time writer ever since, except for some brief teaching stints here and there. I've never been to college and barely got out of high school, but I wanted to learn to write and simply taught myself how by doing it for years. It took me eight years to publish my first book, and by then I had learned how to write *Dirty Work* and *Joe*. I tell students, if I can do it — I who made an F in English my senior year — then they can do it if they want to work hard enough.

How does your family feel about your writing?

Oh, they're proud of me. They sure are.

You don't use your family in your fiction, do you?

I don't know that I've ever put anybody in my family in my books. It's always been things I saw somebody do or something that happened to somebody I knew or something somebody told me about. A lot of times, it's just been something somebody told me about where I wasn't there to actually witness it, but that it really happened.

The monkey in Father and Son — *was that one of those real things that ended up in a novel?*

When I was working at the fire station, I had a partner named Reuben Jaco. His brother-in-law was Bob Vaughn up here at Abbeville, and he had this monkey that he brought into the fire station a couple of times. This thing was about two feet high and it was as mean as a son of a gun, and he told all this stuff about how it would act around women. Also, when my daddy was out of work sometimes in Memphis, sometimes he would work at the Mid-South Fair and he was telling me about seeing some show one night when these trained monkeys just went crazy and jumped on the trainer and started biting him and clawing and everything and he had to slam them up against the wall. That's where all that came from. Whenever he'd bring that monkey down to the fire station, I'd be sitting there in my chair, scared, not moving a muscle. So I just put him in that bar.

There's a car-wreck scene in Fay, *and a scene in* Father and Son *where they drag the river for the body of a drowning victim. Did you draw upon your experience as a fireman to write those scenes?*

Sure. I saw plenty of terrible things when I was with the fire department. The worst things are the wrecks. The fires were the scariest and most dangerous for you, personally. But the wrecks were the hardest things for me to deal with. I had to run the crew. Sometimes I was the captain and if my assistant chief was off, then I had to run the whole show. We would have to respond—usually out in the county was where the wrecks were. We have had some bad wrecks in town, but mostly they are out in the country. You've got to drive a ways, and by the time you get there, the highway patrol is already there, the ambulance is already there, and they've determined that they can't get the person out without the extrication tool. So the fire department is the last resort.

Those are hard scenes to read. In fact, there are a lot of hard scenes in your books. There's that scene in Father and Son *where Glen rapes Erline, for example. You describe what happens in such an even tone, but it's suffocating to read. Would you talk about what it is like to portray such violence? How do you steel yourself against the truth that you know?*

I got up in a bookstore in Lexington, Kentucky, in 1996, when I was touring for *Father and Son*, and told those people that I was going to read this passage that was going to hurt them to hear it. But it had hurt me to have to write it, but it was something that I had to write to put in the book to be part of the character. They needed to suffer through it the way I suffered through writing it. They needed to hear the way I felt when I wrote it because it hurt me to write it. Sometimes in fiction you have to go into places you don't want to be in, or never have been in, and try to cover the whole range of human experience and emotion. Even if you've never done all these things, you've got to at least try to put yourself in the character's mind and get inside his skin or her skin from whatever point of view—I'll become that person. That's what I try to do. I try to be honest. I sometimes get accused of being brutal. But I say "Well, that's okay. At least it's honest."

In all of your novels, the characters seem to be searching for someone it is safe to love, someone who will love them and at the same time let them be who they are. Would you talk about that?

I think that it's something that everybody needs and can hardly do without. I think some people spend their lives looking for that and never find it—or never find it happily. But I guess it's just the idea I have about people in general. That people are generally good, not bad, and after you write enough, I think you discover that no character is either all good or all bad. Because when you think about it, even the person who goes around putting pistols to people's heads and executing them might have a little five-year-old niece that he is just nuts about and goes out and buys teddy bears for. People are so complex and have such different sides to them and have such a range of emotions.

Is that what fiction does for you—allows you to figure out folks?

Yeah. The people I'm trying to write about—I'm trying to figure out what they are up to, what they are about, what their story is, what their connections are to family, friends, loved ones, and lovers. How they survive whatever situation I put them in. I'm interested in that. I am interested in seeing what they do when I load them up with all this trouble. And how they react. That's why I do that. That's a conscious decision. But I also think that that is what draws the reader into the story and makes him or her forget that they are reading a story. I think that's the illusion that the writer is trying to pull off. Trying to make the reader forget that they are reading.

The opening scene of Joe *certainly seemed real! You nailed that little girl, Fay. Did you know that she would show up as the center figure in her own novel?*

No, I had no idea. Originally, I thought *Joe* was going to be about this migrant family, and then Joe cropped up and the story became about Joe *and* this family. But I didn't see any of that coming. I just let Fay walk out [of the novel] that day. She was disgusted with that situation; it was just one more bad thing that happened to the family. But in the back of my head, I always knew that eventually one day I'd sit down and find out.

What was it like, writing that book?

It's such a messy process, writing a novel. You don't know where you're going. You don't know how long it's going to take you to get there. Halfway through, sometimes, you get to feeling like, "Oh, shit, this ain't gonna work." About the time you've got two years invested in it, you can't just stop. You've already taken some money. You got to finish it. So whatever mistakes you make have got to be fixed. You keep working your way through, throwing away pages, writing new ones. I know I went one four-month stretch when I was finishing *Fay*, I didn't do anything. I would get up at seven in the evening, fix me some breakfast. I would go to my room and work until about twelve or one or two, fix me something else to eat. Then go back and work until usually past daylight. Then about seven, when the kids were getting up to go to school and Mary Annie getting up to go to work, I'd be sitting in there eating some ice cream, watching TV or reading, getting ready to go to bed. At seven AM. And I did that for four months straight. That's all I did. But I can do that when I have to. I mean, that's not my normal routine, but when I've got a big piece of work nearing completion . . .

How did you know when you had come to the end of the novel?

Endings are hard. Sometimes, I have to do them five or six times. I didn't have the ending to *Fay* right when I turned in the second draft. I'm talking second draft, but I'm also talking like each page had been revised six or seven times. That was last spring, February or March, and I was headed out to Austin for the music festival. I had turned in an 880-something-page draft. Long for me, and we had already sent pages back and forth, so I was finishing the second draft and I said, "Well, I'll worry about it when I get back from Austin."

I was sitting out there in the parking lot of the hotel one afternoon, waiting for a cab to come, and I had already written this other ending that didn't work, where Aaron got killed by some guy he had burned on a dope deal. People came in with shotguns and killed him and his brother both. Fay came in and found them. It didn't work: then her and Sam never did get hooked up. Then it just came to me, in that parking lot, waiting on that cab. I was sitting on the curb right there. I can remember, I had a piece of paper in my pocket and a pen, and I just sat there and in just a few minutes I just wrote it down the way it all had to go. It fell through just like a ton of bricks and I said, "I got it." I went on and caught my cab and went on to the bar and heard some music.

Will Fay's brother Gary get his own novel eventually?

Well, that will be on down the road.

Are you as interested in him as you were in Fay?

Sure, sure. Yeah, eventually, it will be a trilogy. But Gary's story will take place in modern times. He'll be older. He'll be a man. I think he was about sixteen, and *Joe* and *Fay* are set back in the '80s. Yeah, he thinks he's sixteen, doesn't know for sure; he doesn't have a birth certificate.

Your characters are people who, in some ways, are so far removed from the experience of most readers—for example, in this day and age, it might be hard for some people to believe someone wouldn't have a birth certificate. Does this concern you?

No, not really. Because I know that there are people like that in the world who don't have a birth certificate, who don't know how old they are. They were born in some shack in the north woods of Alabama or somewhere. They are beyond the reach of society. They don't know what the real world is like. They are so . . . primitive, kind of.

So you don't think about your audience?

No. I think I have to please myself first. I think that if I like it, maybe somebody else will like it. That's the premise I operate off of.

How do you go about pleasing yourself? How do you get the work to the point where you feel good about it? How do you revise?

I just go back to the beginning and write until I get to a place that I figure I need to go back and start correcting things. So I go back and start cutting out things, adding things, retyping new pages. I don't like to get too far ahead without knowing that everything is right. That's probably the main reason I go back.

I can only stay with the first draft for about two or three hours. That's about all I can handle. But when it comes to revision, I can stay with it for about twelve hours. I can do it. I'm just sitting there. I've got the story and I'm just improving it.

If you get stuck, how do you get a novel moving again?

I really don't get stuck very much. What I do is make mistakes. What I do is put things in there that I shouldn't have put in there, and then I have to go in and take them out. You do one thing wrong and it's going to cause problems two hundred pages down the road. So that's another reason I go back and revise. I want to make sure that everything is progressing correctly. I don't want to get to page five hundred and see that I made a huge mistake on page thirty.

What's a good day of writing for you?

Five or six pages is probably a good day for me. I write pretty slowly and think about it as I go along. But in another way, I don't worry about it. Madison Bell says that he doesn't do much revision because by the time he gets set to sit down and write, he pretty well knows what he's going to say. And he's published eleven books already and he's a lot younger than I am. He's just got it down and he knows what he's going to say. But I'm not like that. I have to discover what I want to say by going back and changing things, trying different things. I'm always trying to get the best sentence, trying to make things flow smoothly. I guess you just have to find your own system. But it just takes so long to find it. You make so many false starts when you're starting out and you don't really know what you're doing. But I think that's because you've got to write enough words. I think that a young writer has to write x number of words, but nobody can tell him or her what that number is. They'll know when they get there, and until they get there they just have to keep operating on blind faith. That's the apprenticeship period.

What do you read when you are writing?

God, I read everything. I read fiction, nonfiction, novels, short stories. I read everything.

Is there anything you can't read when you are writing yourself?

I try not to copy anything by Cormac McCarthy because I'm so crazy about his work and I've read all his novels so many times that I have to consciously watch it that I don't repeat one of his sentences that's buried in my brain, that's imprinted there forever. And I've caught myself doing it and had to go back and take it out.

Does teaching affect the flow of your work? Are you likely to continue doing it?

I hope not, because it takes a full-month chunk out of writing. I was by myself the whole time in Montana. I bought me a new truck and drove out there and I only flew home one weekend. You know what I did for my students one day in Montana? I had about fourteen or fifteen in my class, and I took about ten of my unfinished short stories in there and just threw them out on the desk. They had red marks all over them, none of them was finished, and I said, "This is what my stuff looks like in progress." That impressed them so much: that I would show them unfinished work with all the crap and the red marks and the misspelled words all over it. I said, "My stuff is not perfect by any means when it's under construction."

How did the students respond to the unpredictability of process, all the revision and polishing?

They don't want to hear that. They want to hear who the good agent is. Who can get me the most money. I say, "First you need to write something worth publishing."

What makes you think a student might get to that point? What in a student manuscript conveys talent?

I look for something original, something you haven't seen before, something that shows that they are doing something with the language on their own. That they aren't copying anybody. That they are trying to develop their own voice — and I think that voice will always come through in a piece of fiction. You are able to identify with it in the first paragraph — it needs to be in the first paragraph! That's the way I judge a book. I know by the first page if I'm in the hands of a good writer or not. Not always, maybe, but usually. But then, you think some student's a dunce and three months later, they turn in a brilliant short story. So, in some ways, it's hard to tell. Sometimes, they just get fired up and decide to dedicate themselves, and then the ones you thought were really hot at first, they kind of fizzle out. To me, there's nothing better than coming up with something new, that hasn't been done before, a new thing that's added to the world, that you did, that didn't exist in the world before you did it.

Did you feel that you had talent when you were starting out?

If anybody could look at my early work — Ole Miss bought a lot of my early manuscripts and I've still got a good bit of it myself — the ones that didn't get published and all the early stuff, you'd have to say that I had no talent. It was that bad. You would have no choice. That would be the only decision. "Larry Brown has no talent."

So what kept you writing?

I always just had to believe that if I just stayed with it long enough and dedicated myself to learning my craft, I would eventually learn how. If I wanted to suffer enough and pay the dues and the price to continue to write and have it rejected. After a couple of years, I began to see that there was a process and an apprenticeship period that a writer had to go through. I read enough to see that Faulkner had one that lasted about five years. Even him. So I just said, "Keep on going." I would get depressed and sad, of course, when all my stuff came back. Mary Annie always said that the worst thing was to see me go down to the mailbox and pick up all those manila envelopes when the stories had been rejected and then see me come back up the driveway. She said she'd kind of watch me and I'd read them for a little while and then I'd sit down and start writing something else. So I just had faith that if I could work hard enough, eventually I would learn how.

Peter Cameron

Peter Cameron is the author of five novels and three collections of short stories. He was born in Pompton Plains, New Jersey, and grew up there and in London, England. A graduate of Hamilton College in New York State, he sold his first short story to the *New Yorker* in 1983, and published ten more stories in that magazine during the next few years. Beginning in 1990, Cameron stopped writing short fiction and turned his attention toward novels. He has taught writing at Oberlin College, Columbia University, Sarah Lawrence College, and Yale University, and worked for Lambda Legal Defense and Education Fund, a legal organization that protects and extends the civil rights of gay men, lesbians, and people with HIV/AIDS. Currently, he works for the Trust for Public Land. He lives in New York City.

One Way or Another, 1986 (stories); *Leap Year*, 1990; *Far-flung*, 1991 (stories); *The Weekend*, 1994; *The Half You Don't Know: Selected Stories*, 1997; *Andorra*, 1997; *The City of Your Final Destination*, 2002; *Someday This Pain Will Be Useful to You*, 2007

Would you talk first about how books gather for you? What is the process by which book ideas appear, develop, and evolve in your mind?

I don't understand the process very well. It seems mysterious and also very much beyond my control. I often go years in between books simply because I don't have an idea for one. A very gradual accumulation happens during those periods, ideas appear and develop. The ideas that I originally had for both *Andorra* and *The City of Your Final Destination* were more intellectually and architecturally ambitious than the books turned out to be. *Andorra* was going to be a novel within a novel about this man participating in a prisoner-mentor writing program, corresponding with a prisoner who was writing a novel. You'd see the mentor's life and the scenes around him, and then you'd see the correspondence between them and the chapters of the novel the prisoner was writing. I worked on it that way for a year or two and it was sort of nowhere until I realized that the only part I really liked was the novel the prisoner was writing. So I jettisoned the frame. I conceived *The City of Your Final Destination* as a book that would explore the nature of biography. You would see scenes from the lives of Gund [the subject of the biography] and the people around him. Omar would come and you would hear how they would talk about their lives. Then there would be scenes from Omar's subsequent biography [of Gund]. It was about looking at how life gets lived, how it gets remembered, and how it gets recorded. Again, I worked quite a while and realized what really interested me was the very human story of the people there. So I reformulated the book as a much simpler story. It seems to me that to get an idea I have to conceive of a book more ambitiously than it turns out to be. Then in process it gets simplified and scaled down. Part of the reason might be that there's always pressure to write a big book, a more complex book—and I'm not that kind of writer. I think I'll always write pretty conventional, not terribly ambitious books in terms of scope. But I think I feel that pressure and I conceive of these ideas that could potentially turn into a big book. And they don't.

Your style, your use of language is so careful and beautiful. Are you a slow writer?

I am a slow writer. It's interesting. The idea for *Someday This Pain Will Be Useful* just came. I knew it was going to be a small book that would take place over a few days. I thought, since that was so clear to me, it ought to be a fairly quick book to write. But no. My original idea for the book was not so different from the book it ended up being, but it took me just as long. It just takes me a long time to write a book. I keep going back and rewriting what I've done before I go forward, so that what's there seems very solid, in as good a state as I can get it.

So you don't have to revise much at the end?

Usually by the time I get to the end I've reworked what's there and gone through it so many times that it's in pretty good shape. Of course, you get to the end and things have changed, so you have to get it to work.

Your first novel is really a comedy of manners with all these funny things taken to extreme. But there's that underlying ache in it that I see in all your work. The title Leap Year *reflects the fact that the characters' lives are out of balance. Would you talk about that book?*

I had written a novel a couple years before *Leap Year* that never got sold. A lot of publishers saw it and liked the writing. The problem was, nothing happened. There were characters and place . . . but no plot. It was a very discouraging experience. I thought, I can write stories, but I'm never going to be able to write a novel. Around this time, a friend of mine, Adam Moss, was starting a magazine, *Seven Days*. I saw the prototype a few weeks before it was launched and there was no fiction in it. Sort of kiddingly I said, "You should have fiction." He said the only kind of fiction he could imagine working into the magazine was a serial novel, and asked, "Would you be interested in doing that?" I thought, after writing this novel in which nothing happens, I'm the least qualified person in the world to try to write a serial novel, which would be plot intensive. Then I thought, well, this would be a way to force me to make a plot. I had written a novel my senior year in college that took place in New York City, involving all those characters. It was my fantasy about coming to NY, being an adult in NY. So I took those characters and began writing the novel. It was a great way to be forced to write a novel very quickly because I had to write a chapter every week. I had to make things happen. I didn't know where a lot of things in that book were going to go, but I realized you could trust action. If you throw a lot of balls up in the air, eventually you figure out what to do with them. It was sort of amazing to me how it all just worked itself out.

Juggling is exactly what that book feels like — all those balls in the air. How did you work with the multiple points of view to make that happen? How did you know when it was somebody's turn?

It was something I had to plan out. There were so many characters and so much action I needed to keep track of it in some way. So I kept this notebook — a musical notebook with staffs. There was one staff for each character, to track in a linear way what they were doing. For every week there's a page with everybody on it. It was a way of visually looking at the book, mapping it out in a way I've never done with another book.

How was the book received?

It was a very curious book to publish first. My reputation was a very literary writer of *New Yorker* short stories, and it was not the sort of book that people were expecting of me. I was comfortable with it, but it made me realize how people have expectations, and when you don't meet those expectations, critics, especially, can be disappointed.

Still, it has in it all the things that show up in your later novels in varying proportions. There's always art and the question of what's original and what's absurd. There's love and vulnerability, honesty versus proper behavior, the importance of words and how words fail. These elements are in Leap Year, *though maybe in a lighter way.*

Yes. I wanted it to be a comic novel, but I hoped it could fluctuate between being gently comic and overtly melodramatic — and also have these moments when the characters take on dimension and didn't seem cartoonish. That was a hard thing to try to modulate. I wanted it to go back and forth between a very silly book and a serious book.

Your next novel, The Weekend, *was completely different. It is a book about grief; it feels like grief. Lyle, John, and Marian, still grieving over Tony, who died the year before of AIDS, are sometimes numb, sometimes sideswiped by small things that devastate them. And there's that interesting problem of the continuing presence of the lost person in disconcerting ways. The sequences in which Lyle's memories of Tony overlap with the present day he's experiencing in the same place with his new love, Robert, are particularly effective.*

I wanted the uncertainty about whether you were in the past or the present. I'm glad the book felt that way to you, that there was some confusion about where *are* we? In the film they made of *The Weekend* they shot all the flashback scenes of Tony in this blue and white haze, so they looked very different from the rest of the film. That seemed like a real mistake to me.

Marian's anxiety about her baby, Roland, adds a different dimension to the way grief plays out.

I wanted Marian to be in some way channeling her grief. I felt like she was someone who just worried about things and that the baby focused her worry. He was so young that you didn't know and you were anxious about it. She could have been totally wrong about the baby or her concerns could be real.

She was reminiscent of the mother in Judith Guest's Ordinary People. *In some ways you really didn't want to like her, yet there were these moments when you knew that she was the one who was probably in the most trouble emotionally. The scene in which she embarrasses Robert by offering him the grape scissors, as if it's a kind of criticism of the way he's eating the grapes, comes to mind.*

When I think about that scene I think about the last line, where Marian takes the scissors and says, "They were my grandmother's." The scissors seem ridiculous and pretentious to the reader, but to her they have this incredibly sentimental feeling. They're not ridiculous to her. I wanted that shift to come at the end of the scene. You might think that she was being this pushy, awful hostess, but at the same time everything she was doing was coming out of the place of feeling and sentiment and memory. It's so easy to condemn people when you don't understand what's motivating them.

Another very compelling moment is when Robert overhears John and Marian talking about his relationship with Lyle. The reader is as surprised and mortified as he is. You actually create that "shriveling" feeling on the page!

Before having written *Leap Year*, I probably would have thought it was too bold, too melodramatic to have someone overhear something. But the book was all about politeness. I wanted the reader to see how shocking it was to a young person who hasn't learned to be duplicitous like that.

The dinner guest Laura Ponti cranks up the tension and helps bring things to a head with Lyle and Robert.

The Weekend was written first as a short story called "Departing." It's the only time I've ever written a short story where, when it was finished, I felt still connected to those characters, still intrigued by them. The conception of *The Weekend* was at first, again, very ambitious in terms of architecture. You would read the short story first and then you would read different versions of it, each one longer and deeper. I would show the surface of the story and then excavate.

But I realized that I just wasn't interested in formally experimenting like that, and it turned into a very conventional novel. I just expanded the story, taking longer to look at every moment—adding flashbacks and adding depth to every scene.

In the story Laura is a genuine Italian, the only character that really changed. When I was rewriting it as a novel I realized that the idea of somebody who was sort of posing as an Italian, somebody who had to come to terms with her own self-image and deception, would make her a more complex character in the novel. I always like having young characters, like Kate (in *Leap Year*) and Portia (in *The City of Your Final Destination*); but I also like to have these older characters who have a different perspective than the [young] adults in the novel, who comment or have the wisdom — or think they have wisdom — the other characters lack. So I liked having a character like Laura Ponti because she could make those pronouncements.

Her kindness to Robert in the end was unexpected, but perfect. It added something really interesting to that thread of the story.

Rapport often skips a generation. People can see each other more clearly and appreciate each other more when they're a little bit further toward the ends of that spectrum.

The time frame of The Weekend *is really short. Would you talk about the flow of time in this novel, and generally?*

Leap Year takes place over a year, *The Weekend* takes place basically over two weekends, and *Andorra* and *The City of Your Final Destination* both take place over a couple of months. I can't imagine writing books that take place over years and years. I can't imagine knowing a character well enough to do that. People change so much during the course of their lives that the idea of writing convincingly of their whole lives is something that seems incredibly challenging to me.

Tony describes an ideal city in The Weekend *that seems like the seed for* Andorra. *Is that where the novel comes from?*

That certainly introduced the notion into my mind. But when I was thinking about writing the book I realized it couldn't just be that idea. It needed plot. I thought it had to be more ambitious. So I thought, I'll write this book that's a book within a book that has these frames — again thinking a book would be one thing and then it turned into something else.

The ending of Andorra — *the shock of everything you thought you knew being turned upside down by what's revealed — is reminiscent of Ian McEwan's* Atonement. *How do readers react to it?*

I didn't like the ending of *Atonement*. I don't have a high tolerance for books that manipulate. So the whole time I was writing *Andorra*, I was thinking, I *can't* be writing this book. It's the kind of book I really hate. It surprised me. I had never written a book that had that element of mystery. It was something I didn't think I was good at or would be able to pull off.

I knew all along that there was this person in prison writing the book and projecting his past into this narrative. But the problem was, when I took away the frame, how would I come out of the book? That was a little tricky.

The main character, Alexander Fox, falls in love with two women, Ricky and Jean, who are opposites in many ways. There's interesting tension in that.

I wanted him to be falling in love with two people at the same time—and two very different people, both appealing and sympathetic in their own ways. There's something bad about that; you're supposed to fall in love with just one person. So I was trying to create these two women so the reader would understand what was compelling about each one.

And also, writing this book, I was always aware that it's him creating these characters. It's all about him feeling so rejected and unloved, so he creates this world in which he's immensely appealing to people. Everybody in this book immediately falls in love with him. I wanted these two women who were interested in him and were interesting to him, too. Even Nancy, Jean's sister, finds him appealing in a sexual way.

In this book writing and the act of writing are, in a way, a big part of what it's about. Right from the start, he's writing in the journal and he says that calms him down. At the end, there's the sense that writing is the process by which he was able to tell the truth to himself.

I think that book is in some sort of subtle way all about the comforts of reading and writing. There are all these allusions to other books in there. The act of writing that book goes back to Tony saying he wants to write a book and invent another world. When we write books, that's something we can do, and when we read books it's about entering another world that takes us out of our own. So in some ways that's what that book was about for me: getting out of your own world and entering a world that's better or more comforting. But that illusion can't sustain itself because the book ends.

The Weekend *takes on AIDS and is fraught with grief, yet there's a loosening in the characters at the end. They're not happy, but they seem to have moved a little bit. In its own way,* Andorra *is about grief too—and the end is devastating. You come to a grinding halt with the realization that his life is completely wrecked. He's going nowhere.*

It's odd to me because I realize in retrospect that they're both about grief, but that's not something I was conscious of thinking about when I was writing either one of them. I feel like I've been very fortunate being a gay man, living in New York for the last twenty-five or thirty years. I know so many people who lost people they loved, and I didn't have that experience. I've been lucky in terms of my family and friends, too. That overt grief over losing someone I love has not been a part of my life. So it's interesting to look back over those books and wonder, where did that come from?

The City of Your Final Destination *seems to resolve some of the issues you explored in* The Weekend *and* Andorra. *Omar behaves recklessly, ultimately abandoning words and explanations to step out of his life into a whole other world—and he's a happy guy in the end, as happy as anybody can be as a human being.*

The whole time I was working on that book I did not think there was going to be a happy ending. I didn't think Omar and Arden were going to end up together; I thought, he's going to have this experience and go back and move on. But as I moved through the book, I was more compelled and convinced by his love affair with Arden. It turned into something larger and more solid than I had thought it would be. As I was getting near the end of the book, I was thinking maybe he should go back there. Then I'd think, I can't write a book like that. I don't believe in happy endings. Then I thought, again . . . you can. That's what I love about all my books. I make these sort of intellectual decisions and then the characters dictate their fate and therefore the fate of the book. I realized that Omar and Arden were going to end up together and there wasn't anything I could do about it.

Your most recent novel, Someday This Pain Will Be Useful to You, *is a book for young adults. What made you decide to write for this market?*

I didn't write the book thinking it was a YA. My editor at FSG was disappointed in it. At first they wanted me to rewrite the book, make it bigger, but I realized I couldn't do that. The book was what it was. We sent it to another publisher and got the same response. This wasn't a Peter Cameron book they wanted; it wasn't as elegant or ambitious as my other books. I got discouraged—these were two editors I respected, who were good and sympathetic readers and who liked my work. Then it occurred to me that maybe people were reading it with the wrong expectations. I thought, what if somebody read it with a different set of expectations, thinking of it as a young adult novel? So we sent it back to Frances Foster, the children's book editor at FSG, who read it and liked it very much.

The book was cross listed in the adult and young adult markets, which rarely happens. Did that give the book some advantage?

It didn't actually work out very well. You can only market a book effectively in one market or the other. The book was published by FSG children's division—that was the imprint. So the only place the chains will put it is in the children's book section. The independent bookstores will put a book wherever they want to, so I reached out to a lot of independent bookstores, asking them to put it in both sections. But you can't do that with Barnes and Noble.

It was frustrating because, remembering my experience of being a teenage reader, it seemed much more likely for a teenager to find this book in the adult section than for an adult to find it in the children's section. But I don't have a large readership, so I felt like the small group of people who had read my books would find this one—and it turns out it's sold much better than any of my other books.

So in a weird way, it is the breakout book that editors were looking for—and will probably send a lot of young people to the adult section of the bookstore in search of your other work. As a young reader yourself, what kind of books appealed to you? Did you read the perennial favorites of teenagers, like The Catcher in the Rye, A Separate Peace, Lord of the Flies?

When I was a teenager I read all the books you mention, although the ones that had the greatest impact on me were *The Catcher in the Rye* and *To Kill a Mockingbird* (of course). I don't remember reading many YA books at that age, except for Emily Neville's *It's Like This, Cat* and Constance Greene's *Leo the Lioness*, both of which I liked (and continue to like) very much. I started to read "adult" books very young, and I wasn't particularly interested in books about young people. In high school I was reading Fitzgerald, Hemingway, Doris Lessing (*The Golden Notebook*), Margaret Drabble, Virginia Woolf.

Probably, many serious young adult readers are like this. Which brings us to an interesting question: what is a young adult book, after all?

I don't really understand that.

You're not alone! Maurice Sendak said something useful on the topic, though. When asked for advice on "writing for children," he responded, "I don't write for children. I write as a child." There's a rawness and urgency in Someday This Pain Will Be Useful *that makes it feel as if it's been channeled from your teenage self.*

Logically, it would have been my first novel. A lot of the short stories I wrote in my early twenties had teenage characters like James, and I guess I felt I had dealt with that particular kind of coming-of-age story, that teen angst. I wanted to do something else in a novel. But I also felt I was too close to all of that. It's taken me twenty-five years to get some distance on that time. To be able to write a novel I had to take that experience and reconceive it, invent a character—and that was something I couldn't do when I was younger.

What do you think finally made the material available to you?

I grew up in suburbia in New Jersey. Once I made the shift and conceived of James as an urban character, someone who was born and grew up in New York, which made his experience of being a person very different from mine, I felt freed. I had attended a student-government thing when I was in high school. Actually, when I was seventeen, I tried to write a novel about that. I wrote about three pages; it was terrible. So I liked the idea of not having the novel be about that experience, but having the novel reference it as something that happened in the past, and then inventing the plot, what little plot there was—John, the gallery, his family.

Also, having written *Andorra* and *The City of Your Final Destination*, which took place in Europe and South America, [respectively], the idea of writing a book that's set in NYC was very appealing. That was another liberating thing about this book, I was writing about my own backyard.

There's that thread of imagining an idyllic world, though—in James's fantasy about buying a big house in the Midwest.

New York City people are obsessed with real estate. You can go on the Internet and look at these beautiful houses that are incredibly affordable. That's something I fantasize about. Like James, I have an affection for houses. He thinks, with all this money they're spending to send me to Brown, I could buy this beautiful house.

It's very similar to Alexander Fox in *Andorra*, who thinks that if he moves to a different country, a beautiful country, his life is going to be beautiful. James thinks that if he moves into a beautiful, authentic house, like his grandmother's, his life will take on authenticity and meaning. He thinks it will make him happy.

James has such a strong, idiosyncratic voice. Did you get it right away?

Yeah. Pretty much. I like James, which made it fun to write the book because the voice was there from the beginning. I've heard from a fair amount of people about this book, and some don't like James. They find him unsympathetic. I can see that; he's a spoiled rich kid. But he's very aware of who he is and how privileged he is. He knows that his sadness doesn't make sense, that it's not earned. But that doesn't make it any less painful to him.

Like all good young-adult novels, Someday This Pain Will Be Useful To You *is a coming-of-age story, and a big part of growing up for James is coming to terms with his sexual identity. This is brought to the forefront of his life when he creates a false identity to impress the manager of his mother's art gallery, John.*

James is very attracted to John. He finds John very appealing in many ways. He has no way to express that; the only way he can imagine attracting John or expressing his attraction to John is to do it by creating an alter ego that he knows will appeal to John. When you feel unloved and unlovable it's very hard to express love or to acknowledge those feelings, so you have to do it in this covert, sort of warped way. Because he's in such turmoil he doesn't think at all about the ramifications of what he's doing.

Other things are troubling him, too. There's his crazy family, his anxiety about starting college, his general fear of any kind of intimacy, his chronic sadness—along with all the usual difficulties of adolescence.

Sadness is, at least in my experience, not specific. It's general, it's not just one thing. I didn't want it to be a book about James suffering over his sexuality or suffering over the divorce of his parents. There are a lot of reasons why he's feeling the way he's feeling. *Ordinary People* is a book that I read and loved when I was a teenager, but there's this one event that causes the character to be feeling what he's feeling. I didn't want James to be that reducible. It's all those things, and it's more. He's just a solitary, depressed person, and he's going to go through life that way. Although people change as they grow—and get perspective, which you don't have as a younger person.

For New Yorkers, 9/11 is lurking out there, too—which you treat in a wonderfully subtle way. James thinks, but doesn't say, "We did see everything from the windows of our classroom," which tells us all we need to know.

I realized that if I was writing this book and it was set in the summer of 2003, 9/11 would be something James had experienced. I didn't want to write a book about somebody responding to 9/11. I wanted that to be one of the many things that had turned him into who he was. I felt like his avoidance of it helped me as a writer. I wanted it to be something that's there, but partly submerged.

It's simmering in there, along with everything else. Maybe the fact that a book, like real life, is about so many things in a character's life that can only be looked at honestly, not explained, is what makes it literature—whether YA literature or just plain literature. It's certainly what makes a book appealing to a serious reader, regardless of age.

One of the reasons I was really happy that this book was being published as a YA novel is that I remember the effect books had on me when I was that age and how thrilling reading can be then. I continue to love reading books, but it's not that same experience. It doesn't change my life. At that age, you feel very disconnected from the world. You don't realize what other people are feeling or that what other people are feeling what *you're* feeling. Through reading and encountering characters, you feel that you're not so alone.

Do you think you'll write for young adults again?

I don't. I feel like this was my telling of this story, and I can't imagine how I could do it again in an original or necessary way. But I never *really* know what I'm going to write.

Michael Chabon

Michael Chabon is the author of six novels, two collections of short stories, a novella, and a collection of essays. Born in Washington, D.C., he received a BA from the University of Pittsburgh and an MFA from the University of California, Irvine. His first novel, *The Mysteries of Pittsburgh*, was submitted for review in a workshop led by MacDonald Harris, who liked it so much that he sent it to his agent, Mary Evans. Evans surprised Chabon with an offer to represent it, and the book was published shortly thereafter to great literary acclaim. He received the Pulitzer Prize for his novel *The Amazing Adventures of Kavalier and Clay*. Other awards include a National Magazine Award, an O. Henry Prize, the Nebula Award, and a Lila Wallace–Reader's Digest Grant. Chabon is a screenwriter as well as a fiction writer. He lives in Berkeley, California, with his wife, writer Ayelet Waldman, and their children.

The Mysteries of Pittsburgh, 1988; *A Model World and Other Stories*, 1991; *Wonder Boys*, 1995; *Werewolves in Their Youth*, 1999 (stories); *The Amazing Adventures of Kavalier and Clay*, 2000; *Summerland*, 2002; *The Final Solution: A Story of Detection*, 2004 (novella); *Gentlemen of the Road: A Tale of Adventure*, 2007; *The Yiddish Policemen's Union*, 2007

Your first novel, Mysteries of Pittsburgh, *was completed while you were working on your MFA. What was it like to work on a novel in a workshop setting? What kind of feedback did you get during the drafting process, and from whom?*

I started writing a novel because I thought that everybody else at the UC Irvine workshop, when I got there, would be writing novels or would already have written novels. I began *Mysteries of Pittsburgh* out of self-defense, in other words. Of course when I arrived, with a hundred pages in tow, I found lots of people focusing exclusively on short stories and others whose first novels were still in the future.

I showed my hundred pages, soon after arrival at Irvine, to the great Oakley Hall, one of the two writer/professors then in charge of the program. He told me, essentially, with typical bluntness, "You have far too many characters and nowhere near enough story." And I saw at once that he was right. So I went back that afternoon and cut all but about fifteen pages, and spent the next week reconceiving the book much more in terms of two stories — the Art-Arthur-Phlox love triangle and the Art-Cleveland-father plot — committing myself at that point, without being sure how I would do it, to have the two stories intersect.

After that I turned the novel in to the workshop three times, roughly at one hundred pages, two hundred pages, and three hundred pages. The first time, the workshop was led by the other main Irvine guy, a man named Donald Heiney, since dead, who wrote some extremely interesting Steven Millhauser-ish novels under the pen name of MacDonald Harris. He began the workshop by saying, basically, "This is brilliant, it's wonderful, and clearly Michael knows what he's doing here. Anything any of us says to him beyond encouraging him to go on will only foul him up." So he essentially forbade any discussion. Needless to say, that rankled the other members of the workshop considerably. This came back to haunt me the next time I submitted it to the workshop — they were pretty well lying in wait! The third time, it was a finished manuscript, which I had already shown to Don Heiney. Without telling me, he had sent it to his agent in New York. A few weeks later, I got a call from Mary Evans, then at the Virginia Barber Literary Agency, saying they were going to take me on. So when the workshop started chopping it up the third time, I already knew that I had an agent who was pretty enthusiastic about her chances of selling it.

I don't want to give the impression that there was anything like a hostile environment in that workshop, by the way. We all got along very well, for the most part, socialized together a lot, etc. But they were an opinionated group and very articulate, and that first experience of being gagged by Don Heiney just sat very badly with them.

Did you know that Mysteries of Pittsburgh *was a novel right from the start, or did it start as a short story? If the latter, would you talk about how you came to realize that it was a novel? What is the difference between a short story and a novel, in your opinion?*

I began the book with the conscious intention of writing a novel, which I tried to pattern loosely after two of my favorite novels, *The Great Gatsby* and *Goodbye, Columbus* (which latter was, I believe, patterned to some degree on the former), in that it would take place over the course of a single summer.

A short story is a commando operation. It has a specific objective; you have to get in quickly, set your charges, and get out, leaving the reader to be caught up in the blast. A novel is more like a war: always begun in the highest enthusiasm, with full confidence of right, and of the certainty of it all being over by Christmas. Two years later you're in the trenches and the mud, with defeat a real possibility, doubting everything, in particular the wisdom of the commanding general.

Would you describe the genesis of the novel and the process by which you found and wrote the story? What did you know when you began? What surprised you during the writing process?

All I knew when I began work was "I'm going to write a book about summer." What surprised me most, I suppose, was the realization, about two-thirds of the way through, that I was actually going to finish a novel!

You had the experience that all novelists dream of having with a first novel—great reviews, great sales, comparisons to Dickens, Salinger, and F. Scott Fitzgerald. What was that like? In what ways was that kind of success not all a blessing? How do you think it shaped you as a developing writer?

It felt even less real as it was happening to me than it does now. And there were factors in my personal life, in my first marriage, that conspired to make every good thing that happened simultaneously a burden. I think that, in retrospect, that may have been a good thing. It was hard to feel too proud of myself. I'm not sure how it shaped me, although I think I have unquestionably benefited from having the sense, after *Mysteries*, of there being a real audience for my writing, small but loyal—I mean my gay readers. They have always been there for me and I have taken a lot of heart over the years from knowing they were there.

Though Wonder Boys *is your second published novel, it is not the second novel you wrote. Would you describe that second novel — what you were attempting with it, why it was so difficult, and what ultimately happened to it?*

I feel as I've talked about this book so much by now that perhaps I ought just to have published it and thereafter shut up! It was a novel called *Fountain City* and was primarily concerned with the attempt by a developer, an architect, and his apprentice, to build the perfect baseball park on the Gulf Coast of Florida. But there were lots of subplots and sub-subplots dealing with Paris, French cooking, environmentalism, and a plot to rebuild the Temple in Jerusalem. I think I started out telling a fairly simple story about an architect who lived in a kind of classical dreamworld and then [I] got more and more reckless in adding ingredients to the brew . . . just tossing in all kinds of stuff I was (and remain) interested in, and trusting — wrongly, as it turned out — that it would come out not merely edible but tasty and nourishing.

For many novelists, the second novel is actually more difficult to write than the first. Why do you think this is so?

I don't know; it took me twenty-two years to write my first novel, but only seven to finish a second, and four for this latest one — maybe it's getting easier!

What was the genesis of Wonder Boys? *Would you talk about the process by which you found and wrote that story? What did you know when you began, and what surprised you?*

I was terrified by the ongoing failure of *Fountain City*. Five and a half years into it, I began to worry that I would never finish it, that I would keep on writing it for the rest of my life. I didn't think I had the guts to walk away. But then one day my then fiancée, now wife, announced to me that she was going to take the California Bar Exam six months earlier than she originally had intended. Which meant that between studying and her job as a clerk for a federal district judge, she would be completely unavailable to me for the next six weeks.

It was a like a bolt of lightning. Something inside me said, "Now's your chance." I went down to my office under our house in San Francisco, opened a new file, and just started writing. I wrote the first five or seven pages in a night, pretty much as they are in the final book, and just kept on going. It was very strange; I have no idea where any of it came from, beyond my apparent desire to create, in Grady Tripp, a writer who had screwed himself even more than I had. It was as if, once I had made the decision to use this six-week period to "cheat on" *Fountain City*, some story-telling part of my consciousness was liberated. Seven months later I had a solid first draft.

Did you imagine the scene in which Grady Tripp's novel blows away when you conceived of your novel, or was it something that came to you in the process of writing it?

I think that episode pretty much arose out of the moment. I didn't really know until I got there what was going to happen to Grady's manuscript, to his work on the novel.

Was James Leer based in any way on yourself and your own experiences as a young writer, or on the experiences of someone you know? Do other characters in the book have counterparts in real people?

James Leer was sort of an amalgam of me and a couple of other "boy genius" writers I had known in school, and I use the quotes advisedly. And real people usually manage to work their way into all of my characters, somehow or other.

Wonder Boys is hilarious, but also powerful because it is true on the most fundamental level. Any writer who has been through an MFA program or even just attended a writers' conference recognizes the basic truth in your depiction of that world. To what degree do you think that the work of a serious novelist is helped and/or hindered, either as a teacher or student, in these programs? Can writing be taught? For you, what is the benefit of having earned the MFA degree?

It really all depends on the program, which in turn depends on (1) most importantly, the amount of financial support the program offers to students, so that they can concentrate on their writing; (2) the quality and commitment to teaching of the faculty; and (3) the tone of the workshop itself, which grows in part out of (2) and in part from the nature of the students. If you get yourself into a program that supports you both emotionally and financially, with teachers who inspire by example and help you past some of the shoals and rocks that confront the young writer, then you can really blossom.

What is talent, in your opinion? How does it fit into the mix?

Talent is, with luck, one of the two out of three required elements for success, both artistic and material, as a writer, over which the writer has absolutely no control, and for which he or she can take no credit at all. The third absolutely required element, and the only one the writer can both ensure and take pride in, is discipline.

My view of talent is like that of the catcher Crash Davis in *Bull Durham*, when he's lecturing Nuke LaLoosh on the importance of discipline in pitching: "God reached down and turned your right arm into a thunderbolt. It has nothing to do with you." Literary talent is an accident of birth, like the ability to spot four-leaf clovers, and about as meaningful in the absence of hard work.

Your novels have become longer and more complex; each one is a completely different kind of story, yet certain things show up again and again. Would you comment on the idea of a writer's material? Where does it come from? How do you recognize an idea as your own? In what ways does your own material reflect the experiences that shaped you as a child?

That's what Henry James called "the figure in the carpet." It's a kind of an inherent signature—a watermark—that can be seen in every work by a particular writer when you hold it up to the light. I'm sure that the explanations lie in my childhood and adolescence as a lonely, dreamy, socially outcast child of divorce, but beyond that I prefer not to think about it too much, to be honest. I'm just glad to know it's there.

My ideas are just . . . my ideas. I've never had one that I didn't like, that didn't just seem to arise bearing the promise of being very interesting — to me.

The Amazing Adventures of Kavalier and Clay *moves into the heads of characters who seem purely invented and who live in a completely different time. Where did the idea for this book come from? How did it develop? How is the book you wrote the same as and different from the book you imagined at the start?*

This book ultimately grew out of an ongoing conversation between me and my father, all through my childhood, about the world of his childhood, in Brooklyn, which he remembered in deep and fond detail. The comic books, the movies, the radio programs, the political and social history, the music, the games, and landscape of his boyhood; he brought them to vivid life in my imagination. I guess I just wanted to do the same thing for readers. From the start I knew that I wanted to try to cover the entire period of the so-called Golden Age of Comic Books, circa 1938–1954.

It's funny. When I finished the book, I felt that I had really wandered very far from my original ideas about what kind of a book it would be. That I had made all kinds of surprising discoveries and decisions along the way that I never could have foreseen. And then I came across a brief note I had written to myself, four and a half years earlier, as I prepared to start to work. In this note I laid out my intentions for the book and for what I thought it would be like, what kind of territory it would cover. And it was remarkably like the final draft! I was amazed.

Creating the character of The Escapist, Sammy asks Joe, "What is the why?" This seems to be fundamental to creating characters that are believable and compelling. Would you talk about this idea in terms of how you go about creating the characters in your novels?

I guess I'll just say that when I get into trouble working on a book, it's almost always because I don't understand my character or characters' motivations; there's a disjunction between the behavior of the character as dictated by the needs of my plot and what he or she really would do in the situation, whatever the situation is. And until I sort out and get a very firm grip on "the why," I can't really proceed.

How do your characters most often show themselves to you in the beginning stages of writing a novel? How do they clarify and begin to shape the action of it?

It depends. Some characters come together, from their aches and the sources of those aches down to their smallest particulars of speech and dress, very quickly and effortlessly. And once I have a good sense of them, I can sort of sit back and let them do what they do. Other characters go through endless permutations and revisions, turning from wicked to kind to whimsical to mad and back again, and I'll struggle from draft to draft to draft to get to the heart of the character and to what his or her function in the book must be. In this latter case, sometimes the problem character will just one day abruptly pop into place, and I'll say, "Oh, of course!" And sometimes he or she never comes together, and I just have to cut him or her out.

You gave the reader the "why" of the comic-book character Tom Mayflower in a separate chapter early in the book. Later, Judy Dark's "why" was given a chapter. In each case, the stories are in large part woven of issues and memories that their creators are grappling with at the moment of creation, and real-world details that they encounter going about their day-to-day lives while the story is percolating on an unconscious level. Would you talk about how these chapters describe the process by which the novel itself was made? What issues, questions, memories, and details of your real life made their way into the fabric of the story during the process of writing it?

This is a very good question, but unfortunately I don't think I can give it a very good answer. It's such an intuitive process that for the most part I'm not even aware that it's happening, and often it won't be until later, when somebody points it out to me, that I see how much of some real-life experience or concern of mine has been reconfigured in the fiction. And yet, as the examples you give suggest, it's a process that I'm fully aware of, that, in fact, I rely on.

My life, my memories and desires, are the bits of string, colored paper, yarn, tinfoil, etc. — not particularly interesting in themselves — that I assemble into the collages of my novels and stories.

The practice of magic is a thread that runs through the book. Would you discuss the ways in which you think magic is a metaphor for the process of writing a novel? What rules of magic apply to creating a novel?

The magic, to me, is in the enjoyment of a work of art, not in the creation of it. In other words, the novelist has not performed any magic at all until his or her book is in a reader's hands, is reaching directly into that reader's mind and is transporting the reader out of his or her own soul, the suffering and tedium of the reader's quotidian life. Everything up to that point is craft.

In The Amazing Adventures of Kavalier and Clay, *you regularly intro-*
duced new elements, building on what had come before to torque the tension
of the novel. How did you create the plot of the novel? Which twists and turns
of the plot did you know at the outset and which ones revealed themselves as
you wrote? How did you keep all the various strands of the book straight, both
in your head and on the page?

It was pretty much a long, often painful and dull process of trial and
error, groping my way along, writing and rejecting long passages that went
nowhere. I subscribe to the perdition theory of plotting: you just have to
get very, very lost, a lot. I know very little, when I'm starting out, about
the plot, and in fact a lot of the things I think I know end up getting dis-
carded because they turned out to be not germane or simply superfluous.

But at a certain point I will begin to get caught up in the story myself, almost the way a reader does, and the things that happen next will
have this marvelous sense of inevitability. And then, as I'm closing in on
the end of the first draft, I will sit down and plot out the last part of the
book. After that, I try to figure out where I'm going. Before I begin the
next draft, I make a very thorough outline. At this point, for the first
time, I start to question myself about the dominant motifs of the book,
the themes that seem to be emerging, and I try to use the answers to these
questions to help guide the plot choices I make, discarding elements and
episodes that seem beside the point, and trying to forge new links for the
chain, tempered by my deeper understanding of what it is I seem to be
trying to say.

But I'm making the process of revision outlining sound much more
articulate and drawn out than it really is. It's really a matter of about a
half-hour's work, and my notes to myself are very fragmentary, and later
often turn out to be not especially helpful.

Would you describe the research you did for The Escapist? *Did you do most*
of the research before you began writing, or as you wrote? What rules did you
set for yourself in your use of the real people, like Salvadore Dalí and Al Smith,
who appear in the book?

I did a lot of library research, poring over old back issues of the *New*
Yorker, going through back issues of the *New York Times* on microfilm. I
read histories of comic books, histories of America during the period. I

spent a month in New York, doing research at the New York Historical Society library—especially looking through their collections of old photos of the city. And I had the 1939 *WPA Guide to New York City*, which I carried around, trying to see the city as it was then. I interviewed a lot of surviving Golden Age comics creators, trying to jog their memories of the time. And then as I wrote, subjects kept working their way into the book that obliged me to go back to the library: the Antarctic, Houdini, the Empire State Building, the golem.

I had some reservations about using "celebrity characters." It's a widely [used], perhaps overused fictional "trick" nowadays. But ultimately I decided since these people—Dalí, Al Smith, Orson Welles—kept cropping up in my research, over and over, they were a legitimate part of the cultural landscape of the time, as much as the smoke-ring-blowing Camel sign in Times Square, and that it would be not only silly but mistaken to leave them out. So my rule was just not to let them be anything more than minor characters, taking cameo roles. I kept them in the background.

A number of things in the book either mirror or are reminiscent of real events of that time. For example, Hans Hoffman's failed effort to bring the Jewish children to America on The Ark of Miriam *echoes the incident in which a shipful of Jewish children actually reached America, but were turned away at immigration. How did these real things work their way into the book? In what ways did your research discoveries shape character and/or plot? In what ways did you transform real events to suit the needs of the story?*

The research really did drive the plot. For example, I was reading about comic books in a magazine devoted to older, "vintage" comics, and there happened to be an article about this 1960s comics artist named Jim Steranko who had had an earlier career as an escape artist. When I read that, a light just came on. The idea of escape just felt instantly right, though I wasn't really sure, yet, why.

That was an experience that got repeated over and over again: some little tidbit in my reading would just ring a bell, and the shape of the book, the destinies of the characters, would change.

Why did you decide to use the occasional footnotes throughout the book?

I was trying to confuse the reader. I wanted him or her to have moments of very serious uncertainty about just how fictional this book, and in particular the characters of Kavalier and Clay, really were. Footnotes are a weirdly effective way of lending an aura of fact to your lies.

What were the pleasures and perils of research for you?

It was pretty much all pleasure to immerse myself in the history, images, and atmosphere of this era that had always meant so much to me. The peril was, first of all, that it was always more fun to go to the library and read old *New Yorkers* than to write; and, second, that doing too much research sometimes started to make me feel imprisoned by the facts. There always comes a point when you have to put research aside and just start making shit up.

What is your process of revision? Do people read for you? If so, what kind of feedback do you depend on them to give you?

I revise as I go along, and then from draft to draft. Generally, I begin each night's writing session by going over what I did the night before. My principal techniques for identifying the parts that need work are (1) listening carefully to the sound of the words with my "inner ear"—I can usually hear the wonky parts; and (2) attending to the feeling in my gut: a clenching, uneasy, anxious clutch of dissatisfaction that seems to bloom whenever I'm reading my way through a weak section.

My wife is always my first reader, and over the years I have trained her to be harsh in her judgments. And for this latest book I gave drafts to a lot of people, far more than had been my practice in the past. I think I was worried more about this book than about previous ones—it was so big and complicated, and plus there was the whole period element. And I got some very helpful readings. It was like being back in workshop again. I think I'll probably do the same thing with the next book.

Have you ever experienced writer's block? What is writer's block, in your opinion?

No. Like Grady Tripp, I don't believe in writer's block. If you're disciplined about your work—meaning you do it at the same time every day, for the same amount of time—you'll have bad days at the keyboard, days when you struggle and it all comes out crap. But it will come out, because you will have trained your writing organ to wake up when your butt hits the chair.

After living intensely in the world of Kavalier and Clay, *what was it like to finish the book and think about moving on to another set of characters, another world? Would you talk about what it's like to live in a novel—how it impinges on your real life, how your real life funnels into it?*

I was mostly just relieved by the time I finished the book. There was a little bit of sadness, because it had been a pleasurable experience, and I knew I was never going to have quite the same relationship again to Glenn Miller's music, Jack Benny, Eleanor Roosevelt, etc., that I had felt while writing the book. I was back in my own time again, for the foreseeable future. But mostly I was just relieved.

What is it like to let go of a book and send it into the world of readers and reviewers? Would you talk about how you deal with the business end of being a successful novelist?

It's an extremely anxious time. And again, as the reviews come in and are, hopefully, mostly good, what I feel is largely relief. But it's very exciting and wondrous to hear from readers, to hear what they liked in the book, what made them laugh or cry, what their favorite sentences are. I deal with the business end of being a novelist by trusting in my agent, Mary Evans. And so far this has proven to be a very wise policy.

Michael Cunningham

Michael Cunningham is the author of five novels and one work of non-fiction. He was born in Cincinnati, Ohio, and grew up in La Cañada, California. Cunningham received his BA in English Literature from Stanford University and his MFA in Creative Writing from the University of Iowa. His novel *The Hours* won the Pulitzer Prize and the PEN/Faulkner Award. Other honors include a Whiting Writers' Award, a Guggenheim Fellowship, a National Endowment for the Arts Fellowship, and a Michener Fellowship from the University of Iowa.

Golden States, 1984; *A Home at the End of the World*, 1990; *Flesh and Blood*, 1995; *The Hours*, 1998; *Specimen Days*, 2005

Your first novel, Golden States, *is a straight narrative, a coming-of-age story that covers just a few weeks in the life of a twelve-year-old boy. Would you talk about that book, about how the characters in it were, in a way, prototypes for characters that you in explored in later books, particularly in* A Home at the End of the World *and* Flesh and Blood?

It's true. The books often tend to contain a boy on a journey and a woman trapped in a tower. *Golden States* was a funny thing. It is my first novel. I wrote it very, very quickly. I was about to turn thirty, and I realized what I had for my years of writing thus far was seventeen abandoned beginnings. I began to realize that this was where old failures come from. First they're young failures, then they're middle-aged failures, then they're old failures. I was working in a bar and I suddenly had this vivid image of myself at sixty, still in the bar, still talking about the novel I was going to write someday. So I said to myself, "Sit down now and finish something. It doesn't matter what. Just start it at the beginning, write through the middle and reach the end and then stop." And that was that book. It came out very quickly. And it's true. It does contain some of the people I seem to have continued to write about. Boys looking for something, women looking for a way out. I never felt good about that book, because I wrote it too fast. Because I knew it wasn't the best book I could write. I've always felt that literature and reading have so many enemies—and writers are the very least of the enemies of writing and reading. But I do sometimes find myself looking through the books in a bookstore and galleys people have sent me, thinking, you could have done better than this. You did not put your ass on the line. Here's just another book taking up space in the universe, and this is part of what is making it hard to keep books alive in the world. They just stack up like cordwood. I'm so much more interested in some kind of grand ambitious failure than I am in someone's modest little success that achieves its modest little aims. I felt that I had written a book like that, and I wasn't happy about it. My publisher very generously allowed me to turn down a paperback offer and it has really gone away.

You don't list it with your novels.

Not listing it, frankly—though I didn't fight this—was a sort of marketing ploy, when my second book came out. It's much, much easier to sell a first novel. [*Golden States*] had sold about seventeen copies and nobody knew about it. The irony, of course, is now they sell for several hundred dollars on the Internet.

The next two books, A Home at the End of the World *and* Flesh and Blood, *are similar in theme and in the way the stories are told. They're just plain "good reads" in the traditional sense. Would you talk about the relationship between the two?*

I've always felt like I want to sit at the table with Susan Sontag on my right and Pia Zadora on my left. I want my books to occupy some sort of tricky zone between the dead serious and the—I wouldn't want to say pulpy or even frivolous—but you know what I mean. Books you might want to take on an airplane. I wrote *A Home at the End of the World* and *Flesh and Blood* during the early years of the AIDS epidemic, when I was very much involved with ACT UP, when the presidents were Ronald Reagan and George Bush, Sr., neither of whom ever used the word "AIDS" in public. Never even said the word. I had a lot of friends I had seen perform heroic acts who were dying. It was a remarkable time. You saw people who outwardly appeared to be disco bunnies, boys in hot pants without a thought in their heads, crazy old diesel dykes with tattoos everyplace, and I watched them take care of people whose families couldn't do it, or wouldn't do it. I watched these people go to the hospitals, hold the hands, get the bills paid, see that there was food if they went home. I watched them call the people you need to call and have the body taken care of. Then I watched those people get sick. I wanted to take them books. I wanted to shut off their TVs and give them something to read. But a lot of these people, who I loved, were not serious readers—not the kind of readers we are. It was late in the game to try to convince them that Chekov was writing about them, and there weren't many books—there weren't really *any* books—that I felt especially good about, in which these people could recognize themselves, in which they didn't have to see themselves by extension or by analogy. That I could bring to them and say, "Here's a character exactly like *you*." I wanted to write a book like that, and then another one—for all kinds of reasons. [Books] that would be easy to walk into. I didn't dumb them down, but I felt that they should have straightforward, traditional structures. They should be good stories, easy to follow, if they were going to provide the kind of company I wanted them to provide for certain people.

The structure of those books is interesting because in a way it mirrors a theme in your work—the power and importance of single moments in a person's life. Defining moments that Woolf called "moments of being." Many of the chapters in A Home at the End of the World *and* Flesh and Blood *feel like "moments of being." Not exactly stories in their own right, but sharply focused on one or several scenes in the characters' lives. For example, the scene in* A Home at the End of the World *in which Bobby's brother dies when he tries to run through a glass door.*

The boy running through the glass is something that actually happened. I was at a party, I guess I was fourteen. It was just one of those parties kids have. Somebody's parents are out of town and so everybody goes over and we're all drinking beer and getting stoned and there was this older kid, who we just all loved. He was great. He was in a band. He was just the coolest of the cool. And some little kids started throwing stones at the house and we all ran out to chase them away and came back in and I shut the sliding glass door. He had stayed outside and a minute later came running back and didn't see that the door was closed and ran through it. And died.

Do you find that details from the real world—things you overhear, things you remember, things people tell you—often work their way into your characters' lives?

They do very much. But I always put them in a box and sort of shake them up and see what comes up. It's funny. It seems to be a strictly temperamental question, the one about the extent to which a writer either works from life or works from imagination. I know people—Mona Simpson, Harold Brodkey—who literally can't write about something they haven't seen. They would be making it up. Anything in their novels, though they are fiction, has been observed happening by those writers. I find if I adhere too strictly to any [real] person, I either want to defend them too much or nail them too hard. It's best if I use a little bit of this and a little bit of that and develop a person. I don't know. It seems like a lot of us dream of people who don't really exist. They may even be . . . like your sister. But it's *not* your sister. It's a very vivid person that you dream, just not somebody you know. It's a little like that.

Where do you go from the image? How do the characters develop?

It's slightly mysterious. I have some actor friends in New York, where I live, and the process I undergo with my characters is a little bit similar to something I hear from them. It's as much physical as it is anything. I think about the person, I associate for the person, I just sort of let the details start to accumulate. Carriage, manner, tone of voice, hair, shoes. But they remain a sort of welter of disconnected details. If I'm lucky, if it works there's a moment when I say, "Oh! There he is."

Does this happen in the writing process, or is it something you work out before you start?

I work it out before I start. But, of course, [I write] the first draft to see what I'm writing, no matter who I'm writing about. The person gains tremendous weight as I go on. But in order to begin to write about a person, I need to get to the point where I'm writing autobiographically.

From the point of view from the character.

Yeah. Though that person may be a suicidal fifty-nine-year-old woman.

Once you have the characters in mind, how do you develop and sequence the scenes?

Very much the way I always work, by trial and error. It's always a question of what's going to work best for this book. I never approach a book with anything in the way of formal conviction. I just try to see what the book is and how it's going to be best told. I certainly found that in *A Home at the End of the World*. It was told initially from Bobby's point of view. I wanted to write a book about a friendship—a big, profound, even catastrophic friendship, which I don't see written about all that much. It's, like, romance: ten thousand; friendship: point one. In that way, I don't find that the body of literature entirely expresses the range of my experience. Believe me, I'm all for love—in all its forms. I just feel like what happens in love can happen between friends, as well.

Love is really a charged friendship—if it's good.

Yes. And friendship is sort of a sublimated love affair. I tried the book with two voices, but I just found that having the two boys talk about how much they loved each other was a little cloying and a little claustrophobic. I always flirt with the sentimental, but this was a heavy flirtation. I felt like I needed to open it out and bring in other perspectives, other people's takes on these boys and on their own lives. I went voice crazy for a while. Everybody had a voice. Every character did. Appliances had voices! And then I cut it down to four.

It has kind of an ensemble feel, comparable to a movie like "Grand Canyon."

Yes. One of the things I'm always aware of when I write—and as I read—is the fact that any character in any novel I write, no matter how minor, is visiting this novel from a novel of his or her own. It isn't written. But somewhere, at least in theory, there exists a really gripping novel about the passions and frustrations and comedy and tragedy of a person who's in my book just long enough to drive a cab, who doesn't even have any lines. I try to get as many people in as I can.

You made a leap with The Hours. *There's richness in it, too—but spare, elegant richness. The characters' lives are connected in a completely different way than the characters' lives in the other books. What was the genesis of that book?*

Here's where it came from. I read Woolf for the first time when I was in high school . . . in Southern California. I was not an especially precocious student. I didn't really read, except what they forced me to read. I was much more interested in movies and music. I was preparing for my career as a rock star, which I intended to pursue—I think, admirably undaunted by the fact that I had no talent. I just wanted to wear leather pants and light my hair on fire. Who doesn't?

I was talking to an older girl, the pirate queen of our high school—every high school has somebody like this. She was tall and mean and beautiful and smart. I was yakking away to her about how I thought Leonard Cohen was ultimately a better poet than Bob Dylan, and she said to me—really, not without a certain stern compassion—"Have you ever thought about being less stupid?" And I had thought about it — and had pretty much decided I was happy with the amount of stupid I was. But she said, "Why don't you read some books? Why don't you read Eliot and Virginia Woolf?" I wasn't a complete moron. I knew who Eliot and Woolf were, I just didn't think that I would ever read them. But I went to the library—the bookmobile, the trailer on the cinder blocks where they kept the books. They didn't have any books by Eliot. They had one book by Woolf, which was *Mrs. Dalloway*—which no one had ever checked out but me. I tried to read it. I didn't know what it was about; I literally didn't know what was going on. But I did get something about the density and complexity and musicality of those sentences, and I remember thinking, "Oh, she was doing with language something like what Jimi Hendrix does with a guitar." I still stand by that analogy. Woolf and Hendrix, I think, are more alike than they are dissimilar. And it really excited me.

I didn't finish [*Mrs. Dalloway*] then, but I read far enough into it until I was just overwhelmed and had to take a nap. But I read enough to see how she had lavished these incredible sentences, this miraculous perceptivity on London in the '20s and how incredibly, eternally alive and important London in the '20s was. I looked around at where I lived and, really, a more deracinated suburb is hard to imagine. It was Southern California, with little bungalows and little lawns with patches of brown grass and a little palm tree here and there. But it was my world. It was where I lived, and I thought, wouldn't it be something to be able to do with this something like what Woolf did with London? To be able to create this world of mine which is so plain, but which I know to be sort of magic and amazing.

So did you start to write then?

No, no. I just thought about it for years.

Eventually, you entered the Iowa Writers' Workshop, though. How did that figure into your development as a writer?

I finally applied to a couple of MFA programs after I'd been out of college for a couple of years. I was working at a bar in Laguna Beach and doing my best to write, but living with people who I loved, but who didn't even read. Everyone else was off at the beach and I was inside — *it was a dark and stormy night* — feeling like such a crackpot. I was starting to go down, I was losing my faith in what I was trying to do. And I didn't want to sling drinks forever. So I applied to these programs.

Weirdly — though I certainly wouldn't feel that way now — there was a certain embarrassment. It felt like a kind of desperate effort, to go to writing school — like it was charm school or modeling school. Something advertised on a subway. I didn't tell anybody I was doing it. I got in and really wavered up until the last moment about whether I was going to go at all, but finally went. Got in my car, drove to Iowa City. There it was. And actually, though I don't think I can really credit the man behind the curtain at Iowa — because I think there is some real mean-spirited stuff that goes on there — it made a huge, huge difference to me.

What it really did for me more than anything else was put me for two years in a local economy. It was Iowa City and there was no place else to go; no one else to know but the other writers. There I was among people who were willing to come to blows over questions of sentences, who cared that much about them. There was intrigue about fiction. There were people — a group of them — who I really respected, who agreed that writing a beautiful sentence was a significant thing to do with your life. That mattered to me more than anything. I had some friends there and we sort of educated each other. For years afterwards, I wrote for them. I still write for people — different people now. But it could not have mattered more to me that they were there in Iowa. Then we scattered — but they were still there, and I knew that they were writing and I knew they were thinking of me writing. I think MFA programs, though they can do harm as well as good, are great. It's not like there's anything else out there for young writers. I really don't want to be one of those people who says, "It's better in France," but I've traveled a lot the last few years around Europe, and I can tell you that, in other places, the fact that you are trying to write, even though you haven't published anything yet, is more likely to be treated with the kind of response it deserves. Which is, thank you, hero, for undertaking this very important, difficult work, knowing, as you must know, the odds against it ever paying or giving you anything of any material worth. Here people tend to excuse themselves and get another drink if they hear you're trying to write, and I think MFA programs are sanctuaries, places where it's taken properly seriously.

When you set out to work with Woolf's Mrs. Dalloway, *how did you prepare yourself? There are so many echoes of Woolf's language and her characters' lives in* The Hours, *and I wonder how you were able to accomplish that.*

What I decided to do was read *Mrs. Dalloway* a couple of times, along with pretty much all of Woolf and a couple of biographies, and then close all those books and start to write and not look at them anymore—so that I would be writing from memory about her life and about *Mrs. Dalloway*. I didn't want the parallels to be too exact. I didn't want it to be a little Swiss music box.

Did the book surprise you as it developed?

Oh, yeah. I was continually surprised by that book. Of the books I've written, it was the one that felt most often and obdurately like it was just nothing, like it wasn't going anywhere. That it was just pieces and they weren't going to add up.

So you didn't start at the beginning and move through it?

Actually, I did. I got to the point where I thought I would write about these three different days in the lives of these three different women, but I didn't really see how they connected.

You didn't know when you started what the connection was?

No, no. That came later. In its early phases, I just thought, fasten your seat belt. See if this goes someplace. You have some instinct, though you never know if you can *trust* your instincts. But you have some instinct that something's going to happen and it will come together.

Did you use feedback from other writers or readers as you worked your way through the novel?

Absolutely. Sometimes my students say they hope they reach the point someday when they are sufficiently writers that they will know what's good in their work, what's not good in their work, and they won't need any help. My reaction is always, that day will never come. Nor should it. I think there is a fantasy of the writer as some sort of Bunyanesque figure who strides out into the woods, preferably without any instruction at all, and comes back a year or two or five later with a newborn novel. That's not really my experience. I do the initial work myself in a sort of secrecy. But I show it as I go along to Kenny, the man I live with, and he has a lot to say about it. Then after a whole draft is done I have an actual team, though it changes a little bit over the years. I show it to four other people and listen very carefully to what they have to say about it. Of course I don't do everything they say. But when my friend Stacy said, "You can't just drop Richard out the window. We actually have to see him fall, see the consequences," I thought, oh, you're right.

The idea of criticism as a kind of gift often seems alien to beginning writers. They have trouble dealing with the necessity of revision. Do you revise a lot?

I do a lot, lot, lot of revision. I'm sure there are writers out there—good and great writers—who don't revise. There's always some exception to any kind of rule you try to make about the process. But I feel like maybe what I am—as much as I am anything—is the guy who won't give up. What I do is start out with something that's okay—mediocre—with some nice sentences in it, and then I work it into something alive. It's rather like a painter works, putting down the layers. You get everything there, then keep doing things that don't seem to be large, but make all the difference.

In The Hours, *it's clear that your character, Virginia, is Virginia Woolf and that Clarissa Vaughn is a modern-day Clarissa Dalloway. But what about Laura Brown? How did she make her way into the novel?*

Laura Brown was the last to arrive. I was working with the book as a sort of cryptic, involving the modern-day Clarissa Dalloway and Virginia Woolf writing her own Clarissa Dalloway, and it wasn't working. I didn't feel like enough. What I originally thought with Mrs. Brown was, "Well I have a story about a day in the life of an invented person and an invented day in the life of a real person. Maybe it needs a real day in the life of a real person." And in an early draft, it was my mother. I used her name and I tried to reproduce a day from her life as accurately as I could, but found fairly quickly that I couldn't make it work. I couldn't remember. It was already fiction—but without doing all the little narrative things you do to make it interesting. It was just sort of bad fiction. Then she metamorphosed into Laura Brown and I realized, I have writer, a reader and a character. That's what got it moving.

Here's something a reviewer said about the book: "The Hours makes a reader believe in the possibility and depth of a communality based on great literature, literature that has shown people how to live and what to ask of life." In fact, this is characteristic of all your work, particularly in terms of presenting gay life lived in the mainstream of society. Would you talk about yourself as a gay writer/activist and how you go about going about creating literature that teaches the reader about what it's like to be gay, but at the same time avoids feeling like it has an agenda?

I think about this a lot. I've always wanted, on one hand, not only not to deny but to actually work with what I know as a gay man—just like anyone works with their experience. If they're a woman or an African American—or white. Because books tend to assume that we're white, it's hard to know that you're working with whiteness. But you are. I know a lot of things, I know a lot of people who have very little to do with gay life, and I've always wanted to write the biggest books I possibly can, books that include what I know. I know a lot about gay people's lives, I know a lot about my Aunt Helen's life, too.

This is evident in the way the lives of your gay characters reflect the very important fact that being gay is only one aspect of who they are. Still, reaching a gay audience—particularly young gay people—is so important because good books can teach you how to live. They can help a kid imagine a life for himself that he couldn't have imagined before.

That's the kind of funny doubleness. On the one hand, I want them to be on the shelf with all the other books, not in a special section. On the other hand, if it could be of some help to a sixteen-year-old gay kid, yeah. And if that kid's more likely to find it in a gay and lesbian section—this is where it gets complicated. I get criticized—I have arguments with other gay and lesbian writers—about the relative absence of politics in my books, which is intentional. I feel like, as a citizen, I'm trying to do what I can from keeping Dick Cheney from blowing up everybody. As a novelist, I'm interested in what it's like to *be* Dick Cheney. Part of what's fascinating and difficult about human life is that everybody is the hero of their own story, everybody thinks they're doing the right thing. It seems to me that novels are uniquely equipped to help us understand that.

Is that why you prefer the novel to the short story?

I need a certain amount of space to make things happen. I was a painter for a while, though I wasn't a very good one—and it was very clear early on that as a painter your arm either moves like this [small movement] or it moves like this [large movement]. You are, with very few exceptions, somebody who paints a certain size. It's physical. If you're a big painter, your small paintings are going to look funny. And vice versa. It's the same with short stories and novels.

Like The Hours, Specimen Days *grew from the life and work of an iconic, groundbreaking writer—in this case, Walt Whitman. Would you talk about your interest in Whitman and what made you want to look at his life through the lens of fiction?*

Woolf and Whitman are the two writers who've mattered most to me. There are of course hundreds of other writers I love, but Woolf and Whitman got under my skin in ways no others have. Like any ardent love, it's partly a mystery, and should remain so. It also has something to do with their various insistences on the epic qualities of outwardly ordinary life, whether the subjects be a middle-aged English woman of no particular distinction or a crowd of dock workers having their lunch. That resonates enormously with me, maybe in part because I grew up in a Southern California suburb where, as in so many suburbs, the ordinary was not just respected, but revered.

In *Specimen Days* I set three interconnected novellas in three very dark periods of American history: the Industrial Revolution, the period post-9/11, and an imagined future in which America has essentially crashed and burned. Whitman, in the novel, is meant to be a mitigating spirit of sorts.

He lived in, and wrote about, a newer America, an America that actually looked as if it might be on its way to becoming the most compassionate, generous, democratic nation the world had ever seen. It didn't, of course, turn out that way. I wanted Whitman's paean to that thriving, hopeful America as a counterpoint.

Woolf and Whitman being the two writers most essential to me, I have now written two novels in which one and then the other of them figures. I have no plans to write a third novel that centers around yet another great literary figure of the past.

How was working on Specimen Days *similar to and different from working on* The Hours?

Working on any novel is in some ways different and in other ways exactly the same, and really, the similarities run deeper than the differences. Every novel, for me, starts out with a great burst of energy, and, yes, the illusion that this one will be a departure—it will not only be better than any of the others, it will cause me less trouble, because finally I really and truly know how to write a novel. I've *learned*, and now for the first time I'll just put down one sentence and then another and another and sometime within the next six months to a year I'll have a finished book that towers over anything else I've done.

And then, of course, every single time, I get to a certain point, somewhere around page one hundred, when the whole thing falls apart; when it reveals itself to be thin and foolish and riddled with sad conceits and not, in the final analysis, *about* anything at all. Novelists require a certain level of delusion just to keep going, though it may surprise anyone who isn't a novelist to know that this happens with every book and still, when I start a new one, I believe that this time, it won't.

What's actually occurring, when the books fall apart, is that they're shedding whatever little ideas got me started on them and taking on their own form, their own meanings and directions, which only slightly resemble the plans I had for them at the beginning. I survive two or three very dark months, keep writing even though I've lost all faith, and then eventually, inevitably, enter a sort of phase two, and go on about writing the book that seems to be presenting itself.

I should probably mention this about writing *Specimen Days* versus writing *The Hours*. After *The Hours* I knew, as any halfway-sensible person would, that some readers and critics were going to hate the next book, no matter what it was. It's pretty much inescapable, after you've had a success. On certain days I found that daunting, but more often, I found it liberating. Okay, then. You're writing a book that some people already despise, even though you're not finished writing it yet. You're free.

Reviewers called Specimen Days *"genre bending." The book has three distinct parts, each a novella that stands alone — one historical, one contemporary, and one science fiction. Would you talk about the difference between a novella and a novel and about what, in your mind, makes* Specimen Days *a novel as well as a collection of novellas?*

Frankly I've never been all that clear about the differences between novels and novellas, except that the latter is shorter. And, okay, being shorter than a novel but longer than a story, the novella involves a sort of hybridization of a novel's expansiveness and a story's economy.

Specimen Days is three novellas, or short novels if you will, that involve the same three central characters, more or less reincarnated from novella to novella. I'm interested in how much, and how little, our natures change according to our times and circumstances. Although *The Hours* turned out to be about any number of things, my initial interest was fairly singular: what would Woolf's Clarissa Dalloway be like if she were alive today — if she wasn't so utterly constrained by the upper-class strictures of England in the 1920s? It was really a short step, then, to wondering how an Irish seamstress and part-time prostitute in New York in the 1860s would act if she were a lizard-like woman from another planet in the twenty-second century. Three interrelated novellas permitted those parallels and overlaps.

Did you always know that Specimen Days *would be a series of three connected novellas? How did the structure and the connections between the stories reveal themselves to you in the drafting process?*

Yes, I always did. Well, actually, it was originally going to be five novellas — I was going to include a Western and a romance as well. But five just seemed like two too many.

Would you talk about the particular challenges of working in the historical past and also of writing about the future?

Writing in the historical past isn't all that difficult. You do the research.

All you've got to watch out for, really, is your desire to go into unnecessary detail simply because you've unearthed all this fascinating stuff. You have to remember that most novels don't want or need a lengthy disquisition on garbage removal in nineteenth-century New York, or fashionable women's shoes in London in the 1920s.

Writing about the future is much harder than I'd expected it to be. It's actually, to my surprise, a little embarrassing to posit a nonexistent world. Fiction set in the real world, whether it be the present or the past, involves certain elements that are out of your hands. The buildings are like this, the cafés are like that. Setting a narrative in the future involves taking responsibility not only for the story and the characters and the prose but for all the other particulars as well. People have a habit of saying, of the science-fiction section in *Specimen Days*, that I must have had great fun writing it. I didn't. I felt mostly foolish. I felt like a child making it up as he went along. Still, when assured that I had great fun, I've found it easiest to respond with a shrug and a queasy smile.

There's a Chinese bowl that plays a part in each of the sections—and, of course, Whitman and his work. Would you talk in particular about these elements and how they work in the novel? Which of them did you know when you started and which evolved (and perhaps surprised you) in the process?

There are a number of recurring images, some of them planned in advance and some of them not. I did know that I wanted there to be a central object, something that survives unaltered from story to story and is passed from person to person. The object—I didn't know what it would be at first—would be a stand-in for Whitman's *Leaves of Grass*. A great book is a mix of the animate and the inanimate; Whitman the man is gone but the Whitman of *Leaves of Grass* is still very much here, and will be after everyone alive at this moment is gone as well.

Depicting the book seemed too literal, though, and a little preachy: books are immortal and *alive*, get it? I finally settled on a bowl. Something about the concavity—the fact that a bowl is both an object and a void. And, okay, at the risk of sounding as pretentious as I actually am—there's that business about the Grail, and James's golden bowl. I did want it, at the end, to be revealed to be a cheap souvenir. Its value resides in its longevity, not in its actual substance.

New York feels like a character in its own right in Specimen Days, *the chaos of the city at these different times the main factor in shaping the characters, their circumstances, and the action of the novel. Did 9/11 and its aftermath shape your idea for the book and/or its evolution in any way?*

I started thinking about the book before 9/11. After that tragedy I had, of course, to include it, but it wasn't part of my initial conception.

What are the particular pleasures and challenges of using the lives and work of well-known literary figures in creating an original work of fiction?

The main pleasure is expending all that thought, and spending all that time, on people you love and admire so.

It's difficult to write fiction about anyone who's actually lived, and the difficulty is of course compounded if the person is a great and celebrated artist. The fundamental problem, though, isn't really about greatness—it's about trying to produce a respectful, accurate, unsentimental portrait of a real person, as opposed to just knocking around with your corps of the invented.

I'd been expecting a lot of criticism of *The Hours*, from academics and from the many people who love her almost to the point of worship. That didn't really happen, though. If anything, the people I met who adored Woolf were glad to see her have a further expanded life in the world. Which only points up the fact that you never know what's going to happen, so you might as well just go ahead and do whatever you want to do.

Would you talk about what kind of material you're interested in exploring as a source for fiction now, and your thoughts about your evolution as a novelist?

I'm afraid this is the sort of question the novelist is not all that well qualified to answer. I have no master plan, I live from book to book, and when I'm writing one I generally have no idea whatsoever about the next. If you live long enough, and write enough books, certain leitmotifs begin to present themselves: I have, it would seem, abiding interests in familial relations, and in the ways history, especially the history of art and literature, creates the present and the future. But I never for a moment thought consciously about either of those themes as I was writing.

I can only say, rather helplessly, that I hope to get better with every novel. By "better," I really mean, more than anything, better at the craft of writing, better at conveying what it's like to be human, what it's like to walk down a street on a Tuesday afternoon, and at selecting and accumulating enough of those details that I'm able to shape them into a larger story, that resonates somehow. I think we spend our lives learning how to write novels, and die still learning. A writer's body of work is really a chronicle of his or her long attempt to learn how to write, by writing.

Robb Forman Dew

Robb Forman Dew is the author of five novels and a memoir. The granddaughter of poet John Crowe Ransom and goddaughter of Robert Penn Warren, she came to the literary life early, spending her childhood summers with her grandparents in Gambier, Ohio. Her first novel won the American Book Award. Dew has taught at the Iowa Writers' Workshop at the University of Iowa. She lives in Williamstown, Massachusetts, with her husband.

Dale Loves Sophie to Death, 1981; *The Time of Her Life*, 1984; *Fortunate Lives*, 1992; *The Evidence Against Her*, 2001; *The Truth of the Matter*, 2005

Growing up and becoming an adult is a theme that runs through all of your novels. What draws you to that material?

Well, growing up is such a surprise. I remember when I was just married; I was twenty-one and suddenly had a house, a car, was considered responsible. And I was driving somewhere, listening to the radio, and the news came on and suddenly I thought, "Oh, my God! The President of the United States is just a grown-up!" I was horrified, because I had discovered that you don't know much more than you ever have just because you're considered an adult, but you can do pretty much anything and it's perfectly legal!

I think I'm really interested in power. And in responsibility. Children don't have any power; they're at everyone's mercy. In fact, up to a certain age, a child doesn't even have a choice about who he loves. Or maybe I mean who he needs love from, which is more or less the same thing, I suppose. A child will love [his] parents; he has to, it's a matter of survival. And later it's a matter of being able to find a way to love your own parents—or convince yourself that they loved you—or you aren't able even to care much about yourself.

When you have children of your own, you develop great pity for your parents—I think this is easier and more common for women to do than it is for men. But when you become a flawed parent yourself, you finally realize that whatever misery you felt your own parents visited on you was unintentional—in most cases. You are suddenly filled with dread for yourself. You know you won't escape your own children's wrath and disappointment no matter what you do. It breaks your heart.

I had two children by the time I had written *Dale Loves Sophie to Death*. I called my mother and said, "I want you to know before you read this that you're not Polly," who I actually believed she was at that time. And she said, "Well, of course I'm not. You only know me as your mother," which stunned me. And my mother isn't even remotely like Polly, in fact. But the few little details that were similar had convinced me that I had based the character on my mother. Of course, none of us can really write about our parents. And that's what really interests me—how elusive and unreliable memory is, and how puzzling and complex the relationship between parents and children will always be. Getting at the truth is so hard because it shifts, and it's not really there anyway. There's no real truth, for instance, in one person's portrait of another except maybe a few facts.

How old were you when you started to write?

When I really started writing I couldn't even write. I was about four. I would sit and do pages and pages of squiggly lines. Thinking of that now it seems to me that it must be just as genetically imperative to have to do that as it is for people who have to paint. I wrote all the time when I was young. I remember renting a typewriter when I was in college and working on stuff that was really not good. The first thing that I wrote was about an account I read in the newspaper. A little girl and her sister, they were four and six years old, were walking along in the woods. The four-year-old got her foot caught in the railroad track and a train was coming. Her sister just hugged her, and they were both killed. I was nineteen, I didn't have any experience, and I wrote the most god-awful story. I made the parents a kind of a Fitzgerald couple, so careless to let their children wander off from this mansion to the railroad tracks.

It's so interesting that you spun it into a story about careless parents. It's reminiscent of the relationship that Claudia and Avery have with Jane in The Time of Her Life.

I hadn't even thought of that until you mentioned it! Our subconscious is so sly, isn't it? But, even then, I knew the parents had no idea of their accountability. It's that particular intersection of intention and responsibility that fascinates me. That theme is probably always my theme.

I just realized that, in the novel I've just finished, a young woman who has had careless parents marries somebody whose parents' flaws I've made clear. But this couple, who mean to be terrific parents, are, of course, having all sorts of evidence collected against them by their children and by the narrator of their own failures at being parents. And certainly some of this is based on my own life—well, of course it is. But none of the details are autobiographical, really. But . . . well, for instance, I remember once, when I was in about the seventh grade, coming home and discovering that my mother had painted all the walls with blackboard paint and neighborhood children were all over the place, standing on ladders drawing on the walls with pastels. I had brought my Junior Miss Club—a sort of junior-high sorority—home. They thought it was great. But I was mortified because it was so strange.

What I wanted when I was growing up was to be really, really normal. I didn't want my children ever to come home and have to explain their house. So I did just the opposite: I tried to become so bourgeois. When I first moved to Williamstown, another writer and I were asked to entertain Rosellen Brown, who was in town to give a reading. She was perfectly polite to me but absolutely uninterested in anything I had to say. When my friend told her that I had a book coming out with Farrar, Straus, and Giroux, she said, "Oh! I thought you were just some Junior-League person." And now I can't even pull that off; I'm just a frumpy little grandmother type. But I think it almost embarrassed my children that we *weren't* more eccentric. Or, no, they probably thought we were very eccentric. In ways I'll never know. You can't win either way.

No, you can't win. And that's what your books are about.

In fact, you find out it's not even a contest. It's just surviving, trying to be happy. A housepainter was here, working, the day I finished my book.

I opened a bottle of champagne and we sat at the kitchen table and had a glass, and just chatted about this and that. Eventually he said, "So, your book. What's it about?" And I said, "Oh, it's about the pursuit of happiness." He said, "I've been pursuing that all my life." I said, "Everybody has." But it was the first time I had really registered that fact. I think that must be what all fiction is about.

Yes, or about what you have to look at or understand in order to be able to pursue it. In your novel Dale Loves Sophie to Death, *Dinah goes back to her hometown every summer in search of the happiness she missed when she was a child. She doesn't find it. But she does finally realize that that time is over, lost, and that allows her to make her husband and children her center.*

Well, pursuing happiness and finding it, of course, are not the same thing. Sustained happiness isn't possible for anyone. That's a pretty big shock to discover—especially in a country like this in which so many of us have the luxury to contemplate our own state of mind. And even though Dinah understands at the end of *Dale Loves Sophie* that her family is at the center of what she needs in her life, it doesn't prevent her from failing them. In *Fortunate Lives*, she fails them.

And the nature of a writer's role is so odd. After I wrote *Fortunate Lives* I was giving a reading in Iowa to a group of women who all seemed to me to be nice, very bright people. But as we were finishing and they were asking questions, a woman raised her hand and said, "I'm a pediatric nurse! Do you realize that Toby might have died?" I thought, "Well, of course I realize it. That was the point." But I didn't want to embarrass her, so I said, "Oh, really?" Which later made me feel like a fool. I'm no good at public appearances.

But it made me realize that, in fact, the book had worked—at least for that woman. Because once the book is in the reader's hands, it's no longer about what the author intended. The reader should never be thinking about the author. I felt like a fool for not explaining, but, in fact, the whole thing was gratifying. But I knew I had created a character in Toby who was doomed. I knew when I started *Fortunate Lives* that it had to be Toby who died. It wouldn't have been the same story if had been Sarah or David.

When did you realize that Toby would die?

I knew he was going to die when I finished *Dale Loves Sophie*. It's so odd, and I hate it when writers say stuff like this, but those people really are alive in your head and they keep going on.

But you didn't write the book for nearly ten years. And when you did write it, you wrote about a time that was six years after Toby's death. Why?

I was too frightened to tempt fate. I knew I needed to write that book, but I waited until my children were older than Toby was when he died. It's interesting. A child dies in my new book, and when I started to tell a friend about it, he said, "Don't tell me, don't tell me. I have a ten-year-old." I think of that passage in John Irving's *The World According to Garp*. The death of the little boy. He remembers the little boy taking a bath. Such a small thing. But it's just incredible.

It brings to mind the moment in Dale Loves Sophie *when Toby calls his father and tells him that he's afraid he's dying. Did you know all along that Toby was going to do that?*

No. It happened as I realized how much Dinah was not understanding, and I thought, "What would a child do?" No, that's not right. I thought, "What would *Toby* do?" I think Dinah was like most mothers, threatened by her children's illnesses. Mothers still feel that they are being judged and blamed and held accountable for any misfortune of their children. I think Dinah was scared and angry.

The anger carries over into Fortunate Lives. *Both Dinah and David are angry in that book.*

One of the things I was working toward, writing about this woman and her children, was the general rage men have—not all men, and I don't mean they're even conscious of it—at women. I think it must be so hard. You have incurred a debt that you can never repay just by being born. I think it's part of the reason you see so many men enraged at the idea of abortion, although I also think that's, of course, about power.

But it must be maddening. If you're a woman you can feel mad at being in any way beholden to your mother, but you can have a child, too. It's not quite as loaded a dynamic. I don't mean, though, that I think people sit around thinking about things like this. Well, maybe they do—clearly I do! But I don't mean I'm particularly interested in men's rage. I'm not. But it's puzzling. If you have sons, and I do, their determination to separate so absolutely at a certain age is such a surprise. You think, "What did I do?"

Certainly, Dinah feels this way in Fortunate Lives.

Yes. That's what *Fortunate Lives* is about. She just can't bear it. And I think a lot of women go through a terrible time of their lives when their first children leave, but it's an idea that's made—oh, amusing—in our society. The sort of cute "empty-nest" syndrome.

These feelings are heightened by the long-term effect of Toby's death on the family. It's interesting, though. Usually the "good" child dies in a novel, and the other children are left to try to take his place. But in Fortunate Lives, *the difficult child died. Did you do that on purpose?*

Well, Toby was difficult, but I adored him. He wasn't as successful at being Dinah's child as the other two were, but he would have made a great adult. And he was a valiant little boy. Family dynamics fascinate me. There are myths that we all have, stories we've heard a million times in families.

For years I heard a story about my grandmother riding her horse. She grew up in the wilds of Wyoming. Her father was a lawyer, and he had bought an outlaw's horse for her when the man was convicted, and she thought that was terribly glamorous. One day in her teens she decided she wanted to impress this particular boy who lived in town, and she gave that horse a bath using some of her mother's scented French-milled soap. Anyway, she rode into town and the horse started lathering. She had on this beautiful skirt and just sheets of perfumed soap slid off her horse and soaked her skirt, and whatever impression she made was certainly not the one she had in mind.

Everyone in the family knows this story about my grandmother, and it somehow sums her up. She was a very athletic, gutsy sort of person. Very beautiful. But she could make fun of herself. That story has defined my grandmother over all these years, and I don't know why. There are so many things more important to know about her. Things like that fascinate me, because they become how you know who you are. Yet it's all so slippery.

How does that affect the way you make a character? How do your characters form for you?

They're generally there. For instance, Netta, in *Fortunate Lives*, is an actual person. I changed everything about her, but she actually did come to my house when I was having all these people for Thanksgiving dinner. She was in the middle of a divorce and she was terribly lonely, and I liked her very much — except for that one day. She arrived at four o'clock — we were serving dinner at six — with a bag of unpeeled chestnuts, a red cabbage, and a bottle of wine.

So that cooking scene in the book was real, though you changed it from cabbage to beet soup.

Yes. I actually had to go buy beets to see if they were as messy as cabbage, and they are. In fact, messier. I've never cooked a beet since then. And I never will. Everybody loved this woman — all the men. And that was reasonable. In real life she isn't a "Netta" type. She's quite a remarkable and self-sufficient woman. But I was wrestling with this cabbage, and I heard this one man say to her, "Any man who was stupid enough to lose you . . ." At that moment I was ready to kill both of them. But in the book I turned her into a sort of woman you run across in academe. Probably you run into them everywhere. They're somehow appealing to men, needy and manipulative, though they don't mean to be.

The formation of this character seems related to what you said about the myths. You get one thing like that and invent out from it?

Yes, it's that one thing that suddenly defines a person and then you go from there. That one little detail is like a magnet. It pulls together all the little bits and pieces that eventually make up the whole person. But the creation on my part isn't conscious. It's inescapable, in fact. I have characters wandering around in my head that I don't know what I'm going to do with.

Do characters come first for you?

Yes. The characters, and then visual scenes. I have images in my head. People say, "What about the plot?"

What is plot?

Anything I can figure out that can happen. Anything that will move my characters to reveal who they are. I don't think there's a story I need to tell; it's the people I want to reveal. But I want the reader to figure out what these people are like, and that can only be done through action. As you know, the action in my books is not very great. I don't really know that

I'm a storyteller at all. One of the curses of being southern is that people assume you're a storyteller. If you're from the South, you're bound to have somebody in your family who is a fabulous storyteller. You'd just sit and listen. But I'm not a tale teller. I wish I could tell tales, but I can't.

But there are wonderful moments where things torque. Like the scene in The Time of Her Life *when the huge hanging plant crashes down onto the table in the restaurant. The way the characters react to that is very revealing. Claudia just sits there and Maggie wants to take photos to use in a lawsuit.*

That was lots of fun to write. Some scenes are lots of fun to write; some are torment. That one actually happened, though nobody responded in that way.

Did it happen while you were working on the book?

Yes. I thought, "Oh my God, this was meant to be." You really think everything is revolving around your book. Everything seems to be happening for a reason. What can be more seductive than that?

There's another revealing scene at the end of that book. Claudia and Avery are hiding, peeking out the window, and you see how these two characters are at the same time so wrong for each other and absolutely destined to stay together.

I had the toughest time with that book. I love it best, but one of the things I'm trying to address in the trilogy I'm doing now is to illustrate both the grimness and the pleasure of any life, which I didn't manage to do in that book. I think it was very hard for people to read, and I can understand that. In fact, my original editor, Bob Giroux, wanted me to kill Jane. He said that if she didn't die there would be no redemption for the parents.

But there is no redemption for them. It's Jane the reader really cares about, anyway—and there's that great moment in the book, both tragic and liberating, when she understands that her parents will never change. She's on her own.

Once you know that, you can face almost anything. I think that anybody, almost anybody, if they thought about what it was like to be a child, would think that it is rarely a happy situation. It's not the time of your life! But Jane survived. She's taken all these pills, but she's okay. In fact, I think she'll be in the third book of the trilogy I'm working on. I don't know if I'll be able to call her Jane. Right now I think her name is Maddie.

Were you like Jane?

I suppose so. But I was more politic than Jane. I would never have messed up that Thanksgiving; I didn't have the courage. Even in despair I would have been very careful to cultivate everybody's good opinion. I was quite a politician. In the first grade I discovered that at the end of the year we were going to vote for most popular and best all-around girl and boy. In the first grade! I started campaigning, and I managed to win every year I was in grade school. It was the only way to prove to myself that I was okay. In the seventh grade, we changed to a bigger school and, suddenly, I was pretty enough and popular. And I managed to keep up having a "good personality" for about three more years. Then I got too tired.

But when I could still manage it I also knew that I was filled with terrifying thoughts. If my friends had known what I was thinking they would probably have been appalled. And my mother and I were at loggerheads about everything just then, and her opinion of me was the one that I believed, of course. When my children were the same age I forgot that, of course, and I imagine I lashed out when they hurt my feelings. Thirteen-year-olds have no idea of their power to hurt their parents. But the discrepancy between how I was thought of by the person who knew me best, as opposed to what I had managed to convince my friends I was—well, it was too extreme. I became convinced that there was something terribly wrong with me. I believed that all my schoolmates were being nice to me and electing me to various things to keep me from knowing about some terrible deformity or disability I suffered from. I really believed that. I remember looking at my hand on my school desk and thinking "Oh, my God, is it a claw?"

Many writers describe similar feelings of alienation and separation. Do you think it is an inevitable, perhaps even necessary, part of a novelist's life?

Actually, Anne Tyler and I were talking about this yesterday. She was saying that, in a way, writing novels is a terrible thing to have to do, and people around you who aren't writers don't get it. They'll say, "Oh, I wish I had time, I'd write a novel." And you just want to say, "I wish I didn't have to write a novel." You are working in solitude on something that you get no feedback on until you have committed so much to it and made yourself so vulnerable that there's no going back. We have all written stuff that is just terrible. You feel great when you finish a page, and then the next morning you look at it and say, "Oh, God, how could I have thought this was good?" It's terrifying.

People think it's about talent.

I think it is about talent. You'd give up if you kept failing at it. But I wonder if that's true? Look at Faulkner. He thought he was great, but nobody else thought he was for a long time. Emily Dickinson wrote and wrote. I'd probably be writing and just putting things under the bed if I couldn't publish them. I think it's also a compulsion.

You'd do it, no matter what—which has interesting implications in defining success and failure. Maybe failure is looking at something you wrote and thinking, "I just didn't capture it."

Yes. With every book there's a little euphoria and then you think, "Well, I didn't get it yet, and I don't know if I ever will." And of course you never really do. And even worse, you invent the perfect reader and you're writing for that reader, and you never find him. You find really good readers, but nobody's going to read a book exactly the way you want them to.

Which is another kind of alienation, really. Eudora Welty described being a writer as standing just outside a circle in which everyone is holding hands. Even if they let you in, you wouldn't be truly in the circle. You'd still be watching. That sense of detachment is a novelist's natural state. You have to learn to use it.

I wish I could once in my life be that eloquent! I always feel that there isn't anything I ever do that that little part of my mind is not considering and judging simultaneously. I've always thought that it really might qualify as some sort of mental illness if it couldn't be put to use somehow. In fact, if you don't use it, if you don't somehow wrestle it into some sort of shape that you can look at objectively, I think you suffer terribly. My mother had that judgmental detachment, for instance, and didn't continue to write. And I think not writing was really damaging to her. She has some wonderful poems in a collection called *The Kenyon Poets*. But it must have been hard on her, because my grandfather [John Crowe Ransom] was fairly famous. I imagine that was intimidating.

What was that like for you?

Well, I was once-removed, of course. Red Warren was my godfather; Robert Lowell, Peter Taylor—they were around a lot. Lots of writers were around all the time. My family spent several summers in Gambier with my grandparents. All these people were just around, so I assumed that everybody wanted to be a writer. It seemed to me that if you weren't a writer, you were somehow a failure. I think my mother had that same idea, although I doubt she ever realized she felt that way. It must have been hard on my father, always, who was a neurosurgeon. But I didn't start writing until my grandfather died. I mean, I wrote. But I didn't show it to him, which is a shame, because he would have been an ally, I imagine. He really probably saved my life.

I think now that I was close to suicidal when I went to live with him and my grandmother in Ohio. I was seventeen, a senior in high school, and my parents were in the middle of once again possibly getting a divorce. I really wanted them to split up. I couldn't stand it anymore. The constant arguing—terrifying, dangerous rages toward my mother on my father's part, and often probably a ricochet syndrome of enormous rage at me on my mother's part. I don't know how either of them survived it. Well, actually I guess my father didn't. He died at forty-eight.

My mother and sister and I had moved out—we were staying in a motel, as we often did for weeks at a time. But this time it was in preparation for my mother and sister and me to go stay with her parents in Ohio. And then, of course, my parents reconciled. I couldn't stand it anymore, and I wired my grandparents and asked if I could come stay with them.

Now that I know more about how difficult teenagers are and how old they were by then I can't imagine how they stood it. I was really a mess. But no one ever said anything to anyone else. The whole family just pretended that this was sort of a whim on my part. My grandfather would get up every morning to fix me breakfast—grits and ham and eggs and toast and coffee. Every morning I would come in and light a cigarette and say, "Pappy, I think I'll just have some coffee." He would say, "Well, Robb, these are fine fried apples, here, and this bacon's mighty tasty." But I'd sit with him and drink my black coffee and smoke a cigarette. But every school day he'd be there and make the same offer. On Sundays he would get up, put on a suit, and say, "Robb, would you care to have me escort you to church?" Neither one of us was religious, but I didn't know that, and I was worried he'd be disappointed if I told him I never went to church. So every Sunday I'd say, "I don't believe I'll go to church today, Pappy." He would change to his gardening clothes and tend to his garden if it was warm, or disappear into his study in the winter.

One evening we were watching *Gunsmoke*—which was an occasion for my grandparents, they always had an Old-Fashioned with the show; it was sort of ceremonial. But one night he said, "I'll tell you, Robb, I've been thinking about it and I have a proposal to make to you." I had no idea until years later the kindness—the gift—this offer entailed. He was a wonderful grandfather. He said, "If you'll give up smoking your cigarettes, why, I'll give up smoking my pipe." And I was so careless. I said, "But Pappy, I don't care if you smoke your pipe. I love the smell of your pipe."

I just hope that my living with them for that year didn't utterly ruin that time for them, but I suspect it did. I was so self absorbed and probably clinically depressed. But they were unfailingly kind.

Do you think he knew you had it in you to become a writer?

I don't think so. The first thing I published was about being in Gambier in the summer, when all these poets would come. I was the only grandchild for a long time. It was just magical. I never mentioned John Crowe Ransom in the piece. So I actually believed it was fiction and I sent it to the *Sewanee Review*. George Core was the editor. He wrote me and said that it wasn't for them, but that he had sent it to the *Mississippi Quarterly*, because they were doing a special issue on John Crowe Ransom. I remember being amazed that he had figured out it was about my grandfather. Anyway, the *Mississippi Quarterly* published it, and the next year my husband was a visiting professor at the University of Virginia and I saw Peter Taylor, whom I'd known all my life, and he said, "Robb, why didn't you tell us you were such a writer?"

Dale Loves Sophie to Death is set in a fictional town in Ohio. Is it fashioned after Gambier?

Yes. My mother and sister live in Gambier, and Charles and I spent summers there until the children were about six. We'd rent a house from some professor who spent the summer away, just like Dinah did. In fact, the house in the book is a house we once stayed in. There actually was a picture of a girl jogging there.

What about the title? Was there graffiti on the bridge going into town that said, "Dale loves Sophie to death?"

We were moving from Missouri to Williamstown via a summer in Ohio, and a friend of mine, John Breithaupt, was helping me take all these boxes to put them on a bus and send them to Massachusetts. We were driving into Mount Vernon, and he said, "You know, if I ever write a book, I'm going to name it *Dale Loves Sophie to Death.*" I said, "What?" He said, "Didn't you see it?" On our way back, he showed me the graffiti on a bridge we'd passed under. About two years later, when I'd finished that book, I called him and said, "John, are you going to write a book?" and he said, "No, I don't think so. No, I'm not going to write a book." So that's how I got the title. A lot of people sent me photographs of the bridge. It really was there. I wish I had invented it, but I didn't.

There are these wonderful little nuggets of reality in all novels. Often, they're the best stuff. Real life is so strange. You couldn't make up some of the kinds of things that happen or that you observe.

No, you couldn't. I don't know quite what happens when you're writing, but I believe that it's like depression. I don't mean that you're depressed, but there's some kind of real change, so that everything seems to be charged. I remember driving in Missouri once, seeing a tree, and thinking, "Oh my God, that tree! That's supposed to be in my book." Everything funnels into your book. It's as if you've gone mad. It's a strange absorption about this alternate world and the way it mixes with your real life.

If you hadn't been working on the book then, you probably wouldn't have noticed the tree at all.

I wouldn't have. When I'm writing it's as if everything's in more vivid colors. Things are just more fraught.

It's one of the great allures of writing novels. Once you've been in that sort of heightened state, you want to go back to it. You want to live in that other place.

Yes, you want to get back to the place where everything is significant. I don't know why, then, you need to weave it into something, but you do. It's like being hit by a barrage of conflicting sensations. I grew up very uncultured—I mean, in terms of music and art. I knew lots of writers and I read a lot. But the first time I ever went to a real museum—other than the Louisiana Museum of Natural History—I was twenty-two. I was completely unprepared and I couldn't sleep that night, or for several days afterwards. The images were too much for me. I was on overload. I thought, "This must be what it's like for a baby when it's born." It was also incredibly exciting, although I didn't think so as we were going through the museum. I was very pleased and I was fascinated, but I didn't know that it would have that effect.

How do you use what comes to you in this heightened state? How do you go about balancing the conscious and unconscious, what's real and invented, what you know and don't know, in the process of getting the book on the page?

Oh, I wish I knew how it happens. Or why it happens. I really think it may be a way to stave off some sort of mental breakdown. But it's not exactly a choice. I've never said to myself that I am beginning to perceive things in ways that are about to overwhelm me and so I'd better get busy. When I start to work on a book, I'm only in a state of hope. And I do think that it's also a process of finally understanding that you can simply assume your own authority. That you have every right to say exactly what you think and expect that people will hear it. That's the part that's so hard at the beginning. With *The Evidence Against Her* I finally thought, "Okay, I'm not going to mess around anymore and just admit part of what I know, I'm going to try to tackle everything. I'm fifty-four, I have the right to be an authority in my own family." The narrators in all my books are omniscient, but this time the narrator is so bold. The narrator is like God. It was a heady experience while I did it, but in retrospect I'm amazed I had the courage to try something that might be such a spectacular failure.

What was circling around in your mind, contributing to what eventually became a kind of historical novel?

You know, I never think of *The Evidence Against Her* as an historical novel. My grandfather was born in 1888, which is when the book begins, and it seems to me that when you know a person well, have heard them talk about growing up, about their own version of their lives, then that time they lived through is yours as well.

I've discovered that when you're writing a book starting in 1888 and you do a lot of research, two things happen. You have to be very careful not to let your research show—my knowledge of a Corliss engine, for instance, should just be assumed. And you cannot use props. In previous books, I had done things I hadn't realized—careless, sloppy shortcuts. In *Dale Loves Sophie*, the family drives a Volvo, which signifies a certain thing. If they were driving a Mercedes it would be a different story. Or a pickup truck. Now that I recognize it, I've begun to resent this shorthand in other people's work, and I'll try never to resort to it again in my own writing.

Such details are very freighted, and you can't use them in a novel set in another time. I couldn't say a certain character rode an Appaloosa, for instance, and assume that that fact would convey anything at all to a reader. So imagining the people in this book was an entirely different experience. It was like the surprise of falling deeply in love—luxurious and surprising and absorbing. I didn't realize that I was getting tired of writing the same kind of book, dreading starting another book that would span a single year. I thought, "I don't have to do that."

Generally, what sorts of things do you know when you begin a new novel? What don't you know?

When I start writing, I never have any idea where I'm going. In fact, I just had to do a synopsis of my next two books, which was like pulling my own teeth without Novocain. I'll have various scenes—little vignettes—in my head, but I don't know how I'm going to get there. I don't know the context, but I start enlarging on those little bits of narrative. I just start feeling very unhappy and uneasy and tired of everything. Nothing amuses me. I don't even enjoy reading after a while. I get really cranky and I know I've got to start working. I know that there's a subject there. I'll start having incredible dreams, very unsettling. And I wake up uneasy. Eventually, I start forcing myself to go into my study and just sit there and be miserable.

So you don't really have a sense of story. You just know that it's time to do something.

I know it's time to do something. With *Dale Loves Sophie*, I started the first chapter as a story and the second chapter I did as a story. The third and fourth I did as stories. I sent all of them to *The New Yorker*, and Chip McGrath said, "This is a novel you're doing." I said, "Oh no, it's not." And he said, "When you're finished, let me see it." It was just so terrifying to think I was writing a novel. I didn't know how to write a novel. But I just sort of went ahead. It was ignorance; it was not letting myself get scared. I just kept telling myself, "Oh, this is just another story," until about the eighth chapter. Then I couldn't escape it anymore.

When you finally admitted to yourself that it was a novel, how did you proceed?

With both *Dale Loves Sophie* and *Fortunate Lives*, I knew that when I got to a certain length, I had to start pulling the chapters together. That sounds absurd, but it was at about 120 pages that I would say, "Okay then, now this much more has to happen." Also, when I knew that I had a certain space left, I started tightening at the front. I tried to pace it as well as I could. I had no idea how other writers did it. I still have no idea how other people do it. Writing a novel is very mysterious; you cannot hold a novel in your head. In fact, probably any novel you could hold in your head all at once wouldn't be very good.

At first when I've finished a book I feel liberated. I get excited about, oh, going to the grocery store, getting a new bedspread, reading especially—without making comparisons. But eventually some sort of peculiar guilt sets in if I'm not writing. Which is strange, because there isn't anyone expecting anything from me. But writing is what I can do, and I guess everyone needs to be occupied. And then I feel a kind of yearning for the complications of developing a whole world. The discoveries. The high! I really want to get back to my people.

The novel is an alternate reality for you.

Yes, it is. And, in a way, it's better than reality because you can step back. You can decide what happens. My life happens and I don't get to control it all. But nothing is better than cutting and pasting a novel to make it right. I used to literally cut and paste. I'd sit in the middle of our bed, and I'd spread out all my papers. I'd need to cut from this and put this over here. I would have some really short pages and some really long ones. Then I'd have to carefully collate and retype.

Do you usually revise as you work through a novel, or at the end of a draft?

I revise chapter by chapter. I can't stand to move from a chapter until I get it exactly right. So it takes me a long time to do each chapter. And of course, at the end I go back and make sure that everything works. I don't rewrite much after that. With *Fortunate Lives*, Harvey Ginsberg, my editor, sent seven pages of suggestions for changes that would make the book work chronologically. I was in such despair. Poor Anne [Tyler]. I FedExed it to her and she read it overnight and she called and said, "Don't touch it, don't touch it!"

You did something really interesting in that book. You would often get beyond the moment and then go backwards to tell it.

That's what drove Harvey crazy, I think, although he was very tactful.

Why did you do that?

It wasn't conscious. I really never thought about the structure of a book, or how I would go about building it. Not until I took on the work I'm doing now. And even now I only think of it as what will make the book have momentum, have power, be clear.

The editorial changes would have made it a completely different book.

Yes. When I looked at what Harvey had sent, I thought, there won't be any psychological layering.

You were absolutely right, even though you sort of broke the "rules" of fiction to do it that way.

Yes, but I didn't know I was doing it. I know nothing about writing. I mean, I write, but I don't know any of the terms or whatever rules there are. I realized that when I was teaching at Iowa in 1982. My students would say Henry James says you can't have an omniscient narrator—or whatever he called them. And I'd say, "He did?"

In an early class some student complained about a story in which he thought that there wasn't a clear "POV." I was really alarmed. I had no idea what a "POV" was, and the story we were critiquing was determinedly erotic. I thought, "Oh, God, that must be some sexual position or something that I don't know about!" But I faked it. I asked him to suggest how he would approach it, and I finally figured out that he was talking about "point of view."

Your prose style has been compared to Henry James's, also to Edith Wharton's. It's lush and evocative, like theirs.

I have to be really careful. I am very wary of being considered overly lyrical.

In fact, you create a wonderful kind of prose rhythm on the page. There's lyricism, but then there will be a sentence that is absolutely naked. This sentence in The Time of Her Life, *for example: "Jane didn't join them for lunch, and they didn't notice." It's almost like a sharp intake of breath. It's so revealing. Do you do that kind of thing on purpose?*

I didn't realize I was doing it until I was reading my grandfather's poems. In fact, I can hear his voice when I write. He had a beautiful, old-fashioned Tennessee accent, not a twang. I had a friend who was reading the poems and she said, "Oh, these are kind of sentimental." But they're really not sentimental at all. They are ironic. The opposite of sentimental. In fact, "Winter Remembered" is a poem that strikes me. At the end is a line about ten frozen parsnips hanging in the weather—and it's really a love poem. I'm trying very hard for that kind of thing. I mean, I want some lyricism, but I don't want to make it romantic.

You don't want people to pay attention to the writing.

That's right. I hate self-consciously lyrical writing. It gets tedious. On the other hand, I love Marilynne Robinson's book *Housekeeping*, which is lyrical. But in her case the language is the vehicle that pulls you into a whole mysterious world. I don't even notice the lyricism. She is so authoritative that you just go with it.

The writer just opens the door and says, come in and explore this world with me.

That's a wonderful way to put it. And you also want to say, "I'll show you all this, but let me explain it." If it works, you get to impose your point of view, your understanding of the world on the reader—or at least the world of your novel.

Richard Ford

Richard Ford is the author of six novels and three collections of short stories. Born in Jackson, Mississippi, he received his BA from Michigan State University. After a brief stint as a law student, Ford enrolled in the MFA program at the University of California, Irvine, where he studied with such writers as E. L. Doctorow and Oakley Hall. His honors include a Guggenheim Fellowship, a PEN/Faulkner Award for Fiction, a literature award from the Mississippi Academy of Arts and Letters, a Literary Lion Award from the New York Public Library, and an Echoing Green Foundation Award. Ford has taught at the University of Michigan, Williams College, Princeton University, and Harvard University. He lives in Maine with his wife.

A Piece of My Heart, 1976; *The Ultimate Good Luck*, 1981; *The Sportswriter*, 1986; *Rock Springs*, 1987 (stories); *Wildlife*, 1990; *Independence Day*, 1995; *Women with Men*, 1997 (stories); *A Multitude of Sins*, 2002 (stories); *The Lay of the Land*, 2006

Do you consider yourself a southern writer?

A Piece of My Heart was set in Mississippi and in Arkansas. When I started writing it, I thought, "This is my subject, this is the thing I have to do. I have to write books that are set in the South, and they have to be about the South and things going on in the South because, after all, I'm a southerner and that's what southerners do. They write about the South." But when the book was reviewed, a lot of things were said about it which didn't make me happy. One of the things that was said was that it was a southern book. I had kind of hoped that it would somehow—even though it was about the South—transcend its southernness, but nobody who talked about the book wanted it to transcend its southernness at all. They wanted it to be right in their Faulknerian mode and the Flannery

O'Connor mode, which in some ways I guess it was. And I thought to myself, I have got to find a way to quit writing about the South, because if I don't, I'm never going to be taken seriously. So I thought, "I am going to write a book in which the South does not figure at all." My little joke to myself was that I went on writing about the South, but it was Mexico now, instead of Arkansas and Mississippi, where I had grown up. So *The Ultimate Good Luck* was a real conscious attempt to try to break the regional and also the stylistic mold and mode of writing about the South.

I'm looking back on this now, maybe seeing things with more clarity than I did at the time. I thought that a book that was also a kind of genre book might be the thing that would sort of clear my palate, which it did. *The Ultimate Good Luck* is a sort of little noir book about some people who go down to Mexico to get a woman's brother out of jail. It was rather purposefully influenced by Graham Greene. I've been a big Graham Greene fan for a long time, and I've admired his books very much, and I thought I could safely write a book that I knew he had influenced. It was during a time in my writing life that happens to all writers—when you know who your influences are and sometimes they take a rather conspicuous stylistic grip on you. I wanted to let that happen to me with *The Ultimate Good Luck,* because I wanted so to rid myself of Faulkner. I wanted to get away from all things southern as much as I could, so I just kind of let myself choose a style that I felt like I could handle. It was also strongly affected, I think, by Robert Stone's book *Dog Soldiers*, which I profoundly admired.

As I say, I'm looking back on it now and maybe seeing things with greater clarity, but I knew all those things. I knew I had to get away from the South or I would never be able to hold my head up as a writer. I didn't think, and I don't think now, that I had anything new to say about the South. Everything that I knew about the South, Faulkner or Miss Welty had already written.

But the other thing is, [*The Ultimate Good Luck*] is a very different kind of book from other sorts of books that I had written and have gone on to write. I think that those kinds of big changes are essential for writers. But sometimes critics or book reviewers or just casual commentators will talk about writers as though they spoke with one voice. It frustrates those people [when they can't] categorize your books. Sometimes that frustration causes them to dismiss you, to say that you're all over the map, or that they can't find anything consistent as you go from one book to the next—as if that were somehow a measure of your worth. Carver's a good example of that. People have said, "There's your Raymond Carver story." Well, if you actually get down and look at the Raymond Carver stories from 1974 to 1986, what you'll find is a much more diverse range of sentence lengths and attitudes and preconceptions and stylistic gestures in his stories, and that just corroborates for me the fact that writers' work—x as they go on and get older and maybe, you hope, smarter and better— will change radically.

So do you feel that writing The Ultimate Good Luck *established you as a writer in your own right?*

Yes. I don't think I ever worried about Faulkner again after that, which was a huge thing. You know, growing up in Jackson and having Faulkner be the eponymous Southern writer felt like a lot to have to get over. I know that a lot of the things that I have learned from reading Faulkner and being influenced by him when I was young still do inhabit books of mine. But I don't care anymore. I feel like I have gotten out of his stylistic twitch, and I've quit writing about the sorts of things that he wrote about, and that whatever I kept I can use and make my own.

Did The Ultimate Good Luck *liberate you to write* The Sportswriter, *which was the book you wrote after it?*

Yes. It was certainly very different for me, though *The Sportswriter* has its inheritances, too. There's no doubt about that. I'm perfectly happy to say what they are. It's a first-person novel told in present-tense verbs, and so all those books that I had read that are first-person novels with present-tense verbs funneled right into it: Walker Percy, and Joe Heller in his wonderful book called *Something Happened*; Frederick Exley in *A Fan's Notes*; John Barth in *The End of the Road*. All kinds of books sort of shoved me along my way, but I felt like I was getting into a way of thinking about stories that was both new to me and was something I was vitally interested in.

I started writing *The Sportswriter* on Easter 1982. I wrote on it for about eight months and I got about 150 pages, and I showed it to a—at the time—very influential editor in New York named Gordon Lish. Gordon was a big influence in my life in a kind of bad way. He was a sort of Mephistophelian character in my life for about ten years.

But when I finally showed him the first 150 pages of *The Sportswriter*, after having been brayed at by him for several years to the point where I thought he would like nothing better than to publish a book of mine, he read about ten pages of it and said, "You can't write this book. This doesn't work, it's no good. Put it in your drawer and never think about it at all." These were the kind of broad strokes he generally painted the world in. That was about Christmas time, 1982, and I had to stop working on the book for about seven months because I was so cast down by such a bad opinion.

But when I went back at it in June 1983, I went back at it with a lot of vigor. I got reconvinced that this, in fact, was a way I could write a book. He didn't like it because it deviated from what he thought I was: a southerner who could write southern books and a kind of hard-boiled book, like *The Ultimate Good Luck.* That's all he could see. I was starting off in some totally new direction, and he couldn't figure out how to take it in. But for me, that's the challenge of being a writer after the first ten years of trying: What am I going to do next? How am I going to surprise myself? How am I going to write about things I've never thought about before and make them logical and whole?

As a writer writing about a writer in The Sportswriter, *how much of yourself appears there?*

I always try not to include things about myself or people [I know in my] characters, because I think that when the lines of my own system of beliefs cross with the character's, then that character becomes less malleable. One of the things that you want in writing characters is for them to stay as changeable as they can be until you get right down to the ending and you think everything is how it should be. If you have things that go into this character's past or into what she or he might say that coincide [with] or directly reflect your own beliefs, then it's less easy to change [the character]. The process of discovery is somewhat inhibited by my own hold on those things I believe.

The more fully a character is occupied [by] or invested with facts out of the lives of someone I might actually know, the less nimbly can I work with the character. Because, you know, you start off writing a character, and maybe, in the most rudimentary way, you write a line of dialogue and then you put "he said" or "she said," and that may be the first little scratch on the empty slate that that character has. You don't know what the character's going to be when you develop him by this sort of cross-hatch of gestures. So if suddenly into that hit-and-miss process comes a whole bunch of stuff out of an old girlfriend of yours or somebody you knew as a teacher, well, then the process is moored in a way that I don't like it to be moored, because I think of characters as always being little expeditions that the writer makes.

Then there are other problems with putting big dollops of human characters into fictive characters. The character himself, the person in life, almost always is going to be resentful and hate your guts when you do it. No one likes to have another person take dominion over her or his life, even if the person turns out to be sanctified. Nobody ever likes it!

Has that happened to you?

Oh, yeah! Oh, yes.

With friends?

Well, they're always ex-friends. My wife is the only person who forbears on that. I've never actually written a character that I thought bore any resemblance to her, but she is quick to point out that I snatch lines of hers all the time and put them into some other context. She always says, "Well, it's true you never wrote about me. But you've raided my life for its best lines for thirty years." I always say, slightly unconvincingly, "Well, that's my homage to you." I've never actually sought to write a character that I thought was physically modeled on her and the truth of the matter is, I'm not sure I could. If I were to try to write a character who was like Christina, I think I would have to make certain kinds of decisions about that character in limiting the range of her reference, which I don't find I can do when I deal with Christina herself, who has always had the kind of consummate ability to surprise me.

How do you know what the time frame of a story will be?

I don't let the story determine anything. I determine everything. These people who say, "I just start writing and the characters kind of run their own life"—not in my books they don't! I decide, I choose, I am responsible. I am the author of everything. That's what authorship means. Now, it may very well be that you sit down and you don't know what, for instance, the time trajectory for your book is, and you may figure it out by a process of eliminating other possibilities. I didn't know that I wanted *The Sportswriter* to take place in that four-day period, but I did know that I didn't want it to take place over a year, and I knew that I didn't want it to take place in a day, and I knew that I wanted it to start on the Easter weekend sometime. So I may have kind of come at it backwards, but finally I had to decide.

Did you see Frank Bascombe as a reliable narrator as you were writing from his point of view?

I guess I would have to say yes. But finally, in the larger sense, I think he's like any other character. He has attitudes, and he says things that he believes are true, and he contrives and orders the world in various ways. I think the reader will make up her or his mind about how reliable Frank is. I mean, I'm never trying to make Frank a liar. I'm never trying to make him seem so insincere as to be dismissible. But I do think that the reader has to bring his own intelligence to bear upon what he sees and what he therefore should believe. So in that way I suppose Frank is unreliable; but he's no more unreliable than you or I.

Maybe I've been a novelist so long that I no longer know what the truth is in a received sense. My view as a novelist is that it's my obligation to create the truth, not to receive it. So no received truths have the same profundity to me as the truth that I can create. Every time I affirm something to be true based on prior knowledge, I always kind of wonder to myself, "Do I really mean that? Do I really think that's so? Do I really want to go to the wall with this?" Whereas when I get to the end of a story and I find myself making those concluding gestures that are typical of the end of a story, I feel no such doubt. Everything floating around in the world that I understand, that is sayable in life, seems to me to be highly provisional.

Did it surprise you that you wanted to write another novel about Frank Bascombe?

It didn't surprise me in one way, because I so liked writing in his persona. But it worried me because sequels have a hard path to follow in the literary world. The reason for this is that a sequel is often just a retelling of the first book, or a better working out of a book that was ill worked out originally. So I was afraid that I wasn't on firm ground. Even though I was comfortable writing in Frank's persona, that very comfort gave me pause. I spent a year preparing to write it to be sure that I really did have a book that was whole.

Once the characters begin to develop and you figure out the time frame, what do you do to prepare to begin writing the book?

One of the things you do is you tell yourself that you're writing a book, but you're not going to write it right now. What that means is that you think about the book all the time and you collect information. As I realize that I'm going to have to write a book that wants to go to the Baseball Hall of Fame, where I've never been, then I get on the airplane and go up and rent a car in Albany, New York, and drive the route that I think Frank's going to drive. I have my tape recorder and I just kind of talk into it while I'm driving and look at the things on the side of the road—sort of, you know, barnstorming in a sense. Then I come back, get a typist to transcribe all those notes. I did it for the Baseball Hall of Fame and I did it all over Connecticut. I went down to the Jersey Shore. I went back to Princeton and looked around Princeton and Hopewell and Lawrence Field and all that central New Jersey area, just accumulating impressions.

I get one of those big ring-bound notebooks and I put the little dividers in. One will say "Frank" and one will say "New Jersey" and one will say "Baseball Hall of Fame" or "Independence Day" or all of the names of the secondary characters. As I go through that year, accumulating material, I put that material where I think it belongs. Sometimes I'll particularly seize on a line of dialogue that I like, and I'll think to myself, "Gee, someplace in this book I would like Frank to be a character who could say this line. I don't know how or where, but I like the line so much I want to put it in my stock of available quotes." But sometimes it seems so good that I think, "Well, I'd like to have several people say it." So I'll put it in all their folders. Now, they won't all say it, obviously. Only one person will say it. But sometimes one person will say it and then I'll contrive a way to have another person throw that line in his face; so she gets to say it, too.

As you do the research for a book, do scenes come to you?

Absolutely. When you're driving along, you're basically living in a kind of virtual reality, which is the book that you hope you'll write. In that virtual reality, certain things begin to seem sort of prepossessive: "Ah, that would be a nice place to set a scene." So you do a lot of the doping out—I do, anyway—and accumulate what you think would be good scenes long before ever getting around to trying to write them. I find this to be one of the most highly vertiginous parts of planning a book. It's the part when you ain't got a book and yet you're having to go along as though you did. Somehow those two realities, the virtual reality and the real one, clash so profoundly. Sometimes it can be very disheartening.

What about voice? For instance, the voice in Wildlife *was so strong. Was it like that from the start, or did you develop it?*

I just nailed that voice from the beginning. It was a voice that I had written other stories in; and, in fact, I was slightly embarrassed by the fact that I was willing to write a whole other book using certain tonal conceits that I felt I'd pretty well perfected. I thought, "How do I think I'm going to get away with this?" But then I thought, "I'm just *going* to get away with it because this is a book I have to write and can write and want to write." It was never hard, though I think I've just about squeezed all of the words I can out of that particular attitude. I'm not going to write any more stories that use that ploy. Once *Wildlife* was written, I thought, "Well, okay, that's the full fruition of that preoccupation of mine." I do believe that's one of the reasons I'm principally a novelist and not a story writer. I believe that the obligation is to use it all up. Don't leave any behind when you're finished with a book.

We talked about the use of time within your novels. Time often jumps within a chapter. Things are taking place in the present, then you bump into another time, ten years before. Then you go back to the present.

I think that that kind of narrative strategy is a sort of standard operating procedure for writing books, and it probably adheres to a conviction that I have about what novels or stories are about for me. Stories are, for me, principally about the way in which the past impends upon the present and prefigures the future. That's the sort of moral architecture of my books. It's highly Faulknerian in its preoccupations. That's what *Absalom, Absalom!* is about. That's what *The Sound and the Fury* is about. It's my sense of how morality is finally corralled. If morality is about how we are able to choose to do good or choose to do bad in our lives, the way in which that choice can be explained and understood and cast in a plausible way is in terms of how the past has impended upon the moment of deciding, and then having the future be its consequence. So I'm always putting in little dollops of the past as a way of creating that sense of moral [linearity] in a story.

It also is true that that's really the only way I understand fiction that I can write myself. It's just so fundamental to how I understand the world that it would necessarily be the way my books were structured and conceived. I do think, on a more technical and superficial level, perhaps, that it is good for the rhythms of the book to have the long girth of a narrative trajectory be interrupted and resumed and interrupted and resumed. It creates a sense of consequence, it creates a sense of rhythm, it creates a sense of suspense.

Do you write a novel all at once?

I write it all at once, in order. The only thing I have ever done differently is to decide, at the end of a time of writing a book, that something will be sort of outsized. There'll be a passage, say like Chapter Four in *Independence Day*. It was the hardest chapter for me to write because it's the chapter that has to do with the past. It's the chapter that has to do with what Frank did since *The Sportswriter* was over. I can't actually remember precisely how I wrote it, but I remember writing it in such a way that bits of that past were sort of scattered through the book. What I did as a last gesture was to decide to consolidate them and to put them in one chapter, which I thought when I did it and still think was a little ham-handed of me. But I didn't like it scattered through the book because it made the past slightly more ephemeral than I wanted it to be. I wanted that little passage between the end of the last book and the commencement of the action of this book to be well articulated and well expressed in the book. I ran the risk of diminishing it and subordinating it by scattering it through the book, so I put it back together so it would be clearer and inarguable. That caused me to really have to work on the passage hard. I thought it was a little blunt the way I did it. I still think it's something that is rather inelegant in the book.

When you're making decisions like that, do you have friends that you send the manuscript to?

No. Most of my friends are my age. They don't have time to read my books. They're writing their own books. I just couldn't imagine asking a colleague or friend to read a book just for general reasons. I might show something to somebody and say, "Would you please tell me if this that I have done here is successful? Or would you tell me what I should do better than I have done?" I haven't done that, but I think I would if I had such a friend.

What about editors?

Now, that's another matter. I have a wonderful editor; he's been editing my books since 1984. He's such a good guy. He edits stuff of mine so ravenously: 70 percent of the sentences he'll make some comment on. I like to have my work submitted to somebody else's opinion that I trust. One of the things that happens is you get sick of a story. You finish it, in the sense that it has a certain little veneer on it. To make it better, even if you know you've made it pretty good, you have to break that veneer. You have to sort of crack it and get back into the things that are integral to the story, but it's very hard to break that veneer when you worked so hard to create it in the first place. Sending it to an editor is the best way to do it, because the book always seems like a draft to him; it seems provisional and unfinished.

But my editor has his little quirks and foibles and flaws. He is never going to question the structure of the story. He's a great line editor and will just beat lines till they sing. But he's never going to be interested in what follows what. For instance, I wrote the ending of *Independence Day* and I thought, "Probably there's something about this ending that's not quite right," but I couldn't at that moment figure out what it was. But when I showed it to him, he loved it. He said, "Don't change this ending," and he showed it to Sonny Mehta and to lots of people, and they all said it was the right ending.

What I understood was that they wanted it to be the right ending; but I felt that it was not the right ending. They said, "I think you're going to make a mistake if you put a new ending on this." So I just said, "Well, if I do, at least it won't be because you've decided something. If it's the wrong ending, then it'll be Richard Ford's wrong ending." It means everything to me that I make all the decisions. I'm the one who's going to take the rap for the book, so I have to be satisfied and pleased with everything.

At what point did you know that it would take three books to tell Frank's story?

It isn't (or wasn't) that three books were required in any way that was proportionate with "Frank's story." At the start there wasn't a Frank, and once there was a Frank he didn't have a story until I'd dreamed it up. I finished *The Sportswriter* not thinking I'd take up Frank Bascombe again. I wrote books one might say "singly." And one was all I imagined. Later, when I was thinking of another entirely separate novel I might write, I realized I could tell it in Frank's speaking voice; and so that subsequent book—which became *Independence Day*—became a sequel. Frank as its narrator was a somewhat late arrival. So, it wasn't as though, again, that Frank had a story and I had to figure out how to tell it. With *The Lay of the Land*, I imagined that book from the start as a sequel to the other two. But as with them, I started with nothing and gave Frank the story which that novel comprises. Frank, as you can see, is just a formal feature of the books—although he's one I've come to like.

When and how did the issues that Frank deals with in The Lay of the Land *reveal themselves to you?*

I'd have to say the issues arose out of the normal practices I employ as a story writer: I write notes down over time, and then refer to them when I decide to write a book. The idea of "independence" was a lot in my thinking prior to writing *Independence Day*. I can't remember why; but I wrote a lot of notes about it. "Acceptance" was in my thinking prior to writing *The Lay of the Land*. Who knows why? I suppose a scientist would say that the discovery of these significant elements of these books came by way of "normal science." Or I might say, somewhat more affectedly, by the habit of art.

All three books that Frank narrates are set on holidays—why?

I set the books on holidays because in the first place I started writing *The Sportswriter* on Easter Sunday, 1982. And it was a particularly vivid day and seemed to offer me a chance to engage what were probably vivid Easter memories in my readership—in case I found a readership. I had nothing directly to do with the issues that came to dominate that particular novel — rebirth, renewal; although one could certainly say that the coincidence was rather a strong one. When the later books came along, it occurred to me that setting them on a holiday was a bit of the same good idea. Namely, that I could engage the experience of my American readership, all of whom would have vivid Fourth of July memories, and Thanksgiving memories. I suppose the idea behind such a choosing is that if I can make the temporal setting of my novel a plausible formal feature — i.e. make the time when it takes place real to the reader — then I've done something rather easily that many other novels have to struggle with: getting the time setting to signify to the reader. If I set my novel on the ninth of March, for instance, the typical American reader's going to say, "Fine, but why then?" But if I set on Easter, then some of that answer is provided.

What was it about Thanksgiving that you felt particularly suited the mood of The Lay of the Land?

Well, Thanksgiving was available, you might say. I had those vivid memories, and supposed most Americans did, too. I knew the conventional Thanksgiving explanation — giving thanks, sharing with others, plenty, something kind of both patriotic and back-door spiritual (as if God provided for those poor pilgrims — which seemed actually sort of funny to me). I thought I could dedicate some language to the whole notion of Thanksgiving, and in doing so provide myself something potentially interesting to write about: namely — what is Thanksgiving? What has it become? What is it really? As always, I was looking for a chance to write something that hadn't been written before.

The issues and events in that shape the three books that Frank Bascombe narrates about his life happen offstage: the death of his first-born son, his divorce, his diagnosis of prostate cancer, and the desertion of his second wife. It's in the buildup of small moments during a limited, defined slice of time in their aftermath that we see their effect. Why did you choose to approach Frank's life that way?

I chose to do it this way (if choosing is really the right word . . . it seemed sort of intuitive) because I think that in terms of ongoing human morality, it's the consequences of our major actions that are the most interesting and important. It's how we react, how we heal ourselves, how our mind understands the things that happen to us, or the things that we do, which properly define us as humans. So, I concentrated on that.

Why the present tense?

I probably just stole the present tense from Walker Percy and Joe Heller. In their two wonderful novels *The Moviegoer* and *Something Happened,* that verb tense is used. I supposed it seemed quite immediate and dramatic, but was also actually quite accommodating for inserting bits of the past should I need to do that. In other words, it seemed easy. And is. Wittgenstein wrote once "He who lives in the present, lives in eternity." I'm not sure I know what Wittgenstein meant by that, but I wanted my characters' lives to persist without end in the reader's mind.

Early in his life, Frank published a critically acclaimed work of fiction and was considered a promising young writer, but he gave up that ambition to become first a sportswriter, then a real estate agent. Yet he is compelled to tell the story of his life in these three novels. Would you talk about this paradox at the heart of the trilogy?

I'm not aware of a paradox. He's not "compelled" to tell his story. I make him tell his story. I wrote him. He's a piece of artifice. I might want the reader to engage in some kind of illusion that Frank's a real person—because if I can do that I can get across all the other fictive things I want to do. But I don't believe the reader really thinks Frank's "real." I think the reader always has in mind these two differing parts of the illusion of character—the seemingly real and the artificial—and that holding these two things in mind is uniquely pleasurable. If that makes a paradox, I hope I took full advantage of it.

The Lay of the Land *happens during what Frank calls the "Permanent Period" of his life, "when very little you say comes in quotes, when few contrarian voices mutter doubts in your head, when the past seems more generic than specific, when life's a destination more than a journey and when who you feel yourself to be is pretty much how people will remember you when you croaked . . ." Yet the reader is left with the sense that Frank is very much alive, moving into the next, probably last phase of his life. Are you working on or considering another book in Frank's voice?*

I'm intent that *The Lay of the Land* be the last of these books that Frank

Bascombe narrates. This is largely because—as with the other two novels in the little series—when I finished it I was entirely empty of anything else I wanted to write about Frank. But as distinct from those other books, this last time I felt I'd had to work too hard to make the book right. I made myself pretty sick working on it—by which I mean sort of physically exhausted, and also exhausted in some way I can't quite describe. So, I thought, I don't want to do that again; don't want my work to make me sick. It didn't seem then (nor now) that I could ever mount a Frank Bascombe book without having to expend that kind of effort. So I decided I wouldn't do it.

What issues has the completed trilogy resolved for you as a writer?

As to finishing with issues, or resolving issues for myself as a writer, that's not what writing novels does for me. The issues that the novels take up and bring along, aren't reflective of issues in my own life. It's true that I recognize the books' concerns as being potentially important human issues, and encountering them as subjects to write about does indeed set a strong commotion going on in me. But I'm unaware that Frank's life concerns in any but the most general ways reflect my own. And indeed there are plenty of Frank's issues I don't share at all—parenthood, divorce, the vitiation of one's vocation, encountering fatal illness. These are matters I just project into these books out of surfeit of, I suppose, empathy and curiosity, and out of desire to make something where before there was nothing.

Ha Jin

Ha Jin is the author of five novels, three collections of short fiction, and three collections of poetry. Born in Lianoning, China, he joined the People's Liberation Army in 1969 during the Cultural Revolution. In 1981 he graduated from Heilongjiang University with a BA in English studies, and three years later obtained his MA in Anglo-American literature at Shandong University. Ha Jin was on scholarship at Brandeis University during the 1989 massacre in Tiananmen Square, which hastened his decision to emigrate. Ha Jin's novel *Waiting* won the National Book Award. Other honors include the PEN/Faulkner Award, the PEN/Hemingway Award, the Flannery O'Connor Prize for Short Fiction, a Guggenheim Fellowship, and a Lila Wallace–Reader's Digest Fellowship. He teaches at Boston University.

Ocean of Words, 1996 (stories); *Under the Red Flag*, 1997 (stories); *In the Pond*, 1998; *Waiting*, 1999; *The Bridegroom*, 2000 (stories); *The Crazed*, 2002; *War Trash*, 2004; *A Free Life*, 2007

When did you begin to write? Is your impulse to write purely political, or is it intrinsic? Do you think you'd have been a writer regardless of the experiences you had coming of age in Communist China?

I began to write seriously since 1990. I have never been a political writer. In fact, for years I was halfhearted about writing. Regardless of my experience in China, it's the American experience that forced me to be a writer. I have to survive and to exist here. After the Tiananmen Massacre I decided to emigrate, but psychologically I was not ready to live in this country. I didn't know what I could do. Having failed to find employment related to Chinese, I concluded that English was the only means of my survival, since all my degrees were in English. Also, I realized that I wouldn't starve here as long as I worked and was in good health, but what was hard would be how to live meaningfully. It took me more than a year to decide to write in English only. Before coming to the States, I had written some poems in Chinese, but I had never had an audience. It would have been suicidal for me to write in Chinese here. In this sense, I began to write out of necessity.

You have said, "As for the subject matter, I guess we are compelled to write about what has hurt us most." To what extent is your work autobiographical? How do you go about transforming autobiographical material to fiction?

I don't write my personal story in my fiction. Occasionally I may give my experience to a character, but my fiction is never autobiographical. For example, in the story "Love in the Air," all the knowledge and experience of telegraphy are my own, but I used them only to produce the texture of the protagonist's life to make him convincing. On the whole, my life is limited, and my own story cannot give enough room for imagination, so I don't write my personal story.

For many years, I was hurt by China. Because of that stubborn, mad country, I landed here, having to struggle for a different kind of existence. Then, gradually, China became less overwhelming. The immigrant experience is essentially a traumatic experience to most people, which involves truncation of one's old life and the painful creation of a new life. I have been hurt by this experience deeply. Often I feel crippled, but I am not complaining. The American experience has toughened me up and turned me into a different man.

You have said, "Very often I feel that the stories have been inside me for a long time and that I am no more than an instrument for their manifestation." How do these stories gather inside you, present themselves, and take shape?

Usually I don't have enough time to write what is in my mind, so the seed of a story will stay a long time in me until I begin to work on it. Mostly they have the form of a key event, which gradually sprouts into the shape of a story. For instance, the story "Saboteur" originated from two key events I had heard and read long ago. One is that some workers in Shanghai contracted hepatitis, and that the moment they knew they were victims of the disease, they went out to eat at different restaurants to spread the virus. The other event was reported in a newspaper: in a county town, the police chief had a lawyer tied to a tree and let his men slap the lawyer by turns because the lawyer represented a man they had arrested. I strung these two events together and created an intellectual as the main character. Of course, I added lot of other happenings to flesh the story out.

What do you know when you begin a novel?

A piece of material has more weight and dramatic power in it. Writers by instinct know what is suitable for a novel or for a story. I can feel it. In case of *Waiting*, it's about three people's whole lives. The time span and the weight of the subject promised a novel. From the very beginning, I knew this must be a novel.

How are your characters revealed to you in the process of writing a novel?

I have to live with them for a long time. The knowledge about them is accumulated in the process of working on the book. I have few revelations. Or let me put this in another way: I have to struggle for a long time to get to know my characters intimately. For example, in the case of Lin Kong [from *Waiting*], I at first couldn't understand why he waited so passively and why he didn't know Manna well enough to make his second marriage work. Even after I finished the first draft, he was still flat because I didn't know his psychology yet. Gradually I figured out that he was emotionally disabled and he had not grown up emotionally. Even his good nature worked against him, making it harder for him to be assertive and to love devotedly.

The scene toward the end of Waiting *when Lin spends the peaceful evening with Shuyu and his daughter is wonderfully poignant. Did you know all along that Lin would gravitate back to his original family, or did it surprise you? Generally, what kinds of things surprise you in the process of writing a novel?*

I knew that scene would happen before I started to write. Very rarely I was surprised by my characters. Once or twice, I was surprised by the ending of a story.

In the Pond is a straight, chronological narrative, but Waiting *begins about two-thirds of the way through the actual chronology of events covered by the novel and then backtracks to tell the story. How did you hit upon that structure for the novel? Are there ways that you look at an idea to help you structure it in time?*

Yes, the idea of how to start a story helped me construct *Waiting*.

Chekhov advised young writers to break their stories in half, throw away the first half, and start with the second half. The advice implies that a story should start as closely as possible to the center of the drama.

Your novels track the day-to-day lives of ordinary people, but they are page-turners because you do such a great job of cranking up the tension in large and small ways throughout. How do you construct the plots for your novels and pace them to create this tension on the page?

Originally *Waiting* was written as a novella to go with a poetry manuscript. Later I took it back and expanded it into the novel. Writing a novel, I think mainly through scenes and chapters. Again, a writer can intuitively feel the drive and the heartbeat of the book. We shouldn't overload the story with details to drag the story down. On the other hand, if the density of details is too thin, the book will be flimsy. There are no tricks here. It's the labor we put into the writing that makes the words fresh and enjoyable on the page.

The main character of In The Pond, *Shao Bin, appears briefly in the short story "Winds and Clouds Over a Funeral." How did this character appear and develop in your mind? How and when did you know that his story would be worthy of a novel?*

In the Pond originally was intended to be a long story, but it grew too large to be included in *Under the Red Flag.* So it had to stand on its own. That explains why Shao Bin appears in the funeral story. A novel needs more narrative momentum and more scenes and a cast of characters. Once we feel these are potentially present in the material, we can think of a novel.

How do you know it's a novel, as opposed to short stories or poems?

When the narrative drive is not strong enough to sustain many chapters, and the subject doesn't have enough weight to hold the reader's attention for long, the material cannot be for a novel in the conventional sense.

Shao Bin experiences painter's block in In the Pond. *Have you had writer's block?*

I was driven by fear for many years, afraid that my university would fire me. So I couldn't afford to have writer's block and had to write constantly.

How do you work through a novel? Are there techniques or "tricks" you use to keep yourself going? How do you organize your time for the long work of a novel?

There are no tricks. In summer and winter breaks I write a draft, very rough. When I am teaching, I edit and revise the piece.

What is your revision process?

My first draft is awfully rough, embarrassingly bad, but I do rewrites and revise heavily for a long time. For every piece of work, I have reached the point [where] I can't do anything more, though I know that if I put the manuscript aside for a while, I will be able to return to it with a fresh mind and can surely do more revision. In this sense, revision is endless, but we have to stop somewhere. I stop at the point where I cannot improve anything for the time being. In truth, that's not enough. Sometimes I lay a piece aside for later revision. I revised [*A Free Life*] many, many times, at least thirty times. Maybe forty. The original manuscript was bigger. My editor told me to cut one hundred pages, and I cut eighty. Also, the poetry at the back took me forever to finish.

The quality of your English prose is deceptively simple. The matter-of-fact tone you often adopt seems perfect to convey the sense of people pushed to extremes of absurdity, violence, and despair. In your opinion, how does writing in a second language affect both the nature and quality of the novels you write? How would your work be different if you were writing in Chinese?

In English I have to be very careful and patient. If I wrote in Chinese, I might have to invent a different kind of language. Even in Chinese, I wrote in a simple, straightforward style. I hate flowery stuff. That's why my wife often says that the Chinese won't accept my way of writing, which is too plain and too honest. Probably because I study poetry and write poetry, I tend to be more selective than inclusive. This cannot be helped. I am this kind of writer.

Your work informs readers about the conditions of life in Communist China, but the information is always conveyed in the service of the story. As a result, it never feels like fiction with an agenda. How do you accomplish this? What advice would you give to a novelist who hopes to effect political change through literature?

Auden says, "Poetry makes nothing happen." I don't believe in the social effect of literature. I write to tell a good story, which first must delight. To instruct is much less important.

How have living and working in the United States affected the way you see China and/or how you write about it? How do the experiences and concerns of your present life make their way into the novels and stories that are set in China? Do you think that China will always be the subject matter for your fiction?

Living here makes it possible for me to treat China just as a subject. The distance and the feeling of alienation help me become objective and detached. Above all, America has given me a free state of mind. I haven't returned to China since I came. Contemporary China is unfamiliar to me now, so the more meaningful subject for me is the American experience.

While your novels set in China focus on the ways in which the control and corruption of the Communist bureaucracy bring out the worst in people, the perceptive reader looks beyond the extremes and sees all of humanity reflected in your characters' greed and paranoia, their quickness toward cruelty when cruelty is rewarded—or simply ignored. Would you comment on the ways your work transcends its specific subject matter and becomes about all people, everywhere?

I don't believe in difference. Literature operates on the principle of similarity and identity. So I often give some kind of abstraction to my fiction so that it can resonate to most people.

Your most recent novel A Free Life *is the first of your books to address the immigrant experience. Would you talk about why, finally, you felt ready to address this topic?*

I conceived this book fifteen years ago, but I hadn't lived in the United States long enough to write it. I used to think that I would write only about China, but as I continued, I felt kind of alienated from my native land and began to feel that the American experiences were closer to my heart, more meaningful to me. I knew I would eventually leave China and try to arrive here literarily. Having lived in America for more than two decades, I finally felt capable of writing about it, though I cannot completely sever myself from China, which is always my past.

When the seed of this story came into your mind, what did you know about the characters? What questions did you have to answer about their lives in the process of writing the book?

In the winter of 1992, my friend Jennifer Rose showed me a book of poems written in Chinese. It had been given to her by a restaurateur in Waltham, Massachusetts, who was a recent Hong Kong immigrant. I was very touched by the book, not by its content but by the fact that the man had been struggling to become an artist while running a small restaurant. In my novel I wanted to address the metaphysical dimension of the immigrant experience and I wrote against the popular version of the American dream.

In what ways is Nan's immigrant experience like your own, and how is it different?

Only at the microlevel, because I had to be certain of what I was writing about and had to stay with things and events I knew intimately. But the big story is not autobiographical at all. I didn't drop out of graduate school, have never lived in New York, or worked in a Chinese restaurant, or returned to China. I don't have an ex-girlfriend in America either. I have lived a much more fortunate life. In fact, I held [the character] Dick Harrison's job, teaching poetry writing at Emory, for eight years.

You've said that all the details in your fiction are factual and that you create a special order for them. Would you discuss the facts you worked with in A Free Life *and how you found the right order for them?*

The novel is episodic by nature, because I wanted it to reflect the vast American landscape to some extent. Also, the story is an emotional journey and needs time to show the gradual Americanization of the characters. I would still say that many details are factual in the sense that they took place in different places and at different times and to different people, but I pieced them together.

A Free Life *is a straight, chronological narrative that covers ten years. By keeping the reader unremittingly in the present time, you mirror the feeling immigrants must have adjusting to a culture in which virtually nothing that happened in the past is useful in helping them survive day-to-day life. What were the challenges in working with this structure?*

The immigrant experience is not a very dramatic one. It's the slow, small, and mundane changes that define the process. The difficulty in describing this experience partly lies in the fact that compared to people back home, the immigrants are more fortunate and stronger; therefore, their suffering and struggling here must have some kind of spiritual meaning besides good opportunities. Technically, a main challenge is how to write an interesting novel without a plot.

Was writing in English about the American experience different in any way from writing in English about China?

Absolutely. The idiom is different and so are the references. I basically abandoned many of the devices I had invented for myself when writing fiction set in China. *A Free Life* is a departure—I have left my comfortable turf.

Patricia Henley

Patricia Henley is the author of two novels and four short story collections. She grew up in southern Indiana, but she left the Midwest in 1964 and did not return until she came home to teach at Purdue University in 1987. A graduate of the Writing Seminars at the Johns Hopkins University, her first novel, *Hummingbird House*, was nominated for the National Book Award, the New Yorker Fiction Prize, and the IMPAC Dublin Literary Award. When she's not writing, she cooks, visits her children, plays with her cats, and walks the country roads and paths of whatever continent she finds herself on. She lives in West Lafayette, Indiana.

Friday Night at Silver Star, 1986 (stories); *The Secret of Cartwheels*, 1992 (stories); *Back Roads*, 1996 (stories); *Hummingbird House*, 1999; *Worship of the Common Heart*, 2000 (stories); *In the River Sweet*, 2002

You published three collections of short stories before publishing your first novel, Hummingbird House. *How did you make the transition from short fiction to the novel?*

When I first started writing fiction in 1979, I started a novel. Some of the characters that were in my early short stories were in that novel. That was my first effort at fiction writing. It wasn't working. I didn't have a sense of what I was doing. So I turned that novel into stories. Then I wrote the second collection. I didn't really have the idea of a novel in my mind at all until I went to Guatemala.

So the trip to Guatemala came first, before the idea that you would like to write about that place.

I went with a friend in 1989. I had always been interested in indigenous people, the fate of indigenous people, and I followed what was going on there from afar. I had no idea how it would affect my writing, but I was willing to find out. When I went down there, it just seemed like material that begged to be a novel. So I took it on.

Was there anything in particular that struck you that way, or just the general experience?

I felt that somebody reading a short story about that could ignore the historical context, but if you write a novel, hundreds of pages, no one could ignore it. It seemed like really big issues kept coming up. The lives of women and children in wartime, religion. I thought, "This has to be a novel," though I still had no idea what I was doing. One of the hardest technical things I dealt with was switching from writing a tidy, ten-to-twenty-page piece that's finished, to writing chapters, where you want just the opposite. You want a book. You want something that's going to keep the reader reading. Short story writers are used to exposition, conflict, closure, and I found myself doing that a lot with the chapters. I think that's one of the hardest things for short story writers to get over.

Yes, there's a seamlessness to a good novel. It's an alternate reality in a way a short story can't be. You live in it for a while. You want it to feel that way.

I think that's the naive, childlike reader in us. We like to be deeply engaged. We want to have that feeling that we can't put it down. It's kind of old fashioned, I guess. But I wanted that sustained tension throughout. So that's one of the difficulties — and then just sustaining the energy for the project, the mental and emotional and physical energy. My life as a short story writer went like this: I would write a draft in maybe a week or ten days, let it sit maybe for a week or ten days, revise it for a couple of weeks. In a month or six weeks, I would have a story. Maybe I would go back to it in another month or so, but I could have a sense of completion and take some time off. Live my life. Writing a novel requires so much more letting go of the rest of your life.

Another transition comes to mind: plotting, of course. I came to realize that short stories are much more like poems than they are like novels. Plotting perplexed me for a long time. Now that I feel I've learned a little bit about my own way of plotting, at least, I enjoy it very much. It's problem solving, and I've always enjoyed problem solving.

How did you go about learning your own way of plotting?

My son and husband helped me a lot. They were more analytical about [the book] and they helped me see that I needed to arrange the events in a way that continued to raise questions. I looked at what I had and thought, "Okay, where do I want those questions to be raised? How can I keep the reader wondering? How many balls can I get in the air?" I approached it that way, kind of by the seat of my pants.

How did you look at the whole thing?

I would read it over and over again and look at the way one thing inevitably led to the next thing. Screenplay books were helpful to me. It also helped me to look at films and to see how structured they were. The writers who write screenplays have that moment very early on, that instigating event that changes everything, and complications spin out from that moment.

Plot is like a skeleton. I tell my students that our structures can be the same, just like our skeletons can be the same. But nobody would ever look at us and think we're the same, because it's the way we're fleshed out that matters. You can start with that basic structure, that skeleton, but that's the wonderful thing about the novel — it can go off on this cul-de-sac or that cul-de-sac. And every time, it's so different.

Philip Roth said in an interview, years ago, that no matter how long you've been writing, it's not like a dentist doing a root canal. The dentist goes in every day, he does a root canal. But you sit down and you have to face that blank page and start all over again. One thing that helped was that I had these different elements, people, and situations that were dangerous. So lots of different things could happen. I had Sunny with that newspaper and Vida Luz with her husband in jail. I had all these people who had potential danger in their lives, and so I had a lot to work with. I came across these stories or I invented stories that seemed to be a really rich broth.

There's a difference between an emotional plot and an action plot. I think if you write stories with emotional plots, it's really hard to get the other. But you've got to have both. The reader gets attached to all the characters, so there's emotional growth and inner turmoil. But it's triggered by something with such great dramatic possibilities. You have to have that outer tension of some kind. It doesn't have to be something cliché, like a car chase. But you need to have something on the outside. You can't just have inner tension.

So it's translating the inner tension into something you can see and follow and track.

When it comes to plotting, you have to be willing to spend the time in solitude playing out different scenarios in your mind, working it through, daydreaming about it, thinking about whether that's really the way you want it to go, whether that feels authentic enough, whether that's provocative enough. You play these things out and then maybe you back up and think, no that's not it, and try another one. I think oftentimes when we're writing, we think that the first thing we write down is going to be the great thing. It usually isn't. You have to be willing to backtrack and try another path.

When you started the book, what did you know for sure?

I knew that I had Kate. I knew she was a midwife. I've always had an attraction to midwifery. I helped a friend deliver her baby years ago — one of my short stories came out of that, "The Birthing." I wanted a central character who was bringing life into the world. There was so much death and destruction around her, and I wanted that to be part of the conflict and the tension.

I started the material in first person, and I was just writing endlessly Kate's point of view. Then I realized that I wanted a narrator who was more knowledgeable than Kate, who saw a bigger picture than Kate was able to see. So I started writing some third person passages which I was quite happy with. But I didn't want to give up Kate's voice. I wanted her voice to have that ring of the friend who's sitting down with you over a cup of coffee or a beer, telling you, "This is what happened and this is how I'm making sense of it now." I really liked that.

The choice to make her a midwife was interesting because it is such an essentially unpolitical thing to be. This is in so many ways a political novel, yet you avoided any sense of having an agenda behind it. How did you do that?

First of all, I didn't want to come down on the side of any one political group or military group. I just kept reminding myself, "Don't let yourself get bogged down in those things. Pull back and ask the biggest questions you can possibly ask." I kept bringing myself back to, "What happens to women and children when there's war?" That just kept informing my movement through the project.

So I knew Kate, I knew she was going to be a midwife, and I knew that she had had a troubled love life. That's all I knew at the beginning. It didn't take long for me to start thinking about Dixie. I met and talked with and read about men and women of the church who've done a lot of work down there. There's no one exactly like Dixie. But there was a priest in Guatemala in the '80s who was killed, and the people of the village asked if they could have his heart to bury in the churchyard. That stuck with me. Someone told me that story when I'd been in Guatemala for two weeks, and I thought, "I'm going to write about a priest." So I always knew that Dixie was going to die.

And you knew that his heart would be buried in the churchyard.

Yes. I knew I had to put that in the book. You go around like a vulture, stealing these things.

What about the time of the novel? How did you decide when it would take place?

I knew I couldn't set the novel in an era when I hadn't been there. I felt incapable of doing that. So I decided to set it in 1989, the summer when I was there for the first time. I took five trips, researching the book. But that summer was a very intense summer for me, emotionally. I wanted to write what I knew, and I knew the mood in Guatemala that summer because I was there. So that's what I knew. I knew these two people. I knew their lives intersected the summer of 1989 in Antigua, Guatemala, and I just started writing.

When did you start the book?

I started it in 1989, when I came back. I worked on it off and on for a couple of years, but I was also working on *The Secret of Cartwheels* at that time. I completed two hundred pages, abandoned them, wrote a short story about Marta and Eduardo, the orphans. I put that away, didn't do anything with it. Then in 1993, after the publication of *The Secret of Cartwheels*, I got back to the book. I didn't complete it until the spring of 1996, when I was on sabbatical in New Mexico.

So the book was in your mind for a long time.

Yes. And then the book wasn't accepted for two more years. So it was ten years between having that idea and holding the book in my hands. It was a very long time. I changed so much.

Yes. That's another thing that happens with a novel that doesn't happen with a short story. You start out writing the novel as a certain person, but you may very well be a different person by the time you get it finished.

I had to allow myself to be transformed by the material and the experience. I had to just let go. My life was so ruled by that book. The second time I went to Guatemala, in 1990, I went by myself for six weeks. I was a little scared of going because nobody knew what I was doing. It was a dangerous place, where artists and writers, especially, had been killed. I went, and I can remember lying awake—I can picture the place where I was when this happened—thinking, "What am I doing here? Do I really have to do this?" I was really questioning the wisdom of the path I was on. I was just so convinced that I had to write about this in a way that would make the oppression of the Guatemalan people accessible to more people.

Do you find that you write, generally, because there's something you feel you want the world to know? Or is it because there's something you need to know for yourself?

The things I want to figure out for myself are usually the emotional things—thorny issues in my own life and the lives of my friends. But right now I'm in a phase of my life of writing about things that will be provocative. So many people will come to a story. So many people have come to *Hummingbird House* who never would have picked up a book of nonfiction about Guatemala. So that's how I'm approaching my work now. I can pick an issue, any issue, and pursue it in fiction and so many more people will come to it. I'm a very political person.

Passion, really caring about what you write, seems crucial in the mix of talents novelists bring to the page. So does a willingness to embrace the kind of ambiguity of process you describe. What else makes a good novelist?

A compassionate heart seems to me to be very, very important. A willingness to really look closely at human beings and their motivations and their foibles without judging them is really important. To be a novelist you have to be willing to sit there all those hours, just endure. I advise my students to get involved in an endurance sport. It's helped me a lot. I work out. I walk, run. I used to do long-distance skiing and mountain climbing. Anything that pushes you, that makes you push yourself will help you push yourself to get a project like a novel done. That's so much of it, the willingness to be there, to meet with it every day. There's a great essay by Ted Solaratoff called "Going Through the Pain."

What do you do when you're really stuck?

I don't usually get really stuck for more than a few days. I get stuck between sections or chapters, and I'll know that something's cooking in me. I'll get glimmers of it once in a while as I'm going about my day. But it's not ready to spring forth on the page yet. No matter how many times I go through those things, I always find them a little bit frustrating. But I try to have faith. I always say to myself, "You've done this before, you can do it again." I wait it out, and usually when I least expect it the first sentence of that next section will come to me. So I go on about my business and maybe use the time to get a lot of grading done. Or cook. I love to cook.

What surprised you in the process of writing Hummingbird House*? Were there things in the story that you didn't know were going to happen?*

Oh, so much of it. Marta and Eduardo came into the story rather late in the process. I had written this story about them, "Orphans."

So you wrote the story not thinking it was a part of the novel.

Right. My husband said to me several times, "You need to get those kids in the story." Finally, I listened to him, and probably they came into it in the second-to-last draft, when I was really pulling it together. Or maybe third to last. Late in the process. A big question throughout the novel was, would Dixie and Kate sleep together? That was an enormous question for me, almost to the very end. I finally decided that it wasn't consistent with Dixie's character and I didn't want this to be a book about a priest who breaks his vow.

When did you know how the book would end?

I remember the day that the ending came to me. It was probably two or three months before I finished the whole manuscript. I had this wonderful situation. I was in New Mexico, living in an adobe house, and I was set up in the dining room where there were two windows and I could see the mountains, and I could see the sun coming up.

So visually it was like the landscape you were writing about.

Yes, and culturally. Spanish was being spoken, Indian languages being spoken. It was a wonderful place to be to finish this book. I remember the ending coming, those last couple of paragraphs, in a rush, the way sometimes writing will, when you really feel you're accessing something you don't have any control over, almost. It's just there, and you think, "This is amazing." So the ending is pretty much the way it came out.

And did you always know that it would be an ending kind of after the fact? The action of the novel is over a number of years before the actual novel is over.

No! That's another thing that came while I was in New Mexico. I had to have a reason for these first-person monologues to be in here. "What is my reason?" Then I realized that my reason was, she's mulling over her whole life because she's trying to decide whether to go back to the States. But that came near the end. You have to be so patient. If you're patient, I think it will all come to you. But you have to be very patient and realize that there are so many things you don't know, that you can only find out by writing the book. And then you have to rewrite it, sometimes many, many, many times. Even after it's accepted.

Did you do a lot of revisions after the book was bought by McMurray and Beck?

I redid the beginning. Those initial scenes, where I introduce Dixie and the children and Kate, had been written, but they were plucked out. My editor thought it was important to establish the multiple points of view early on. When I sent them the manuscript, it started with Kate in Nicaragua, delivering the baby, which is the real beginning of the story.

Time was muddy in the book. The central action in 1989 takes a year, from the time Kate delivers the baby until Dixie dies. I went through the manuscript and marked any time there was a mention of time and looked at it. It struck me as being such a mess. So much of the book ended up being taken apart and rearranged. It was a very interesting process. It taught me that your work is very malleable. Do not think that the way you write it down the first time or the second time or even the fifth time is the way it's supposed to be to make a good book. I think that's what a lot of beginning writers don't realize. They can improve their projects so much if they realize that and are not attached to one idea.

The publication of Hummingbird House *has an interesting story behind it. You said it was several years before it found a publisher. What happened?*

When I finished the book, I felt that it was good. I was shocked that no one in New York wanted to buy it. I got frustrated and said [to my agent], "I'll take it back." So I took it back and started sending it out on my own. I sent it to a couple of places that were very positive about it, but it just wasn't right for them. Then I sent it to McMurray and Beck. I was away for five weeks that summer. When I got home at the end of July, our house sitter was standing on the porch—it was a Friday, near the end of the business day. She said, "Get in here and call McMurray and Beck. They're trying to get ahold of you. They want to publish your book."

Then the book was nominated for the National Book Award.

I felt vindicated.

What would you say to somebody who's just beginning? How can you think about the absurdity of the publishing world?

You have to have tremendous faith in yourself and you can't get it from anywhere else. My husband saying to me, "There's nothing wrong with it," meant nothing. The only voice that can give you confidence is your own voice, and where a person gets that, I don't know. I've had a lot of adversity in my life. Maybe that's where it comes from. But you have to have faith that you're doing what you're supposed to be doing, that you're working really hard, that the work you do is valuable in the world. You have to love what you're doing when you sit down to the table or computer. You can't be thinking about what kind of rewards are going to come later on. The joy is in the moment of writing. It's not about being nominated for awards or winning awards or even holding your book in your hand.

Charles Johnson

Charles Johnson is the author of five novels and two collections of short sto-ries. Born in Evanston, Illinois, he received his BA and MA from Southern Illinois University and did postgraduate work at the State University of New York at Stony Brook. In addition to writing fiction, Johnson writes screen-plays, reviews, essays, and critical articles. His honors include the National Book Award and the Washington State Governor's Award for Literature; his short fiction is included in the O. *Henry Prize Stories* (1993), *Best American Short Stories* (1992), and *Best American Short Stories of the Eighties*. He was named a MacArthur Fellow in 1998. Currently, Johnson holds an endowed chair, the S. Wilson and Grace M. Pollack Professorship for Excellence in English, at the University of Washington, where he teaches fiction. He lives in Seattle, Washington, with his wife.

Faith and the Good Thing, 1974; *Oxherding Tale*, 1982; *The Sorcerer's Apprentice*, 1986; *Middle Passage*, 1990; *Dreamer*, 1998; *Soulcatcher and Other Stories*, 2005; *Dr. King's Refrigerator and Other Bedtime Stories*, 2005

Middle Passage *has been compared to the work of Melville. What made you decide to shape this material as a kind of adventure story that is reminiscent of early American literature? How did the novel gather in your mind?*

Middle Passage was actually a work of seventeen years. In 1971, when I was an undergraduate at Southern Illinois University, I took a black his-tory course and asked the professor if I could devote my research paper to the slave trade because I hoped to write a novel on that subject. He agreed, and I wrote that first draft of the novel that year, telling the story from the viewpoint of a white ship's captain and in the form of a ship's log. I decided that approach was unsuccessful, because the ship's captain was unable to understand or empathize deeply with the slaves in the hold of his ship. So I put that draft away and worked on other projects, though I continued to gather material on the slave trade until 1983, when I again returned to the book, this time with the intention that it should be, first and foremost, a rousing high-seas-adventure tale—one that delivered more details on the daily life of Africans on those ships than any other novel.

What kind of research did you do for the book? Were there ways in which the discoveries of research shaped the plot and/or characters as you wrote the novel?

As I mentioned, seventeen years of historical research went into the novel. What I didn't have in 1983 was knowledge of the sea and its lore. So, during the six years I worked on *Middle Passage*, I read all of the sea novels of Herman Melville, Joseph Conrad, and Jack London. I went through the Sinbad stories and read nautical dictionaries—that, in order to immerse myself in the language of the maritime tradition. I even had a friend of mine who is an accomplished maker of miniature ships build for me a replica of an eighteenth-century slave ship, one that had twenty feet of rigging by the time he finished it. Knowing the world of sailors and ships naturally helped define (and expand) the parameters and possibilities for what the characters in *Middle Passage* could and would do.

What were the pleasures and perils of research for you?

Research held no perils for me, only pleasures. As a scholar of literature, and a PhD in philosophy, I've lived a large part of my life in libraries, digging through dry texts for those generally unnoticed nuggets of history and thought that lend themselves to drama and new discoveries.

What was the greatest challenge in writing a historical novel?

Actually, I've never seen myself as a "historical writer." My novels and stories that are set in the past are, at bottom, philosophical fictions, but in order to explore certain ideas it was necessary to set those works in a time other than our own.

How did Rutherford Calhoun first appear to you as a character? How was the complexity of his character revealed during the process of writing the novel? In what ways did he surprise you?

Rutherford Calhoun first entered my imagination as a free man, not a slave, a young man who is something of a rogue yet equipped with all the knowledge of a nineteenth-century intellectual, thanks to his former, Christian master. I like narrators who know things, who are sensitive to all the subtleties and nuances of the world around them, so that when they speak it is with eloquence and authority. Truth to tell, I was far less surprised by Rutherford during the process of creating this novel than I was by other characters—Captain Falcon, for example, who is loosely based on Sir Richard Francis Burton, one of the architects of British colonialism.

How did you find Rutherford's voice?

Rutherford's voice—a blend of nineteenth- and twentieth-century diction—was something I first worked out in *Oxherding Tale*, the novel that preceded *Middle Passage*. Both are antebellum-era stories, the former written in the form of a slave narrative, the latter as a ship's log. But these works are, of course, for late-twentieth-century and early twenty-first-century readers, so what I worked to achieve was the textual "feel" of a nineteenth-century document, rather than a transcript of one, which would not have been appropriate for our time.

The shipboard struggles of the slave Ngonyama seem to be a kind of premonition of the collective future of slaves and their American descendants. Would you talk about how you see the character's purpose in the book and how he developed during the writing process?

One of my goals in *Middle Passage* was to fully flesh out the fictitious African tribe known as the Allmuseri. They appeared briefly in *Oxherding Tale* and in stories in my collection *The Sorcerer's Apprentice* ("The Education of Mingo" and the title story), but in *Middle Passage* my goal was to completely render them culturally, to provide them with a language, a society, rituals, etc. To this day there are readers who believe this African tribe is real (as readers of Swift actually thought in his time that Brobdingnagians existed). My goal, in brief, was to create the most spiritual tribe on earth, a whole tribe of Mother Teresas and Gandhis. But I made nothing up for them. Rather, I drew on the details of their culture from several so-called third-world people—from the village of Kerala in India, from Africa, and from China.

The culture of the Allmuseri is nondualistic and shot through with spirituality. The essence of that culture is embodied in the character Ngonyama (whose name means "brave lion"), who is grief stricken by the inevitable loss of his people's cultural *weltanschauung*, when they are forced to engage in violence—a slave revolt—to free themselves from their Western captors. In effect, they become like their captors, like Falcon, and this Ngonyama sees as tragic but unavoidable.

There is a great deal of violence in the book, yet perhaps the most graphic and disturbing scene is the one in which Rutherford helps the slaves put a putrefying, disintegrating corpse overboard. Why did you avoid more epic possibilities for violence, yet give the reader the full effect of this smaller, seemingly less significant moment?

Yes, there is violence in *Middle Passage*. The culture of Captain Falcon and his Yankee sailors is inherently violent, dualistic, and based on conflict. Indeed, the slave trade itself is a study in violence and violation. When Rutherford is forced to toss the decaying corpse of an Allmuseri overboard it is at that moment that he, as a Western, free, black man, fully identifies with the suffering of the Africans on board the *Republic*. As you say, it is in the quieter moments that we often realize the true horror of human oppression.

How do you make decisions about tension and pacing? Are there techniques you use to help you see how the book is moving, how to fix it if it's not moving the way you think it should?

In the six years I worked on *Middle Passage*, I threw out 3,000 pages to arrive at the final 250 of the final manuscript. In this novel (and all my novels), my last draft is usually concerned exclusively with pacing. With eliminating anything that slows the forward movement of the story. The only time in *Middle Passage* that we experience a flashback is when Rutherford remembers his brother, Jackson. Actually, this incident was something I once planned to write as a separate story, but I decided to use it in this longer work, and at exactly the place it appears to give the reader a break—a chance to catch his or her breath—before all hell breaks loose on ship when the sailors mutiny against Falcon and the slaves revolt against them. Yes, I'm always concerned in a novel with maintaining a brisk pace, in fact, with creating a "page-turner," if possible, a story in which the reader is concerned about [asking], "What happens next?"

Baleka, the Allmuseri slave child in Middle Passage, *carries the seed for* Dreamer. *Late in that book, we learn that Chaym Smith, Martin Luther King's double, is descended from her. The ideas and philosophies he shares with Matthew Bishop reflect the Allmuseri beliefs of Ngonyama. To what degree was*

Dreamer *an extension of* Middle Passage *in your mind from the start? What was the process by which* Dreamer *came into being in your mind? What is the unanswerable question at the base of the two books?*

Baleka (in Sanskrit, which I'm in my third year of studying—her name means "young girl") does appear in *Dreamer* indirectly after having a significant onstage role in *Middle Passage.* If there is an underlying philosophical thread that runs through both novels, it is this: how does one realize the unitive vision that is at the heart of Allmuseri culture and expressed so eloquently by Dr. Martin Luther King, who—as this nation's preeminent moral philosopher—emphasized the interconnectedness of all being and the necessity of living our lives with love and nonviolence?

Dreamer came into being because in the 1980s, I realized I simply did not know this man and his legacy well enough, as most Americans do not. By canonizing him, we have reduced him to one dimension only. Please look at my book, coauthored with Bob Adelman, *King: The Photobiography of Martin Luther King, Jr.*, a work I see as something of a companion to *Dreamer*, for in pictures it allows us to re-experience King as a spiritual seeker, a devoted son, a father, and a husband: an American of remarkable complexity who represented the very best in the Civil Rights movement.

The fundamental question at the heart of *Dreamer* is just this: What is the self? Who am I? Where does the Self end and the Other begin? Is it not the case, in the final analysis, that the Self *is* the Other?

The young Civil Rights worker, Matthew Bishop, was an interesting character. When and how did this character enter your mind? To what degree does he reflect your own experience as a young black man during this time?

Well, Matthew Bishop is me and not me. I felt that for *Dreamer* we needed a young philosopher (and a Christian struggling with his faith) who deeply admired King to tell this story, the kind of young man who would be open to the Eastern orientation represented by Chaym Smith (I'm a lay-Buddhist), so that, by the novel's end we have a work that celebrates the life of the spirit, Eastern and Western, as well as King's legacy.

Both Chaym Smith and Rutherford Calhoun are strong, complex, sometimes unworthy individuals in a world that has very specific expectations about what black people should be. What is it about these two men that you feel is important in telling the truth about the African American experience in America?

To a degree, both Rutherford Calhoun and Chaym Smith are Cain figures. They are "outsiders," as black Americans have always been; in fact, blacks (and Jews) were once identified as descendents of Cain by racist white theologians. But, as Chaym points out in *Dreamer*, being thrust "outside" is a phenomenological act that enables one to see what those inside a culture (the Abelites) are unable to see—about themselves, and the world. By contrast, Rutherford is ideally positioned—as a free black man—to understand both the white sailors on the *Republic* and the Africans in the hold, though he truly belongs with neither group.

It is a particular kind of challenge to make fictional characters from real people, as you did with King. What kind of research did you do to help you capture the essence of him? What rules did you set for yourself in inventing Dreamer *around the actual details of his life? Did you have insights about King's life in the process of writing about him as a fictional character?*

Before I wrote a word for *Dreamer* I spent two years reading every biography of the man and history of the civil rights movement I could find. I read and listened to his sermons, read his college papers, went to the Lorraine Motel, where he was killed, and the house in Atlanta where he was raised. I looked at documentary footage of the Chicago campaign over and over, and I brought to this novel everything I've studied about religion since the late 1960s.

With King in *Dreamer* I had to ask all the specific questions that a novelist asks about his main characters. What was his education? Which of all the sermons he wrote were his favorites? What hymns did he love? What did he like to eat? How did he shave? What seldom-reported events in his life—his childhood, young manhood, his marriage—provide telling details that reveal his character and spirit, his desires and fears? I've studied King now for a decade and feel I know him well enough to predict how he would respond to particular situations. That was my mantra during the seven years I worked on *Dreamer*: "What would King do or say in this situation?" By the way, in this novel, I invented almost nothing *for* King—the burden of this book was to deliver in vivid detail what is simply in the historical record about him, which most Americans either do not know or have forgotten.

In what way does the subject material in the two books reflect the personal experiences that shaped you as a child and as an adolescent? What are the life questions you keep trying to answer through your novels?

All my books, I suppose, are forms of spiritual (as well as philosophical) literature. The questions I return to again and again—from my childhood in the black church to my life now as a Buddhist—are, "How does one live spiritually in this world? How does one serve the Good, the True and the Beautiful in a culture that is spiritually corrupt?"

The sections that chart Martin Luther King's process through the last month of his life have an almost biblical feel to them. They also seem to reflect King's own sense of psychological distance from himself, his own life. King is always referred to as "he" by the omniscient narrator, never by his name. Would you talk about how and why you created this effect in the book, and also about the book's structure?

Dreamer alternates between third-person-limited chapters (in italics) where we are perched on King's shoulder, listening to him think and experience the world, and chapters told in first person by Matthew Bishop. I chose this approach after much experimentation because it allows the reader to experience King from the inside as well as observe him (through Bishop) from the outside. The easiest ones to write, as it turned out, were the King chapters, since I didn't have to invent any details for him, as I did with Bishop.

How do you revise your books? Are there techniques you use to identify problem areas? Do you depend upon feedback from others at any time during the process?

How do I revise? My ratio of throwaway to keep is often twenty to one. I revise with two things in mind: the musical and meaning dimensions of a prose line; the sound and the sense. I know a passage or a sentence is done when nothing—not a word or syllable—can be removed or substituted without destroying the sense or the sound of that passage. I revise always with the goal of achieving greater and greater specificity of detail, variety of sentence structure—and I use the rule that every paragraph must contain something special, exciting, or memorable if it is to justify its presence on the page.

Most novelists describe a gap between the novel they imagined and the one they were able to bring to the page. Do you have the same sense about your books? How are the novels you wrote different from the novels you set out to write?

For me, writing a novel is always a process of discovery. There is no "gap" between the novel I imagined and the one I wrote, because I try to enter a new fiction the same way a scientist enters his laboratory: with a hypothesis, which I test through the tools of fiction. The result may confirm or deepen my original idea or thesis (as any scientific experiment can change one's initial ideas), but that is what I expect: to be surprised. If a writer is not surprised by what he or she discovers during the writing process, then I doubt that a reader will experience surprise or discovery.

To what degree did creating a double for Martin Luther King allow you to explore the gap between what any person hopes and dreams his life will be and the life he actually lives?

The use of the double in *Dreamer* allowed me to inform the reader about King's life and vision as Chaym is taught to be his stand-in. Yet, there is a distance between King and Chaym that the latter cannot close simply because he does not possess King's unshakable spirituality until after he takes the bullet intended for King in Chicago.

Eastern philosophy comes into play often in your work. In what ways do you feel that Eastern thought serves the novelist in his work?

As a Buddhist, I feel that for many artists and creators the dharma is a teaching of tremendous value. The concentration required for writing—the one-pointed focus (*ekagratha*) is very similar to the stage of meditation known as *dhayana*. A fuller discussion of Buddhism and American artists appears in my article "A Sangha By Another Name," in the Winter 1999 issue of *Tricycle: The Buddhist Review*.

At one point in Dreamer, *Smith says, "All narratives are lies, man, an illusion. Don't you know that? As soon as you squeeze experience into a sentence—or a story—it's suspect. A lot sweeter or uglier than things actually were. Words are just webs. Memory is mostly imagination. If you want to be free, you best go beyond all that." In what way does writing novels allow you to "go beyond all that?"*

As Aristotle pointed out (and many others after him), words and things are not the same, ontologically. We use words—as writers—to create a "vivid and continuous dream" in the reader's mind. (That lovely phrase is from John Gardner.) But, as every Buddhist understands, we cannot limit ourselves to experiencing the world simply through words and concepts. There are times when we simply must abandon words and experience the poetic and ineffable mystery of Being.

Wally Lamb

Wally Lamb is the author of two novels and the editor of two books of stories written by women in prison. Born and raised in Norwich, Connecticut, he holds BA and MA degrees in teaching from the University of Connecticut and an MFA in writing from Vermont College. He was the director of the Writing Center at the Norwich Free Academy, Norwich, Connecticut, from 1989 to 1998, and is currently an associate professor of Creative Writing at the University of Connecticut. Both of his novels were featured as selections of Oprah's Book Club. Other honors include the Governor's Arts Award, State of Connecticut, and a National Endowment for the Arts Fellowship. He lives in Mansfield, Connecticut, with his wife and sons.

She's Come Undone, 1992; *I Know This Much Is True*, 1998

You have talked about drawing incessantly as a child, and your fiction is certainly visual. How does your strong sense of the visual come into play during the process of writing a novel?

Very often, when the fiction is going well, when it's going without a whole lot of pain and wheel spinning, I'm seeing it almost movie-like in my head or I'm hearing the characters speak the words. It doesn't happen as often as I'd like it to, but it certainly happened with both novels, particularly with the grandfather's story in *I Know This Much Is True*. A lot of that tale told itself almost cinematically. I think it stems back to childhood, when I was not only incessantly drawing, but watching way too much TV, which oddly enough has come back to serve me in a number of ways—not the least of which was the Oprah book club! I watched TV night and day. I didn't do a lot of reading, but that visual stuff! I was saturated with story, visual story, when I was a kid. I still think that way.

When I was having difficulty working on the screenplay for *She's Come Undone,* I sat down in my office and started drawing things out on index cards, scrawling and sketching at the same time, and sort of throwing the cards around—dealing them almost like tarot. Playing with it that way helped: the flow of the cards, the visual thing. Then I went to the wall with those index cards and masking tape. The south wall was act 1, the east wall was act 2—I ended up with a four-act script. I don't think I could have cracked the structural problem of the screenplay had I not been using the cards.

Did you have a scene on each card, or were there also cards with narrative passages on them?

More words than pictures. But sometimes the actual drawing of what would happen, like the surfacing of a whale. Something like that. I did the same thing, or a version of it, with *I Know This Much is True*. I kept spooking myself with that story because the canvas for it kept getting larger and larger and I didn't know if I could pull it off. I didn't know what it meant. Very early on in the process, I had the grandfather's story and it seemed like it was somehow the beating heart of the whole thing; but I didn't know how it related to the story proper. I thought maybe using the cards could help me figure out the meaning of the novel that I was immersed in, but I didn't know how that was going to happen.

When was the meaning of the story revealed to you?

I wrote that novel in a six-year span. Somewhere around the second year, I knew that Dominick was born to discover the grandfather's story. Around the fourth year, I realized that it was sort of a cautionary tale. Years before, I had read an ancient Hindu myth about a proud king who's duped by a beggar—a religious ascetic—and is forced to do his bidding. Forced to humble himself to the task of cutting a corpse from a hanging tree and lugging him to the center of the cemetery. But there's a catch to the mission: the dead guy slung over the king's shoulder starts whispering threats and riddles. Ultimately, it's the answers to the riddles that save the unsuspecting king from the beggar, who is in truth a malevolent sorcerer with a lust for power and a murderous nature. So it's the voice of the dead that allows the king to save himself. It gradually dawned on me that Dominick's grandfather, via the confessional diary he'd left behind, had provided his grandson with the blueprint he needed to save himself.

Did you discover the meaning of the grandfather's story and myth simultaneously, or were you working with the myth all along?

At the time I was working in the university library, writing in longhand, and I would take a break, go to the stacks, and reread the myth of the king and the corpse. It was playing with me. Somewhere in the process, I realized that I was telling a version of it in the novel. Pretty early on, I wrote the grandfather's story and, as I said, I didn't know what to do with it. It came faster and more furiously than anything I'd written before—or since. Little by little, I knew that I was going to put the grandfather's story at the end of the book, if it worked, if it fit into the puzzle. By about the fourth year, I kind of got why I was writing toward this point and how it connected to the myth, how I could pull order out of all that chaos.

In my experience this happens with symbol a lot, too. I'm writing symbol on an unconscious level and when it sort of bubbles up to the surface and becomes conscious to me, then I can use it. The best example is in *She's Come Undone*. I'd been writing for a couple of years and I was thinking of abandoning the novel. Then I sat and began rereading the longhand pages written out in Bic pen on loose-leaf paper, and I noticed, there's a mention of a whale here and there's a second mention of one there. I had no memory of even writing about whales, but when it became conscious to me, I could begin to work with it, sculpt it almost like clay, and use it to help me understand the "whys" of Dolores' story.

Your books take a long time to write. Do you tend to work right through to the end in your attempt to find the story, or do you work to the end and then spend many years to get the story pinned down and revised?

I don't have a satisfying answer to that because it's not an either/or thing. Usually, I'll write the first sentence, I'll fix that six times. I'll write the second sentence, then go back and fix the first sentence half a dozen times. Go on to fix the second sentence. So unless the writing is all of a sudden very visual—almost like a form of madness, where what I'm writing is more real than my real life (usually it's plodding)—I don't go forward easily sentence by sentence. I usually work on a chapter to the point where I know it's not right, but I don't know what to do with it. Then I'll bring it to my writers' group. Since I started writing, I've worked in a regular group. I think that's probably the result of having come out of an MFA program. I entered the program maybe a year after I started writing fiction, and so feedback is really critical to my process.

And you get it all the way along, not just at the end.

Right. Let's say that I'm working on a chapter for two months and finally it's just driving me crazy. That's the point at which I'll bring it to the writers' group. I'll read it out loud and they'll listen. Then I just sit there taking notes on their conversation. I try not to make any judgments because I find that I'm just going to be reacting emotionally — either yea or nay. Lots of times, as I'm taking notes, I'm thinking to myself, "No way, Jose," but I'm writing it down anyway, and two days later, when the experience cools off, I realize that's exactly what I needed to hear. Or sometimes, if there's a discussion going on, one person will say something and another will say something in reaction, and I'll have an "aha" moment. It isn't necessarily about what either person said, but I wouldn't have had it if I hadn't been listening to them talking or reacting to one another.

Sometimes if I am doing a reading in a library, I'll read stuff in progress. I'm not one of these people who keeps my work closeted. I want as much feedback midprocess as I can get. As I read something out loud to an audience, I'm really interested in what they're laughing at, where they seem to be losing attention, and so forth. But also just hearing it in my own voice in a public forum is giving me information that I can't get in silence as I'm looking at the monitor or the page. I think that writers become better writers if they give criticism to other people, too. I think that's a way to hone your craft. It's like anything else: you give, you get back.

Teaching does that, don't you think? So often, writing on a student's paper, you think, that's exactly the mistake I'm making in my own work.

It's funny. The last couple of years, with the foreign translations, I've been doing a little bit of international travel. In Italy I noticed this and in Germany. I just got back from Holland and Belgium and noticed it there, too. In Europe there is this sort of snickering prejudice against writing programs and books on craft. When I was in Amsterdam a few weeks ago, journalists asked about my teaching and about the workshop I'm doing at a women's prison. They'd ask, "How can writing be taught? Don't you feel that a writer really needs solitude?" I said, "Gee, no. I really don't think that. I think, why not get all the help you can get, and give all the help too?" They were openly skeptical. I knew they weren't buying what I had to say. But when I read at the John Adams Institute there—an organization dedicated to the study of American culture—I was swarmed afterwards by writers and would-be writers who were longing for this kind of critical feedback and writerly camaraderie. So there's a real discrepancy between the official thinking on the teaching of writing and what people seem to want.

When you work with people who want to be writers, what traits seem to indicate potential?

Probably more than anything else, persistence. They can't stop doing it, setbacks and obstacles or not. They can't stop forcing writing on to you. They're not put off by criticism, they're hungry for it. They don't think that they already have it right. They want to know what to do. Sometimes it's just a single sentence that sticks out in a bunch of mundane stuff that makes you know they've got it in them.

Here's an example. A couple of years ago, I judged a fiction contest for teenagers sponsored by *USA Today*. There were some impressive entries from all over the country. The story I chose for first place rose to the top of the pile on the basis of a single, striking image of a backyard pear tree whose fruit looked like hundreds of golden sitting Buddhas. You just know that young writer has it in her, if she stays with it, to reach the stars.

If, perhaps, writing can't be taught, you can encourage people to be practitioners. Good writing comes from practice. If you would've told me a year ago that some of these women I'm working with in the prison would be writing the unbelievable stuff they're writing today, I would have said no way. They were disorganized. There was this random stuff coming here and there. They had amazing life stories to tell, but they had no idea how to tell them. For some of them it was too hard, too difficult to face their personal demons and the sometimes-demonic writing process. We started with thirty participants and whittled down to six. But those six who lasted began to feel empowered by their accomplishments. They worked out this special deal with the warden whereby, through one of the teachers, they can send stuff to me by fax. I'll be working and I'll hear that fax machine. I get reams of stuff. They can't stop. I don't know if you've heard all this scientific evidence that people who write about their lives are lowering their blood pressure, curing asthma, and so forth. I see that in these women. They're healing. I'm not healing them; they're healing themselves because the writing matters to them.

How much did your experience as a high-school teacher feed your character, Dolores, in She's Come Undone?

Big time. I heard the voice of Dolores for several months, maybe two or three months. I was kind of interested in her, but I wasn't seriously committed to this character until, one day, I just happened to think of a kid that I'd worked with when I was student teaching, maybe nine or ten years earlier. She was a sad, isolated kid. Her name was Sharon. She was obese. She sat in the back of the classroom at a special desk; she couldn't fit in the regular ones. She came in late almost every day, and she had permission for reasons I don't remember to leave early. She never spoke in class. The other students weren't mean to her, but she made them uncomfortable, so they made her invisible. She was complicit in that because she never participated. If you were a student in that class and didn't look back, she didn't exist.

Of course, in my naïveté, having watched all those old shows—*Mr. Novak* and *Room 222* and *Lucas Tanner*—I was going to come in and save this girl's life. So I would go back there when the kids were doing seatwork and whisper, "Sharon, don't you think—?" Try to lure her inside the circle. But this kid wanted no part of me. Her defenses, her walls were up to stay. So it was a dismal failure; I never reached her. But every now and then I'd think of her and then, all of a sudden that day, I had the visual memory of her sitting in the back of that classroom. When that voice that I'd been working with got married to that remembered image—bam! The story and the character took off. The plotline of *She's Come Undone* is pure invention; it has nothing to do with Sharon's real life. But in some ways I think it was my longing to know what her life was like or what her issues were or how she might be saved that made me invent a life around her.

If you had been successful with her, you might not have written that book.
Maybe not.

Several times you've touched on the idea that the writer in some way acts as a therapist. Your characters are certainly terribly wounded people. Does your writing reflect the desire to understand people who've been wounded, to in a sense give them better lives?

This is Monday-morning quarterbacking or me sounding like my own CliffsNotes, but when I look back at both of those novels I see people struggling with alienation. It's really prevalent in [*I Know This Much Is True*] because I became fascinated with the irony of twinship. I remember as a kid being envious of twins. A built-in soul mate: how cool is that? I grew up in a house full of sisters, lived in a neighborhood with my older female cousins. They all traveled in a pack. There were no boys in the neighborhood, except for Vito Signorino, who would give you a bite of his popsicle one day and take a bite out of you the next. So I was a loner. I wasn't a social outcast or anything, but I had that sort of loneliness that I think still resides inside me.

So when I started working on the twins I became really fascinated with the irony that we are all, even twins, born into the world by ourselves, we die alone. And in between, we spend our lives either seeking or maintaining connections with other people. The theme of alienation versus connectedness, wholeness versus separation, is for some reason key for me. Both of the novels have characters who see therapists who bring them back to the world and make them whole again. So many of the myths do that: send a hero off on a solo journey and then the hero comes back to join the world.

You have studied myths in the process of developing your stories. How did you come to realize the importance of myth to your sense of what a story should be?

When I began work on my MFA at Vermont College, my teacher, Gladys Swan, asked, "What would you like to accomplish?" I said, "Well, I work with high-school students. I know that some novels really work with them and some don't. I would love to write a book that would speak to young people the way that *To Kill a Mockingbird* has spoken to so many of my students and also to me." We also talked about *The Catcher in the Rye* in that conversation. I don't think it's any accident that both of those novels have a prevalent first-person narrator with a strong sense of voice.

Gladys said to me, "The first thing that you have to do is not think about who your audience is." She said, "Write it for you. Make it true for yourself, and let the audience find it." In that same conversation, we talked about a short story I'd just begun about a crazy woman named Mary Anne, who later became Dolores. Gladys said, "You have too many pots on the stove here. There's too much going on here for a short story." That's what I had written up to that point, so I said, "What should I cut out?" She said, "Don't cut out anything. Keep going. Maybe you're trying to write a novel." I said, "Not me. I couldn't handle that. That's beyond what I can do." And she said, "Well, if you want to learn how to write a novel, read the oldest stories. Those stories have lasted because they say things that people have needed to be told over and over and over again." She said, "The world is an old place and all the stories that people need are already out there. You're never going to tell an original story because everybody who's come before you has beaten you to it. Put your own original spin on a story that has lasted."

She came up with a reading list for me, and when I started reading and studying the myths, seeing the cross sections from culture to culture, that's when I saw what she was getting at. And, really, that's been the wellspring that I go back to over and over and over again when I'm starting something new.

What comes first when you're ready to start something new: "This is a myth I'd like to work with," or "I've got a bunch of stuff here, what myth will it fit?"

Actually, it's happening all over the place. I guess the best way to describe it is, I've got my radar up and I'm walking around in life looking for stuff that resonates, vibrates. It might be a story I read years ago, it might be a fragment of something that I'd forgotten about that somebody triggers in a conversation. It might come with research.

Right now I'm studying the myths of the San people, who believe that their creator is a god in the earthly form of a praying mantis. I was reading about them this summer, nonfiction, and teaching in the prison, and one day my youngest son, Teddy, who's nine, comes bursting into the house and he says, "Dad, I'm a father!" He caught my interest, definitely. He was holding this little bug caddy. They had done a science experiment with egg cases at his school, but it had failed. None of the egg cases had hatched. On the last day of school, Teddy, being a nature lover, asked his teacher if he could have the egg case. His teacher said yes. A month goes by and suddenly he looks out at the abandoned egg case that's been sitting outside in a bug caddy, and there are maybe 250 tiny but perfect praying mantises. The eggs had hatched. And I had just been reading all that stuff about praying mantises. That's where my stories begin: serendipitous accidents that I'm tuned into, messages I'm receiving from some frequency I don't fully understand but can recognize as useful.

Where did that take you?

It took me to reading more about myths; and also, as luck would have it, I live across the street from an entomologist who teaches at the University of Connecticut. He gave me a couple scientific books on praying mantises. So I learned, for instance, that when the male and the female meet, the female, in the act of the copulation, bites off the head of the male. The theory is that it makes the experience more gratifying. So, boy, you can take that and run with it!

Where does that show itself in the narrative of the prison novel? Has it yet?

Yes, because for a year and a half now I've been working with abused women; one of them shot and killed her abusive husband. So there are little pieces. It's like connect the dots. But it's frustrating. It wakes me up at night until I figure out how it all fits together. At least I've learned — by the third book — to take a leap of faith and say, "Okay, it's going to come. I might not understand it now, but I'll get there."

One day, I had a wonderful experience with another writer. I was at a really hard point with *She's Come Undone* and I was thinking of giving up. It was one of the many times I thought of abandoning that book. Things were not going right. I couldn't figure it out. For about three weeks I was just stuck, and suddenly I found myself stuck in traffic, waiting to go eastbound at the light, and this woman I know, Anne Levanthal, who's also a writer, pulled up beside me in another lane. We were both waiting at the red light. And she called out, "Wally! How's it going?" And I did my whining, "Oh, it's terrible. I hate this. I'm going to give up." And she said, "You're feeling just about as miserable as you can, right?" I said, "Yeah."

The light turned green and she said, "You're getting ready for a break-through." We both drove off. And sure enough the next day, whatever the conundrum was, it was solved.

It's like a moment of combustion. There's this fact and that fact and then, all of a sudden, you see this tree, and you think, "There's the tree! There's where it happened!" You can't explain it. You simply have to reassure fellow writers that it will happen. You open yourself up to the story.

When you're in the process of writing, how does that radar work?

Often, I haven't even realized that I've filed away things that later come bubbling up to the surface that I can use. In *She's Come Undone*, I had a lot of doubts about my ability to write the story and about whether it was appropriate to be writing in the opposite gender. So in the long process of writing that novel, I found that it was good for me if I shaped chunks of it into short stories and then sent them off to a magazine to get some kind of validation.

Right about the time I discovered the whales, I was sitting around at a family picnic, feeling sort of bored with things. We must have had lasagna or something, because I remember rolling my hands over a container of grated Parmesan cheese that was sitting on the picnic table. Then, all of a sudden, I picked it up and I read on the label, "Keep in a cool dry place." It was like a tuning fork started to vibrate. I don't know why. But that became the title for that story which turned out to be the first time Dolores ever saw print. It was a story I called "Keep in a Cool Dry Place." In that story, which ended up in the novel, there's a box of eight-track tapes stuck underneath the seat of a car Dolores buys after her husband leaves her. On the side of the box of tapes she sees these words printed — and of course the tapes are recordings of the cries of the humpback whales. So she drives around and listens to them. This probably makes no sense —

Actually it does make sense. Most novelists report similar kinds of experiences that seem to be tied to the unconscious. What about the conscious part of the process, though? You've said that you revise chapter by chapter. When you get to the end of a book, is it more or less finished?

The grunt work is mostly done, but there's a lot more work to do. For me, first-draft writing is slave labor and revision is play. After the first draft, which is probably actually draft number seventy-four, I feel a great sense of relief. I think, "I've pulled this off." With *I Know This Much Is True*, there was a lot of pressure to finish because of the Oprah thing. My mother had had a stroke, my father had just fallen and broken his hip, and I had a new job for the first time in twenty-something years, having gone from high-school to university teaching. I had three kids I was trying to be a decent father to. It was really awful.

I remember writing in a frenzy at the end. I had maybe two or three theories about who the twins' father was, but I was writing as Dominick, so I didn't know. I finally figured that out and I worked on the last chapter for about a week. I got to the last sentence—I'd been singing that stupid '80s song by that group, Spandau Ballet, "I Know This Much Is True." For six years that had been in my head. I had no idea why. Then I typed it. It turned out to be the last sentence in the novel. I remember I was so relieved that I dropped to my knees and started to cry. I put my forehead on the rug in front of me and gave thanks to whoever or whatever had allowed me to finish this book without its killing me first. Then I left my office and I couldn't go back for about three weeks. I just couldn't go back there, even though it was way beyond deadline. When I finally did go back, I looked around and saw the place was a shambles. Coffee spilled all over, papers everywhere. Visual evidence of the frenzy I'd been in. Probably the biggest sign of just how much I didn't know or how the story was sort of revealing itself step by step was that on the floor in front of me there was this three-pronged trail of index cards. Almost like dominoes. If Dominick's father is the grandfather, then this had to happen. And if Dominick's father is the translator, then this. I had three possibilities and I didn't know which one it was until the trail went out and I found the one that seemed to ring the most true. It's a goofy business!

Are there techniques you use to help you see the whole draft when it's finished?

Again, it's a visual thing. Earlier on, when the canvas began to expand beyond what I thought I could handle, I began losing track of the story. So I did the index cards and put them all on the wall so I could walk my way through the story.

You use your writers' group as you go along. But when you get finished, do you get a different kind of feedback?

Yes. My editor is my publisher, Judith Regan. She gives pretty much free rein to fiction writers. So, really, you have to seek your own editing because she's not going to sit there and line-edit. Nor is she that much of a master strategist. She's of the new school. Once you submit it to her she's going to take it and run with it. It's product for her. She's not the traditional editor. So I get traditional editing from one of my agents, Laurie Fox, who's also a writer—and very good. She gives me feedback, that holistic kind of feedback. I also get critical feedback from friends, fellow writers, and my wife, Chris.

When you start a novel, what do you know? What surprises you during the writing process?

I know very little. I don't do a lot of thinking or planning ahead. I don't have an ending in sight. I don't know who the characters are. With the first two, I knew what their voices sounded like. I'm figuring out everything from the hurt in the voices. Along the way I'm surprised on a daily basis.

When I began *I Know This Much Is True*, I had a terrible time because I had worked with Dolores and her cast of characters for eight and a half, nine years. I could predict how Dolores was going to behave in a situation by the end of that period. Then, suddenly, I found myself among strangers. I hated it. I didn't know Dominick had a brother, much less a twin. I was really flabbergasted the day I realized that they were identical twins.

Sometimes the research feeds those realizations. I was reading about paranoid schizophrenia and there was a really interesting twin study about shared biochemistry. There's an odd little percent of the cases where one twin gets the disease and the other is somehow spared. When I hit upon that bit of research, I understood Dominick's anger. Until then, I hadn't realized that beneath the surface of his anger were fear and guilt. He was afraid that he was going to get the disease; he felt guilty because he was always the mean-spirited twin, the twin that was playing one-upsmanship. Had he triggered schizophrenia in Thomas? Perhaps he should have gotten the disease, not this kinder, more benign brother. All of a sudden, the doors opened up.

Another moment of combustion.

Right. Exactly. You know, I don't love to write. I don't do it for the money. I'm writing for those surprise discoveries. That's when it's joyful for me.

Readers often comment on the fact that you wrote She's Come Undone *from a woman's point of view. How did you accomplish that?*

My answer to that question is threefold. First, I grew up with sisters and those female cousins, so I lived in that female world. I was always sort of fascinated by it, always looking from the sidelines, but not intimidated.

Teaching high-school kids helped. When I started writing fiction, I had to throw away everything I thought I knew about how to teach writing. I used to be Joe Liberal. I'd say, "Here are five topics. You can pick the one that you like most." But they were my topics; they weren't the students' topics. So I had to cut that out. And I had to stop writing in the margins. I would get quite offended. I teach wholeheartedly, so I'd assign a paper that was due on a Friday and I'd kill a whole weekend writing these copious notes in the margins. You know, comments and suggestions. The grade was on the last page—and, of course, the students would go right to that. I'd think, "I wrecked my whole weekend on your behalf and you're not even reading this stuff." Then I realized, "Why should they give a shit?" They'd already done the paper. Why should they care what they could have done, what they might have done?

So I made my classroom a workshop and allowed young writers to discover and investigate their own subject matter. I started bouncing around from student to student as they wrote, not after they had written. Sometimes we worked in groups, sometimes one on one. Sometimes they worked one on one with each other, and I was someplace else. I began to give verbal feedback in that writing-workshop way and it made all the difference in the world. Suddenly I was on the receiving end of all these great pieces of writing. All these distinctive voices I hadn't heard before because I'd been giving the assignments. Of course, half of those voices were girls—and if you tell a teenage girl to write about whatever she wants, more often than not she's going to write about herself.

The third influence with regard to the woman's viewpoint in *Undone* was my writers' group. The women in the group would say, "Oh, a woman wouldn't think that way," and let me know why it rang false to them. My wife, too. She doesn't know all the buzzwords for critical stuff, but, boy, she speaks up when she hears something that sounds bogus. So if the voice seems true, it's because I had lots of time and lots of feedback to help me sand down the rough edges.

It does seem true. But it's also true that Dolores's voice is a reflection of your concerns, your material as a writer. What do you perceive that material to be? What issues from your own life do you work through in the process of writing novels? Where does that material come from?

I think it's that whole alienation-versus-connection thing. That's definitely part of it. I think it's probably having had an Italian-Catholic mother and a Lutheran father, which created an interesting tension and dynamic within my family. My sisters and I were raised Catholic; we went to church every week. My father didn't go to church. Not that there was a whole lot of religious tension in our household—but a mixed message for sure. Then there is the search for God, a longing for order out of chaos. All of those things are in my fiction.

You've said that you are a questioning Catholic. Does that questioning fuel your writing?

It definitely does. I don't think fiction writers have any obligation to answer the questions, except within the context of their own stories. But I think that, unless we're writing something very packaged and commercialized, we are all in the process of asking questions in the hopes that asking the questions may somehow help fix the world, kick us out of our collective complacency. If I had answers instead of questions, I would probably be a political writer or an editorialist.

Where does a consideration of plot fit into the process of considering unanswerable questions through writing fiction? What is plot for you?

I'm probably not your answer guy on this one. When talking to my students about character, I say that if you boil it down to the lowest common denominator, you're telling a story about what a character wants—and what the character wants on a conscious level may be different than what your character really wants. To oversimplify, plot is the character getting from point A to point Z in pursuit of what he or she wants. But if it's a more complex story, there is the character's pursuit of what he thinks he wants and the eventual discovery of what he really wants or needs. That's what plot is for me.

It would make an interesting graph. Nothing like the traditional rising-then-falling action graph.

No, it's not. There's a wonderful screenplay book by Robert McKee, and it's called, very simply, *Story*. His diagram of what the character wants shows in a hump above — that's the conscious journey, and then what he really wants is depicted in a broken line below — the unconscious journey. Sometimes these wants are in conflict with each other. That's certainly the case with Dominick and Thomas. What Dominick wants on a conscious level is to be the dominant twin, to win the battle. What he wants beneath it, I came to see as I was writing the story, is to be connected to his twin, to be whole. And to be loved by his mother, to be reassured that his mother loved him as much as she loved that sweeter brother.

You mentioned earlier that you did not have a passion for writing when you were a young person. When and how did your interest in writing begin?

If you had told my twelve- or sixteen-year-old self that I was going to become an author of novels, I would have laughed out loud. I was a dutiful student, so I did my regular work. I read what was assigned, but not much beyond that. I fell in love with literature when I went to college. I knew when I was about five or six years old that I wanted to be a teacher, but I didn't know until I was thirty that I wanted to write fiction. I bounced out of the University of Connecticut when I was twenty-one, and I went back to the high school where I had been a student and taught there. I was there for about nine or ten years, not at all burned out. I still love to teach.

But I started fiddling with writing one summer and it just kind of sucked me in. It was the most unlikely time to be starting to write fiction. We were having our first baby, and were very excited about it. When Jared was born, we were up all night in the delivery room and everything turned out fine. Chris, my wife, started going to sleep, and the baby went off to the nursery. So I rushed home. I was going to run a couple of errands, take a shower, make some calls, and then get back to the hospital and play with this miracle. I jumped in the shower, and suddenly I heard a voice in my head that was sort of like me but also un-me. It was just maybe two, three, four lines of dialogue that this character spoke — though I didn't think of him as a character then. He was just a person complaining about his summer job as an ice cream vendor. I jumped out of the shower and ran naked down the hallway, dripping wet, and jotted down what the character said. I just had the impulse to jot it down, I don't understand why. Then I completely forgot about it. Maybe a month, six weeks went by. Then in the middle of summer vacation when I'd gotten pretty good at diaper pins and car-seat straps and all that, I went to clean off my desk and I saw this thing I had jotted down. I sat down and started writing and eventually got a story out of it.

Since then, you've had terrific success with your work—due in part to the attention it's received from Oprah Winfrey. What was that experience like for you?

Back in '92, long before the Oprah book club happened, the phone rings. We're all having dinner. My then ten-year-old son, Justin, picks up the phone and says, "Yeah? Huh?" He's not famous for his phone manners. He passes it to me and the person on the other end says, "Is this Wally?" I said, "Yes." She said, "This is Oprah Winfrey calling." And I'm thinking, "Oh, right—and I'm Geraldo." She says, "I read your book and you owe me two nights' sleep." Now I realize that it is truly she and I'm pointing to the receiver and mouthing the name "Oprah" to my wife, Chris, who's going, "Dope? The Pope?" She's not getting this. Anyway, Oprah was just calling as a reader to say "Thanks."

When the book club started, I had no fantasies that she was going to remember this conversation. Then she called again, on what was probably the most difficult day of my teaching career. I was on a leave of absence from teaching high school, but I had volunteered to work with the kids who couldn't stop writing. So I was going in once a week and running a workshop for them. One of the kids in that group, a wonderful young woman writing way beyond her years, had been walking home from a play rehearsal with her little brother and both of them were struck by a car and killed. This had just happened the day before. It was a tragedy beyond imagination. There were just two children in the family. It was unfathomable. You know, lots of times the kids who are writers are very needy kids. We were all there at school that day, sort of propping up each other, and we went en masse to the synagogue for the funeral service. I got home and

I was totally wiped out. It was a day in January. I still had my winter coat on; I was just walking through the door.

The phone rang and it was Oprah calling to say, "Guess what! *She's Come Undone* has been chosen for the book club." I took a deep breath and I said, "You know, Oprah, I know that I'll be really thrilled in a little while, but here's what's just happened." I explained and she was terrific about it. But she did say to me, "The way it's been building, you're going to have to call your publisher tonight, because they have to start printing more copies of your book if they're going to meet the demand." Gradually, it seeped in. The news got out and it was very exciting, very attention grabbing. But what I remember most is that call, how strange it was that the best and the worst of life could all be happening at the same time.

Valerie Martin

Valerie Martin is the author of eight novels, three short story collections, and one work of nonfiction. She was born in Sedalia, Missouri, and grew up in New Orleans, where she attended public grammar school, a Catholic high school, and the University of New Orleans, from which she received a BA in English. She received an MFA in Creative Writing from Amherst College. Martin worked as a waitress, a welfare worker, a clerk in a children's bookstore, and a high school teacher before turning to university teaching full time. She has taught at the University of New Orleans, the University of New Mexico, the University of Alabama, Mount Holyoke College, the University of Massachusetts, Sarah Lawrence College, and Loyola University in New Orleans. Her novel *Property* won the Orange Broadband Prize for Fiction. Other honors include the Franz Kafka Prize and fellowships from the National Endowment for the Arts. Valerie Martin lived in Italy for three years; currently, she resides in upstate New York.

Set in Motion, 1978; *Alexandra*, 1979; *A Recent Martyr*, 1987; *The Consolation of Nature and Other Stories*, 1988; *Mary Reilly*, 1990; *The Great Divorce*, 1994; *Italian Fever*, 1999; *Love*, 1999 (stories); *Property*, 2003; *The Unfinished Novel and Other Stories*, 2006; and *Trespass*, 2007

In your first three novels, the main characters are intelligent, educated women who live at the periphery of the active world. What fascinates you about these kinds of people?

I don't believe that women in fiction have to be active—or they should be active—in order to be interesting. The novels that I admire are often about women—and men, too—who are outsiders. There's a classic appeal in the outsider as the central character of fiction, because that person is in the position to be the observer. People who are very active are not as observant. They don't see as much and they don't often think as much. They're too busy doing.

These observers speak in voices that are low-key, intelligent, and rational about violently intense sexual experiences, about the lush New Orleans setting. How does this kind of paradox work toward the books' overall effect?

I like the contrast of someone who is rational and calm in a world that's a little bit crazy, because I can lead this character into intense emotional states without the narrative becoming changed by that—without it becoming emotional writing instead of writing about emotion.

When you look at the people who are not particularly emotional, there's a real tendency to think, "Well, then they just don't feel emotion." Whereas, those who are constantly putting on a display lead themselves and the world to believe that they feel very strongly and deeply. But my observation of people has been that the reverse is true. I think my characters have to be sort of passive in order to be able to observe the things I want them to observe. If they were active, they wouldn't know what they know. They wouldn't arrive at the conclusions they finally arrive at.

I think people set too high a premium on being active. I don't particularly value it myself. I think if people would be a little more passive—in some areas, not all areas. Obviously, you should stand up for what you think is right, always. In some ways, I hope that this happens to my characters, that they finally are forced to do that in spite of their natural inclination not to. *Mary Reilly* certainly is a case of that. The narrator in *A Recent Martyr*, who is involved in a dangerous love affair, has to make a choice, which she tries to resist as long as she can because it's much easier just to be passive. My idea of how to put a novel together is to take the character and put him under a whole lot of pressure and see what comes out. In a way, that's how I find my characters.

Given the private, recalcitrant natures of your characters, what do you think it is that compels them to tell their stories?

I think it's the classic guilt motive that so much of fiction is based on. Half, maybe three-fourths of all the world's fiction is written with this notion: the narrator wants to explain "Why I did what I did." Usually, it's because they feel bad about what they did. In the case of *A Recent Martyr*,

[Emma] wants to account for Claire in some way, for what she [Emma] did in this encounter with a young woman who died. In *Set in Motion*, I think [the narrator] wants to explain why she didn't do some things and why she did do other things. There's a certain amount of implicit guilt there. And there's also a desire to figure out what happened, what *really* happened. What did it mean?

The sense that the character is trying to understand what happened gives an authority to the voice. It makes the reader puzzle over what happened, too.

That makes me think of something I've been puzzling over a bit myself, and that is the difference between psychology and philosophy in the development of character. I think that in a lot of American fiction that I read—and particularly in film—there's the notion that psychology accounts for everything. But it never has for me. I think psychology is a sort of bottom level of our consciousness—so bottom that a lot of times we don't even know what it is. But there is a conscious level of thought and decision that we try to ignore a lot; and, for me, that's the philosophy that a character comes to. You only come to that if you stop and contemplate your actions—and, in the case of some of my characters, your failures to act.

I've always been attracted to European novels because the characters do not seem to be simply psychological models: a child is abused, so it turns out to seek abuse. They have experience, and then they try to draw conclusions about what that experience might mean as they move on. They create a philosophy, and in doing so, they create an existence, a being, an essence. It's the existentialist notion: it's not a Cartesian universe. It's not "I think, therefore I am," it's, "I am." We make ourselves, rather than we are made. I keep going back to that. I can't seem to stop doing that.

You don't really give us much about where these people came from. Is that why?

It is one of the reasons. I wanted to avoid the sort of reductionist view of character as being entirely created in childhood, so I just sort of bring them out of nowhere. Here they are, and you have to figure out where they came from. *Mary Reilly* was a case where I did give background. It seemed appropriate. For the experience she was going to enter, I wanted her to have been through a kind of hell in her past, so it was important to mention. But I mentioned it as little as I could.

Except for Mary Reilly, *your novels are in first person. So not only do we not get much of the characters' pasts, we get only one character's view of the present.* A Recent Martyr *is odd, though. It's a first-person voice telling someone else's story.*

It was rejected many times on that account, because the point of view was a little iffy, different. It was all I wanted to do — to bring that off, that particular point of view of somebody imagining their way into somebody else's life. Editors consistently talked about the problem with the point of view. One editor said he would publish the book if I would change the point of view. And I really wanted to publish a book! But I sat down and looked at the book and thought, "The point of view is in every line of the book." He wanted everybody to have a first-person voice, to tell his own tale. But I didn't really think Claire could tell her own story. I didn't think she'd be interested in telling it.

What were you thinking about as that book began to form?

I was thinking about a couple of things. One was that a real saint would not necessarily be the sort of goody-goody, self-sacrificing picture that's often painted, and so I think I wanted to correct that view. Another, of course, was the tie between sex and religion that has existed for a long time. I certainly didn't think it up. Especially in someone like Donne's poetry, sexual ecstasy is very much like religious ecstasy. I had read a lot of writings of, in particular, Saint Theresa of Avila, and the ecstasies she describes are very erotic, the way she describes them. So I was sort of interested in that connection, thinking that in both there's a desire to destroy the self and somehow just be annihilated. Sort of a death wish, but at the same time, it's not really a death wish because it's a wish to be part of something bigger. In the case of love, to be part of somebody else. And in the case of religion, to imagine you can have some kind of community of God. So I was interested in those parallels, and that's basically what the book is about.

Where did it start? How did it gather?

It's hard to remember. That book was ten years old when it was finally published. There's a scene in it where there are a lot of rats in the river. I think that scene was in my mind fairly early on.

Yes, the rats. Rats show up a lot in your books. Why is that?

I think it's partly because I grew up in New Orleans, and they were always there. Of course, they have a lot of symbolic value. I use them because they're useful and I'm familiar with them.

Did you actually see that scene you wrote in A Recent Martyr—*all the rats dying?*

No. But I know from talking to an exterminator that that's what would happen in the case of a plague. I knew there would be a plague in the book, and that image came fairly early on. Claire was not too clear to me at first. I was really interested in the point of view, somebody narrating events that they didn't see. I think the whole book has a kind of retrospective quality. It's all being told from pretty far beyond the action. I was really experimenting with that. I think I was getting ready to move into the third person, but I wasn't quite ready to go. So I found a way to sort of do both.

A Recent Martyr *feels like a transition book, as if it somehow finishes your fascination with certain issues. Is that true?*

It finished my fascination with religion, although I don't know if I'll ever get over it.

Were you Catholic?

No. My mother was. I went to Catholic high schools, and I was very taken with [Catholicism]. I was almost converted during the Cuban missile crisis, but they wouldn't have me. They told me to wait until calmer times. And I did, and I decided not to do it. So I was really fascinated with Catholicism, and I know quite a bit about it. I've been about as close to being a Catholic as you can be. *A Recent Martyr* finished that, and I think it finished in some ways my obsession with a kind of self-destructive character. I began to feel a little less sympathetic for this passion to be dead, which Thomas Hardy, I think, called "the coming obsession." He warned us.

Mary Reilly *is a very different kind of book. What in Stevenson's* The Strange Case of Dr. Jekyll and Mr. Hyde *was so compelling to you that you decided to expand on it?*

I always liked, at the end of Stevenson's book, when we get to Jekyll's true confession. I always liked those first lines when he talks about how early in his life he became divided because he had these secret pleasures that he couldn't let anyone know about. And I'd always wonder, "What were the secret pleasures?" Did he dress up like a woman? Was he a heavy smoker? What was it? And it made me examine my own life. I feel like everybody's divided. We divide early in life because of the pressure of the world around us to appear in a certain way versus the way we feel. That idea is what attracted me to the book. So I just wanted to look at it for a while.

Did you hope to give the reader a different view of Jekyll than Stevenson had?

I wanted to make his predicament more . . . touching. I've always felt sorry for Jekyll. Maybe I felt like he got short shrifted by Stevenson because Stevenson is so interested in his proposition, which is that a man could be so divided—this nightmare that he literally had when he came up with the idea. I wanted to look at the sorts of difficulties that the split would cause Jekyll, not just in the physical world, but in his moral world.

Did your own view of Jekyll change as you wrote the book?

As I wrote the book, sometimes I didn't like Jekyll and I would think he was a hypocrite, especially when Mary was mooning around after him. I would get up from the desk and say, "Can't you see? This guy doesn't care for you." But at other times I would feel sorry for Jekyll, and I thought he was doing the best he could. What really interested me was that I finally really felt sorry for Hyde. In the scene where Mary goes outside and finds him weeping, I just felt terrible. It seemed to me that he represented the only honest force in the place, the only honest voice in the place, which I think Stevenson suggests a little bit. There is an elemental appeal about Hyde and it is that he never pretends to be anything but what he is. He has one interest and that is destruction. There's something attractive about that.

Why Mary? Why did you decide to tell the story from the point of view of a scullery maid?

I had settled on the idea that the story was going to take place in

Jekyll's household, and when I proposed the book to my agent and editor, everybody seemed to like that. I wanted to write from the point of view of a woman. I wanted the point of view to be from the very bottom of the house. I thought it was important to have somebody who would be sort of invisible in the house, somebody who had access to Jekyll but was so far beneath him that he wouldn't bother to keep secrets from her. Mary was such a nonthreatening person.

Was there anything in Stevenson's Jekyll and Hyde *that you decided not to include in* Mary Reilly?

I didn't fool with Lanyon. He's one of the guests at the dinner party, that's all. I didn't want to fool with that whole scene where Hyde transforms into Jekyll. I purposefully avoided that scene, obviously because Mary couldn't have been there. I'll give you an example of something I intended to include that I never did include: the scene where the maid, in the original, is weeping. When I started the book, my original intention was to find out why that maid was weeping. I thought, "What is she crying about? She must know something." It was where the idea for Mary came from. But when I actually got to the scene where they go break the door, Mary wasn't there. I still don't know why.

What about scenes that weren't in the original version? For example, the scene where Mary goes to Hyde's house? Why did you add that?

I had to get Mary out of the house. It is in *Jekyll and Hyde* that Hyde's got another house. Jekyll rents that house, if you remember — the house where they find the broken cane. One of the things that fascinated me about *Jekyll and Hyde* was that Hyde wanted to be a gentleman. Do you remember, in the end of the book, when he goes to see Dr. Lanyon? He's anxious to get his medicine, and he's a little brutish. Dr. Lanyon says, "Well, your manners aren't quite what they should be." He suggests Hyde is behaving a little rudely, and Hyde immediately backs down and says, "My anxiety has given chase to my manners. Excuse me."

I thought, "This is very strange for this great demon." So I like the idea of Hyde wanting to be a gentleman. The other thing in the original book is, when they break into Hyde's house and they find that cane, there are some good paintings in Hyde's room. The furniture is very nice — Jekyll's taste, and there is some good liquor. So Hyde, when he's on his own in his house where he can hide, pretends to be a gentleman. And I loved that idea and I wanted to get into that house. So to send Mary there gave me an opportunity to get a look at Hyde's environment. A lot of people who read the book thought that that house was a whorehouse, but it isn't, actually. It's Hyde's house. I think it probably was—that Mrs. . . . what's her name?

Farraday.

Yes, Farraday. It's been a long time! I think Mrs. Farraday has probably been running prostitutes out of that house, but when Mary goes [that first time], she essentially arranges to empty the house of everybody so that it can be Hyde's own residence. So that's what I picture going on in there. The murdered—or beaten up—prostitute is visiting Hyde there. She's his guest.

Why didn't you add a scene in which Mary confronts Jekyll about Hyde?

I don't think she knew it till the end. [Jekyll] gives her plenty of signs, she's got plenty of clues. You think, "She's got to be daft not to know." But Jekyll really is kind of a father figure to her. He's the father she never had. She's got an investment in not knowing. I think this is fairly true in human psychology. There's a real tendency to invest yourself and to believe the best of a person that you care for, and when the evidence to the contrary starts coming up, I think it's perfectly natural not to see it. In fact, the more you care, the less you're able to see. It happens all the time in relationships. In the original end of the book, she never knows. But my editor said, "No way."

Mary had the opposite reaction to her father, though. She was very forgiving toward Dr. Jekyll, but she didn't ever forgive her father, did she?

I don't think so. She talks a bit about how he probably won't even remember how badly he treated her. I think she even says a little something to the effect that she doesn't hate him. But I think of forgiveness as more than that. I don't think she can ever really understand why he did what he did, although her experience with Jekyll has brought her closer to it. But I don't see her as having sort of Christlike forgiveness, and I don't see the end as redemption of anybody. In my worldview, that doesn't happen. Everything just gets worse and worse. I think she's finally able to write him off and sort of close the door. She knows that if she is going to confront him again in any way, he's going to do a rewrite of the past. If you've had any experience with people who do this, and they are legion, it can really drive you crazy. It's not so much that you can forgive or not forgive. It's that you are forced to accept a new version of what happened. Mary refuses to do that. I think to forgive somebody in a situation like hers is a moot point. Do the people in the concentration camps forgive the Germans? All they're trying to do is just be safe for the rest of their lives, and that's how I felt about Mary. It's not a question of whether she can or can't forgive. It's a question of whether she can or can't carry on.

Did you ever think of putting more of Mary's father in the book? There's something of the Jekyll/Hyde split in him, it seems.

I didn't think of it much, but I was instructed that I should do it. My agent wanted me to have Mary see him and take the money. I received several phone calls to that effect. I didn't want to do it. There were enough parallels, and it didn't seem to make sense to me in what I knew about Mary at that point.

What kind of research did you do to write Mary Reilly?

This is an interesting period because it was really well documented. One book was by a man who did nothing but interview working people and street kids in London. Most of the interviews were with men, but there were a few with women, particularly with prostitutes. I read some diaries of working people, particularly a diary by a woman named Hannah Kolewic. She was what Mary was, a scullery maid. She worked for a man who was a lawyer. He married her eventually. But she didn't want to be a lady and insisted on continuing to live as a maid. Her diary has such a strange quality. She was very proud of being strong and being able to do honest labor. She didn't have a great deal of respect for aristocrats. Her husband was a strange fellow. He spent all day of his time going around photographing working women. He was a kind of Victorian feminist, I guess you could say. He thought women should be allowed to work, particularly at hard labor, like the mines. His idea of fun with Hannah was to have her come over and clean his chimney until she was completely covered with soot. Then he would have her wash his feet.

Her diary was great reading and really gave me an idea about how extremely kinky the Victorians were. It made me understand how very unsurprising it was that Stevenson produced *Jekyll and Hyde*. There were a lot of people living secret lives, and Hannah was a very frank and honest reporter of her daily life. She wrote a lot about what she did all day. That's where I got a lot of what Mary does all day. The constant problems of getting the coal in and out, the kind of cleaning she does, the laundry, what would be done to Jekyll's room. I spent about three weeks in London. While I was there I visited some houses, and I got a list of housemaid's duties that was kept by a woman during the late Victorian period—what she did all day long, from six until six. There wasn't any unaccounted-for period, although there were periods where she had tea and, maybe, a dinner break, and sometimes she had to do a bit of shopping. It was a hard life, with no privacy. I did that research, and then I read a lot of essays and a lot of novels. All the research was interesting to me. It took me about a year.

Did you do the research before you started the book?

I did most of the research as I went along. John Fowles wrote an essay while writing *The French Lieutenant's Woman*, a book that takes place in a similar period. He said that it was best to do the research after you did the writing because if you do the research before, it affects your ability to imagine the world. So I did a little research before, reading those diaries. But I didn't research the period to find out whether they called a chair leg a chair limb. Whether you call gloves "gloves" or something else. What do you call the nightdress? That kind of stuff I did later, just to make sure I didn't make any mistakes. It was very specific. I would go and get a book about clothes and find out what a particular article of clothing was called. I didn't want the book to have that quality of trying to inform you about every detail of the Victorian world.

How did you hit upon Mary's voice?

That was tough. I started a version and it sounded a whole lot like *Jane Eyre*. It had this kind of hypereducated feel. So I concentrated on what her level of literacy would be and what kind of writing I'd seen that would have that level of literacy, and it dawned on me finally that I'd been teaching people for years who were right about there. I used to teach a lot of students in New Orleans who didn't speak English as a native language. People learning English have trouble with the verb "to be." They get that wrong. Mary gets that wrong fairly inconsistently, just the way, I hope, people who are not that familiar with written English have. I found some of her "funny-isms," like the use of "mun" for "must," in Hannah Kolewic's journals. Sometimes Mary is very eloquent. Sometimes I would write a sentence of hers that had a couple of grammatical errors in it, but it was much better than it would've been if I'd put it in my own elaborate vocabulary.

Once you found the voice, how did the writing go?

Once the voice came to me I wrote the first chapter pretty much straight out. It seemed to be coming in pretty loud and clear. The book I just finished, in the third person, was just a devil to write. I'd be lucky if I'd get a page a day. [*Mary Reilly*] went four or five pages a day, sometimes six. I think once I did eight pages, which for me is a big turnout. Once I would start writing in her voice, I didn't think that much. I could hear her real well.

Were there things you did to "enter" Mary, or to help sustain her voice?

I preoccupied myself with things I thought would preoccupy her. For instance, I started cleaning my house. I actually got some blacking and I blacked my woodstove one day. Another thing I did with this book was to keep a lot of photographs of [Victorian] working people around. Whenever I couldn't think of what to do, I'd pick one up. My daughter was very helpful. I made her do things like go down into the basement and knock together some bottles. I was two floors above, so I could hear what it would sound like. I went to the basement and she went to the second floor, and I made her walk around and drag her leg. Then I made her walk around normally to see if I could hear a difference. I made her lie at the top of the stairs with a candle to see what I could see.

I always do that kind of physical stuff when I'm writing a scene; I try to actually in some way work it out. I'm not as bad as I understand Dickens was. There are famous stories about Dickens screaming in his room and his family would come up terrified and find him playing the parts of his characters. I don't go that far, but I do try to enter the characters. Particularly with a first person voice like Mary's, it's real important to forget my world.

Was your writing at all influenced by the film versions of Dr. Jekyll and Mr. Hyde?

I looked at them. They're pretty dreadful. I liked the Fredric March one. It's wonderfully filmed. But the film versions always have Jekyll's split caused by two women. One's a good woman and one's a bad woman. There've been maybe ten film versions, and it's always that. All the film treatments of the book have been really unfair and sort of simple minded. Stevenson was clearly not talking about a split caused by a good woman and a bad woman.

What about the film version of Mary Reilly? *You transformed Stevenson's ideas to write the book, and now those ideas are being transformed again, for the screen. What was that like?*

I think I had more respect for Stevenson than anybody in Hollywood is going to have for me. In fact, I'll lay money on that. I didn't feel bad about what I did to Stevenson because I didn't change anything. I just tried to work inside of what was there. *Mary Reilly* was sold to Warner, and they had Roman Polanski write a screenplay because he said he wanted to direct it. He wrote the screenplay, and the first thing he did was to make Mary illiterate. She doesn't have a mother, she almost never speaks. It's about Jekyll. She has no part at all. Surprisingly enough, the people at Warner didn't like the script and they didn't use it. They got another writer. At one time, they had a pretty nice script, but then they turned it into a pretty stupid script. It hurts me a little bit that nobody would think the book was valuable enough to be faithful to. Yeah, I feel like a jilted girlfriend. I wanted them to be faithful to me, but they were not going to do it. It's not in their nature to do it. But people will go see the movie, then they'll read the book and they'll say, "The book is better." I'm not the first person that suffered this transformation. My feeling about movies is that they sell books.

Do you think you'll write anymore about the Victorian period?

I've been there. [When I finished *Mary Reilly*], I knew I had to get out of that Victorian period, [get] back into the contemporary scene, and find a whole new way of trying to write a novel. I don't want to do the same thing over and over again.

One thing you're likely to do again, though, is to leave the reader wondering exactly what happens in the end. Mary Reilly *is very different from the first three novels, but it is like them in its unresolved ending: we never really learn what happens to Mary. Toni Morrison once said, after commenting on the fact that some readers fault her for her unresolved endings, "I like to leave a reader hungry. I like to leave some questions unanswered, because it's in this hunger that the magic of a book lies." Is this also your stance?*

Yes, I think it's a good answer. Also, in my mind, [this kind of ending is] more realistic. The stories that we live through are almost never resolved, even when we die. Sometimes a character goes through a great change — not often in my books, but in some books. Sometimes it's just a little change, and you know they're probably going to go through vicious circles again, but maybe the circles will get a little wider, maybe it will go a little easier on them.

I think that, essentially, characters and people don't really change much. It would be nice if we could just examine ourselves and say, "This needs to be changed," and change it. But that doesn't happen. I think that readers want to have all the questions resolved because they have a sort of preconceived idea of what a story should do. If you don't resolve everything for them and make everything neat and clean, they're thrown back into the story to try to figure out what it all meant. And what it all meant is the story.

Jill McCorkle

Jill McCorkle is the author of five novels and three collections of short stories. She received her BA in Creative Writing from the University of North Carolina, earning highest honors. As an MFA student at Hollins College, she won the Andrew James Purdy Prize for Fiction. She was only twenty-six years old when she made publishing history in 1984, having her first two novels published simultaneously by Algonquin Books of Chapel Hill. McCorkle's fiction has been selected five times by the *New York Times Book Review* for its "Notable Books of the Year" list, and in 1996 she was included in *Granta* magazine's celebration of the best young American novelists. In 2003 she was elected to the Fellowship of Southern Writers. She has taught writing at Duke University, Tufts University, the University of North Carolina, Harvard University, and Bennington College. She currently teaches at North Carolina State University. She lives in Hillsborough, North Carolina.

The Cheerleader, 1984; *July 7th*, 1984; *Tending to Virginia*, 1987; *Ferris Beach*, 1990; *Crash Diet*, 1992 (stories); *Carolina Moon*, 1996; *Final Vinyl Days*, 1998 (stories); *Creatures of Habit*, 2001 (stories)

There is an "ensemble" feel to a number of your novels. How does that kind of cast of characters gather for you?

This is something I've put a lot of thought into. I have a lot of characters who begin just as a character with a very strong voice. I'm never sure if a character is leading me into a story or a novel. Denny in *Carolina Moon* is an example. I had a monologue that was going to be a story, but it never arrived. Some of Quee's early parts with the Ghost Wall in *Carolina Moon* started as stories. I worked with the character Juanita probably a year and a half or two years before writing *July 7th*. These characters were much better as a part of a much bigger picture. *Ferris Beach* is more a linear piece.

I had intended a straight first person about the protagonist, Kate, and her mother, but I no sooner got started than the family moved in across the street and I was much more interested in them. Amy Hempel once told me that a story needed two things happening simultaneously, so you're not overly attached to one thing. There has to be a way to shift the weight.

You do that in your third-person shifts.

I do. The novels that I'm most proud of — *Tending to Virginia* and *Carolina Moon*—were made of a universe of little tiny vignettes. Both times I felt like I was quilting. I would take a character and focus on what was inside a little square, knowing that it would somehow fit into this larger piece. Usually the larger piece is not something I fully understand until I get to the end.

I think, by nature, I am more a novelist for this reason. When I write short stories, I usually have ideas in batches. I always tell people, I have a litter of stories. I have to keep nursing them all together, pulling threads up a little closer to the surface until I can let them go. I don't know. It's the only way I've been able to feel good about the stories I've produced. I know it's not to my advantage. Right now I'm finishing a collection and there will be very little time to place these stories before the book comes out. But it's very hard for me to just write a story as a story. In my mind, there is something bigger holding these stories together. Right now I'm revising the collection and I have to see what the common variables are between the stories. It becomes important to me as I decide whether a story makes it into the book. Even though they seem completely unrelated to people reading them, it's important to me to get the big sense of the big picture.

You say that you're a novelist by nature, but you clearly love writing stories. Which of the two forms do you prefer?

I love stories; it's the form I've always aspired to. If given the choice, I'd rather read stories. I love to read them because I pay so much attention. I read the first time for pleasure, then I read to see the structure. You can read an Alice Munro story and study and study. So I always wanted to write stories, but I think, naturally, the novel is easier for me. I'm not sure why that is. I once told my students that the short story was like the one-night stand as opposed to the marriage to the novel. I think I really like being immersed in something. I think I feel best in life, period, when I'm right in the middle of something and I know where I'm going next.

There's also a lot of power in the secret connection behind the stories. With a novel, I don't want anybody to see any of it until I've gotten to the end. I may be holding up these stories for the same reason; it may be just total insecurity. There remains the fear that if somebody read one and said, "Ugh," that I would just quit. I feel completely vulnerable showing [any of the stories] until I get to some realization about how they all connect. Then a fresh eye is very helpful. My editor, Shannon Ravenel, is who I show it to, and she comes back with ideas and what-ifs.

Working as you do with these vignettes, how do you come to a sense of the structure of a novel? How do you think about time?

In *July 7th*, I knew I was going to do the day. It was a good way of setting the parameters. The whole idea of *July 7th* was that I would have this kid land in a town for a full day. In that novel, the town itself is such a character, or works as a character. He was the vehicle. By constraining the novel to his trip through town, I could show that the town was going on before he came, that it continues after he leaves. But nobody's the same. Originally, I thought he would move through it, unchanged. I guess I was coming into the novel with a much more pessimistic point of view than I came out with.

In *July 7th* we get bits of people's pasts; it's much more scene-oriented in the present time. With *Tending to Virginia*, I was more interested in thinking about how the past affects the present affects the future. The main idea was to collect these characters' memories of the big topics—love, marriage, birth, death—and see how they all fit together, how they blended into each other, how a person's memory is colored in a different light by the memory of the generation before her. Again, I had all these little stories. When I finished the rough draft, I had all these characters color coded by paper clips. It didn't have a plot. The whole business about Virginia going to her grandmother's house to have the baby came in revision, last thing. It felt like constructing a clothesline to hang all the pieces on. So that time frame came as an afterthought, because there was no other way to hold it together.

In The Cheerleader, *you described a long series of family photographs as a way of moving the reader through the beginning of the novel. How did you come to that device as a way of moving through time?*

That was an exercise I gave myself to understand the character. I just wanted to see where it would go, with the notion that it might lead into a novel. It's an assignment I use with beginning writing students now. I'll say, either get a real photograph or a "memory photograph," and describe that image. But don't let the white square of the photo pin you in. You have the power to say "just before this was taken," or "it wasn't long after this was taken . . ." So you've got the middle of a story frozen, but you have all this power to reach around it, beyond what's visible. It lifts up the constraints. It's amazing what people come up with. It's a good exercise for novelists, too. When you're working on a novel, not just a first novel, there's always the question of where you begin or end a chapter. It can be overwhelming. You can use photographs as a way of setting up natural beginnings and endings.

When I did the exercise, the descriptions of the photos got longer and longer. I think it was a way of tricking myself into writing a novel, though, actually, *The Cheerleader* was my second novel. The first has yet to see—will never see—the light of day. I think the only other copy got washed away when the Hollins library flooded.

Was it your MFA thesis?

Yes, and I learned so much about how I would put a novel together. It was in first person, your standard first novel. Really, *The Cheerleader* was a continuation of that voice. It just kept building. When I got about sixty pages, at the point where Jo Spencer works her way through the photographs to the time of the relationship with Red, I knew it was a novel.

The book stretched out so much from there, telling the story of Jo Spencer's relationship with Red during her senior year in high school.

I wanted, again, the sensation of time. The way that, very often in re-creating time, a moment in your life that was particularly painful snowballs in the retelling. You can't separate out that experience in a clinical way, you can't isolate it.

You switched to third person in the next section of the novel that tells the story of Jo at college the year after. Why?

It made sense to me, and it felt right as I was writing it. It just felt right at the time. I knew there had to be this physical distance. One of the nicest compliments I received about that book was to have someone in the psychology field say that this split, for Jo to think of herself in the third person, was a very natural response.

There was one thing I did with *The Cheerleader* that they didn't let me keep. I had actually done the pagination such that each part started with page one. It was a way of saying from Jo's voice, "Okay, I tried." I didn't find my answer here. And I started all over. I wanted this effect of rethinking. My original title was *Reruns*.

How do you recognize certain ideas and material as your own? Once you know it's yours, how does it spin out for you? What are the things you always find yourself going back to?

You have to pay attention to what story you really want to tell. It's easy to feel pressured by ideas of the kind of story you *should* tell as opposed to the kind of story you naturally *can* tell. For me, that was a big issue—learning how to let go of the reins. The real pleasure of writing comes from getting rid of that self-consciousness that makes you want to sound smarter or more cultured. The most important thing is to strip down and throw away everything that doesn't belong to you. If it feels artificial to you, it will to your reader. You want to be true to the story you *can* tell. Sometimes that means you should put away a story that you really want to write, because you're not ready to write it. I've done that many, many times. There's the story you want to tell, and the story you're able to tell, and when the two come together, that's perfect magic. As a writer, that's always what you're striving for.

I think that my books are always about second chances, being given a second choice in life. Most of my characters are women who fit into different walks of life; by and large they are survivors. Over and over I feel like I've put people in the critical moment. They're either going to fish or cut bait. They survive, but not in a happily-ever-after. For me, a happily-ever-after is coming out of that dark tunnel and seeing a little bit of light.

Juanita is a good example of that. She breaks your heart. She's so vulnerable, so honest about what she's done. She's never defensive.

She's the character I missed. She's the character I physically dreamed about while I was writing that novel. When I finished, I missed her. I realized that Juanita had become a kind of close friend. I could count on her to be funny. It was also my first experience discovering what now I think of as my alter-ego character. I now have these women again and again: the character who possesses no superego, no filter. Quee is like that; Denny is like that. And Misty. Juanita was the first.

That kind of character provides a necessary balance in your work. The reader would be overwhelmed without them.

When you're writing a novel you always hit those lulls, which are scary. I always think if I'm getting bored, I'm going to bore the hell out of my readers. These are the characters you just can depend on. As soon as the book starts slowing down, all I have to do is bring them onstage. It works. I realized that it's become sort of a security blanket for me to have some-body who has the power to come onstage and take over.

You said that you counted on Juanita to be funny, that she was a kind of alter ego. Your books are very funny. Often, you add a comic touch to things that are violent or terribly sad. Maybe the real you is thinking it's not all that funny.

Humor is such a wonderful way to cope and to balance life. The best humor in life is always tied to something very dark. I can enjoy slapstick and physical comedy like the rest, but the effect of that kind of comedy is short-lived. For me the best comedy is the kind that cuts way below the surface, and it's a way of not crossing the line of what would become melodramatic. I say that—maybe I've crossed that line a zillion times, but in my mind comedy is a way to prevent that. You can bring a reader in, pull them in. They're laughing *at* this person, as we do in life. Then you give them something that makes this person human, and suddenly they're not laughing at them, they're laughing with them. It keeps going lower and lower—that's my hope.

Laughter very often is a mask or a remedy. I grew up with that. My grandmother and my great aunt Claudia were the basis for Emily and Lena in *Tending to Virginia.* The facts are not based on family history—they are embellished often and vividly—but the voices of the grandmother and Great Aunt Lena are similar to the voices of my grandmother and my great aunt Claudia. The whole inspiration for writing the book was to capture those voices; so much of the dialogue in the book was just right out of their mouths. While I was writing that novel it was a race, because they were both failing so fast. My great aunt died during the writing. My grandmother actually saw the book. I loved them both dearly. My grandmother was at that point one of the most stabilizing and important parts of my life and she always had been, but yet she did very funny things in the throes of dementia. She'd tell me to go get her cigarettes, when she had never smoked a cigarette in her entire life. You have to laugh. But a lot of people don't, and I don't know how they stand it. I think you have to be able to let those emotions come out. Humor enables you to step closer to what's dark. You couldn't bear it if you couldn't find the humor.

When my dad was dying, he kept his sense of humor as long as he was conscious. One of my favorite memories was, he was on a lot of morphine, he was lying in bed, and he saw my mother's image in the mirror. He said, "Oh my God, here comes that little woman again, and every day she wears an outfit just like your mother's. You know how Melba despises for people to copy her clothes. She'd better get out of here before your mother sees her." I said, "Daddy, that is Mama." And he said, "Oh my God, there are two of her?" How could you not laugh at that? But there's this belief that it's disrespectful somehow.

Living in a small town for so many generations, we all lived together. So we had all this access to each other's lives. As a result, there was an acceptance of death as a part of life. I think that all too often people are removed from having to observe. Older people are not a part of the day-to-day situation. They're sort of tucked away. I find that sadder than anything. So they're demented! They can still participate! I guess that's what I'm striving for in my books with that kind of humor. Misty does it in *Ferris Beach* after her mother has died.

Misty is one of several great adolescent characters in your fiction. What's the allure in that time of life for you?

Growing up in a small southern town, you're with the same kids from kindergarten on. You're labeled immediately. And it's not just the kids who do it; teachers do it. There was this guy at my tenth class reunion and everybody was saying, "Who is he? Who brought him?" It turns out it was a guy we had overlooked. He always did the AV equipment. He was everybody's friend, a photographer. He had moved to Seattle and lost all this weight and was just the best looking thing at the reunion. I remember thinking, "If he hadn't left, this could not have happened." People who leave get that second chance to become who they're supposed to be.

You went away yourself, but you always go back—at least in your work.

I always go back. I go back physically a lot. I still feel very attached.

Have you ever thought of writing a memoir?

I don't know. I can't imagine what I would put in it. I feel like I have drawn on so much of my experience, but it's completely transformed and masked. I think what has always appealed to me about fiction is the mask. Even though someone might look in and say, "Oh, this looks like you did at such and such an age," there's still the loophole. And I'm most comfortable with the loophole, the exit sign. Like in the movie theater when they say, be sure you know where the exit signs are. That's me in life.

I wrote a piece for the *Washington Post* this summer about my dad. It was about this time that these young women appeared in the cottage door in their bikinis, calling, "Is Johnny here? Yoo hoo, Johnny?" We called them the Mullet Girls because they'd caught all these mullets that they wanted to share with my dad. They had been passing by him all day while he was fishing. Then they come up and see this *family*. We'd teased him about this forever. I told my mother that I was writing about the Mullet Girls, and she said, "Do you know something that I didn't know?" I said, "No!" The basis of the essay was that it was the first time I saw my dad as this sexual creature. He was very handsome. I remember, in high school, having people say to me, "Your daddy's really good looking," and it just made me furious. You don't like to think of your parents that way.

And your mom?

She loved the essay and I was totally relieved. It was just—well, I was a little concerned. I felt obligated to a kind of truth that I'm not obligated to in fiction.

Do you think you'll ever write out of that place in North Carolina that shaped you?

I do a little bit in the stories, but I think it's because my children are having this very different experience. And I *am* quite taken with the New England landscape. It's beautiful; there's a lot of history. But still, I really see it from the southern point of view.

To go back to the question about adolescence, Flannery O'Connor said we have all the equipment we need as writers after our childhoods, and I believe that totally. The example I like to give my students is Katherine Anne Porter's "Miranda" stories. You have Miranda as a child, terrified by the circus, and then in *Pale Horse, Pale Rider* you have that same Miranda all grown up, terrified by war and death. If you put it on the scale, given the time and the circumstances, her fear in each weighs exactly the same.

As a child, we experience tremendous loss and joy, just under different circumstances. That's what enables a writer to take an emotion and transpose it to become somebody who's eighty and dying—or become a man or someone of a different race or different culture. My favorite analogy—I tell my students all the time to remember that Crayola box, the big eight box, and you've got the primary colors. Say they're love and hate and sadness and joy. Then you get older and grow into the sixty-four Crayola box—periwinkle blue and burnt sienna. In the name of education and sophistication, everything's muted. Yet you could still take any one of those colors and pull out what is primary. It's blended and much more complex, but the emotions are the same.

I encourage students to look back into their childhoods. Those early deaths of pets, for example, so prepared me. I had one cat who died when I was probably eleven. I dreamed of him and I'd get up and go running outside, thinking he was still alive. I realized when my dad died—I know there's no comparison, but I was having all those same reactions. I hadn't thought of that cat in years, but I realized that I had already gone through that aspect of grief where you can almost convince yourself that the loss is not real. You can almost get them back in a dream.

In considering your material, transforming it, how do you settle upon plot?

Plot is the hardest thing for me; often, I'm accused of having no plot. I would say that plot is the progression from one point to the other, marking an emotional change of some sort—the surface time line that leads to change. Once, someone asked Sue Miller if she knew where she was going in a novel. She said, "Let's put it this way. It's like I know I'm traveling from the East Coast to the West Coast, but I haven't decided which states to go through or where to stop for the night." That makes a lot of sense to me.

So plot is sort of like your game plan, or travel itinerary. How do you go about tying things up, finding the right end?

I don't like endings that feel like they've got a great big bow or a "The End" sign. What I really like in an ending is to feel satisfied that there was completion within the story, and yet, in some way, the story is still open.

What about theme?

With *The Cheerleader*, it was the desire to re-create the past and finding it was impossible to do so without having it affect the present. With *July 7th*, it was the desire to show the effect of one person passing through a town: does he pass through and interrupt the cycle or does he pass through unnoticed? With *Tending to Virginia*, I was interested in how past events color the present. Also, I was so taken with these wonderful stories my grandmother began telling. Were these real stories, or creations of the present? And I was taken by the way she and my great aunt would tell the same story in totally different ways. I was interested in the way we accept on faith certain facts of our own lives.

With *Ferris Beach*, it was originally the idea, very simple, that this young woman would discover that what she had accepted as truth was false. In my mind, that one really was about a kind of second chance. Afterwards, people asked, "Why did you kill that father?" I didn't want him to die, but I also knew it was the only thing powerful enough to turn Kate. If the novel were written another way, I could have let her live to be fifty and experience it then. But I felt there were certain things about her mother that she was never going to see as long as he was there.

Carolina Moon was all about wanting what's gone and can never be found again. It all came from a very real place in my own life, because the whole beach that I loved so much as a kid and where I spent summer vacations is gone. I remember as a kid going out at low tide and being amazed that you could just stand out on this land. Now it's gone. I felt like all of those people were holding on to ghosts. It was the idea behind Quee's Ghost Wall. They were all by the end forced to see reality in a different way and to sort of come out of this kind of death-life back into what is real life.

What kinds of things do you know at the outset, and what comes in the writing process? Jones Jamison's murder in Carolina Moon, *for example. When did you know that would happen?*

Jones Jamison's murder—that's plot. That's vehicle. It came later, in [the] process. Quee's letters came later. After my dad died, I was teaching in Cambridge and, driving back and forth to work, I was writing these letters to him in my head. Even though, luckily, I had every opportunity to say everything I wanted to say to him, it was very helpful to continue this dialogue. It was so cathartic. And I realized one day, that's what's missing from the novel. I had in mind that Quee's letters to Cecil were somewhere, but until then I didn't know they would actually be in the book.

Do you ever get writer's block?

Not yet. I keep a lot of ideas and I rarely let go of something without having something I'm excited about waiting.

What do you think are the attributes of a novelist? What's talent? What do you have to have if you want to do this kind of work?

You have to be able to get in it and sustain something. I think I always go back with my students to the John Gardner thing about the uninterrupted dream. I want a novel that's hard to come out of—and when you do come out of it, it's like coming up from underwater. I don't like a lot of visible strings guiding me. I like to disappear into a novel the same way I do into a film.

And you like that feeling as a writer, too? You have to like that feeling of being immersed in that way?

Yes. And if I don't feel it, I know something's wrong.

Do you find that you are often surprised by what you write when you immerse yourself in that way?

I'm very surprised at what comes out. That's how I can always tell a good day. A good writing day is when I can read back over what I've written and find at least a sentence or two that I have no recall of constructing. That's when you lose all track of time. That's the kind of meditation I'm always striving to find, the place on the page where you momentarily disappear.

It seems that most novelists have many more ideas for novels than they ever write. For you, what's the difference between a good idea and an idea that you stick with and make into a novel?

A lot of times you can come up with a good idea, but whether or not you're emotionally attached to it is what makes the difference. There should be something that resonates, even if it's just some image or a scene that comes back to you, that you can't forget. That's what I'm looking for. I started writing out of purely selfish, self-satisfying reasons. I wrote as a kid, it was entertainment. It was the imaginary friend.

Did you write in high school as well?

I did, but creative writing wasn't such a big thing then. You sort of grow up thinking that writers are dead. I took it up again in college. I stumbled into this great class at the University of North Carolina. I would never be able to these days because it's so competitive.

Did you study under Doris Betts there?

No, Max Steele. I was a slouch of a student and I remember reading the course description, thinking, "Well I've got all these stories I've already written. I write every day. I might as well sign up for this because I've already done the work." Of course, the wonderful backfire was that I just fell in love from the first class, and it really became the whole motivation for the rest of my college time. At UNC you have to get permission to take the next level and the next level. I did the honors level my senior year under Max Steele and Louis Rubin. I never had Doris as a teacher, yet she was still such a major influence.

Then you went to Hollins College to do your MFA. Was that a good experience?

Very good. It was a year to just write. It was not a real structured program, which for me was good because I think I was most afraid of how I would write without being afraid of what Louis Rubin would say. I had gotten so used to jumping the hoops at the right time to produce something. Then, all of a sudden, here's this *year*. You pretty much know that at the end of it you need to have a manuscript.

So you learned discipline—your own discipline as opposed to what was coming to you in a class setting.

It's a once in a lifetime thing to have this year to write with no other responsibilities.

How do you manage to find writing time now?

Aside from caring for my children, writing is the one area of my life that I'm obsessive about. Not obsessive in that I have a rigid schedule. I don't. I don't work that way. But obsessive in that I don't feel good about myself unless I'm doing it. I think one of the greatest realizations I had when my children were real little was that if I waited for huge blocks of time, if I only counted those huge blocks of time as my work, I would be an incredibly frustrated, bitter woman. And it occurred to me that much of my best work is done away from the keyboard. I keep lots of notes and lots of notebooks and save up and trade off until I have a big block of time where I begin typing up everything. As a student, I began working in longhand, then moved to the typewriter. In the past eight years, I've gone back to writing longhand, and I like it. I don't do the actual writing so much as I sit and make notes, so when I find the time, I'm ready to work.

You were successful quite early in your career. In fact, there was a big splash when The Cheerleader *and* July 7th *came out simultaneously. How did that happen?*

I had written *The Cheerleader*, not knowing that Louis had started Algonquin. He had always continued reading my work, and then I heard from him and he told me he had this idea of starting this house. He said he'd like to do the book, but they were just getting started and it would be two years before it would come out. Out of sheer nervousness, I started *July 7th*, which is probably the fastest novel I've ever written. And because it was so linear, the revisions weren't extensive. When Louis saw it, he felt that it was probably the more accomplished novel to begin a career with. But he didn't want to go back on *The Cheerleader*.

I was really frightened by the notion of bringing them both out at once. It's one thing to be afraid of your first novel biting the dust, but if first and second did a simultaneous dive, you'd pretty much be washed up. The closer I got, the more aware I was. But I think the result was that the two books got more attention than either one would have gotten by itself. And people were so interested in Louis Rubin and Algonquin. I was very lucky.

Sena Jeter Naslund

Sena Jeter Naslund is the author of four novels and three short story collections. Born in Birmingham, Alabama, she received a BA in English from Birmingham Southern College and an MA and PhD from the University of Iowa. She is the recipient of the Lawrence Prize in Fiction, the Harper Lee Award, the Southeastern Library Fiction Award, and grants from the National Endowment for the Arts, the Kentucky Arts Council, and the Kentucky Foundation for Women. Currently, she is Writer in Residence at the University of Louisville and program director of the Spalding University brief-residency MFA in Writing. She lives in Louisville, Kentucky.

Ice Skating at the North Pole, 1989 (stories); *The Animal Way to Love*, 1993 (stories); *Sherlock in Love*, 1993; *The Disobedience of Water*, 1999 (stories); *Ahab's Wife, or, The Star-Gazer*, 1999; *The Four Spirits*, 2003; *Abundance: A Novel of Marie Antoinette*, 2006

How did you get started as a writer?

My experience was maybe a little different from the person who says, "I know I have a story in me and I want to write because I want to tell my story." I wanted to write, but I felt I did not have a story in me, that I really couldn't meet the demand of inventing a plot. Yet I loved to read. I'm sure my writing came out of my love of reading. I didn't know what to do with this desire to write and not to have any stories. Then I ran across a quote from Virginia Woolf, who said, "We don't believe in plots anymore." And I thought, "Hallelujah! I can be a writer after all." Sure enough, her novels are very low-profile in terms of plot. Especially something like *To the Lighthouse* or *Mrs. Dalloway*, which are my favorites. So Woolf liberated me to some extent about plot.

Did you start with a novel?

I worked up to the novel form by writing short stories that were basically stories of sensibility and character rather than of plot, so I got some practice that way. Then a novel came out called *The Seven-Per-Cent Solution*, by Nicholas Meyer, who was somebody I knew slightly at Iowa. He had included some historical characters in this spin-off from the Sherlock Holmes canon, especially Freud. I was interested in Freud at the time, and I wanted to see how he'd be treated fictively, where you could give yourself the right to know a lot about the inner workings of characters. So I read Nick Meyer's *The Seven-Per-Cent Solution* for the sake of reading about Freud. I was so entertained by the book—simply entertained—and I thought, "This is entertainment for smart people. I love this. I could do this." So then I embarked on writing the novel *Sherlock in Love*.

How did you prepare to write that book?

I was not a Sherlock Holmes fan, so I set about to read all the Sherlock Holmes stories. I didn't want to make mistakes. I wanted it to be in the right voice. I found from the scholarship, or pseudoscholarship—whatever it is that surrounds Holmes—that the year 1886 was kind of a mystery year. People didn't know what had happened to Sherlock Holmes. So I decided that would be my year. Then I looked for other interesting things that happened in 1886. Like Nicholas Meyer, I have a historical character in that book—Ludwig of Bavaria. And Ludwig II of Bavaria died by drowning in June of that year. The thing that drew me to him, besides the chronology, was that he was a patron of the arts, particularly Wagner. He was devoted to supporting music and opera. I had played the cello growing up, had played in orchestras, and the part of Holmes that most interested me was the fact that he played the violin. He was given a Stradivarius [in the stories] by Conan Doyle, but we don't know how he got it. So there are nice mysteries associated with that.

Were there other factors that came into play?

I wanted to write something that came out of my feminist sensibility. Holmes is seen as such a solitary, cold, rational, domineering figure, but I wanted him to meet his match in a woman. In some ways, that same impulse was in *Ahab's Wife*. Here were landscapes that were exclusively male oriented—the world of Sherlock Holmes, the *Pequod*. Just as some people want to revise history, I want to revise literature to put women on the stage. I don't want to directly attack what's been done before at all. I just want women to be included and respected in a kind of equal way.

And it gave you the opportunity to create a plot!

Writing this novel, which I was writing for fun, helped me to get over my fear of plotting. I don't think I could have written *Ahab's Wife* without that background, when I was just playing. One of the things I think a writer can do for himself or herself, looking at the big project—the novel—is to enter it playfully, to think of a project that's *not* next to your heart and soul. It doesn't mean that you're uninterested in it. I did have some investment in the feminist motif and in the support of music and the love of music in that novel. But at the same time, it seemed to me kind of a lark to do it, and that helped me.

How did you get the idea for Ahab's Wife?

The idea for *Ahab's Wife* came to me out of the blue. I wasn't expecting it at all. I was in Boston. *Sherlock in Love* had just come out and had gotten a fabulous review on NPR, so I was feeling very good. The publisher, David Godine, was wonderful to me. I had never had that kind of success. I was full of creative energy because of all of that, and I was navigating Boston in a rented car. Everything seemed great. And at this moment, I had a vision and I heard a voice. The vision was of a woman on a roof walk, or a widow's walk—a platform on top of a house next to the sea with a railing around it, open to the sky. I just suddenly saw her up there. It was night; she was looking out to sea, hoping to see her husband's whaling ship coming home. But as she stood there and looked, she realized he was not coming home. Not that night, not ever. And with that, her gaze shifted. Instead of looking out to sea, she began to look up at the starry sky and to say, "What is my place vis-à-vis this vast glory? Who am I in relationship to the cosmos?" She was no longer waiting for her husband to come home and define her. So as she began that kind of spiritual journey from her roof walk, for her own sake, the voice said, "Captain Ahab was neither my first husband, nor my last."

So you just got that wonderful first sentence?

Yes. It was a total gift from the air, and from feeling good about what I had already done as a creative person. As soon as this happened, I knew I had a novel—if I wanted to write it. I didn't know who the first husband would be, I didn't know who the third husband would be. I knew only Ahab. But I trusted that voice.

How did you proceed from there?

You know, Hemingway said it was deadly to discuss a story before it was written. You let the steam out. But as I've gotten older, I've found that just the opposite is true. It helps me a great deal to discuss what I'm going to write. So I tried this idea out on a number of my friends, and all of them were immediately interested — so interested that I began to try it out on people I met at parties. The same thing happened. By accident, I had hit upon an idea that had great curb appeal. I could see the light turn on in the listener's eyes about four sentences into describing my projected novel. That was extremely encouraging to me through the whole project.

Weren't you intimidated to go after Melville?

I wasn't intimidated by Melville, I was inspired. I read *Moby-Dick* constantly, all the time I was writing this. I opened it, put my finger down and tried to learn. Whatever the sentence said, there was something there for me to learn — about the craft of writing, the nature of human beings, the nature of philosophical inquiry through fiction. It was the way some people treat the Bible.

Is it a book that you have always loved?

I wrote my first high school book report on *Moby-Dick*. I read it simply because I had heard of it and I was systematically reading all the books I'd heard of. I wanted to be educated. And I loved reading. I can remember taking it off the shelf at the Birmingham Public Library and writing this book report and the teacher saying in a kindly way, "Now, Sena, are these your ideas or the ideas of some art critic?"

I was very surprised. I had no idea what an art critic was. But it was a wonderful question, because now I knew there were art critics and I could read what they had to say. She believed me when I said they were my own ideas. The sentence she questioned said something to the effect that the ocean was such an important presence in *Moby-Dick* that it should be counted as a character. So I think that *Moby-Dick* always seemed special to me on those terms.

Also, the summer before I had this voice-and-vision experience, my daughter, Flora, and I were traveling a lot. She was about eleven then. We listened to books on tape, and one of the books was *Moby-Dick*. She loved it so much. She has a wonderful ear, and she just began to recite Ahab's speeches. That really perked up my attention for *Moby-Dick*. I thought, "What is this book that this little girl likes it so much?" So I was somewhat steeped in recent *Moby-Dick* experience by the time I was in Boston, driving the car.

Then, too, there's a passage within *Moby-Dick* that really inspired me when I reread it again during this nine-month period between the idea and the beginning of writing. This is a scene from the chapter called "The Symphony," and I quote it in the beginning of the book, when Ahab is about to go out after the whale, and Starbuck, the first mate, is trying to persuade him not to do it. Ahab says, "Stand close to me, Starbuck; let me see into a human eye; it is better than to gaze into sea or sky; better than to gaze upon God. By the green land; by the bright hearth-stone! this is the magic glass, man; I see my wife and my child in thine eye."

I thought, "He loves her. I can write the book. He passionately, intensely loves her. It's worth my time to create the character that this implies."

So there were two things, then. That first vision — the knowledge, the voice — then this moment of understanding.

I would really say three things, and include the experience with my daughter, or the deep root, my high school experience.

Once you decided to write the book, how did the story gather?

The structure was all there for me in the first sentence, because I had three romances. I knew the one with Ahab had to end in his death. I was not going to monkey with that. He wasn't going to be washed up on shore and live happily ever after.

Unlike Melville's, your novel deals with everything that was in ferment in that time: slavery, feminism, the movement toward Unitarianism, the expansion of America toward the frontier. Why did you decide to address issues not in Melville's story?

My thoughts formed during that nine-month period when I was asking myself, "Can I do this? Do I really want to do this?" As much as I loved and respected *Moby-Dick*, I did think that some things were left out of the book besides women, and one of the issues that was left out was slavery. *Moby-Dick* came out in 1851, so it well could have included slavery. Melville was against slavery. He was an abolitionist—his heart was in the right place. But it wasn't in his book. He did make a plea for religious toleration in the beginning of *Moby-Dick*, in that Ishmael comes eventually to worship the little pagan idol of Queequeg. It's clear that it's absolutely with Melville's approval, that he sees this as a real act of love and friendship and no act of heresy. I wanted to continue that, because I do feel that so much evil is done in the name of religion in our time. Just look around, and there it is.

Did you take notes or otherwise organize your thoughts as all these ideas gathered and grew in your mind?

I read a lot, and I underlined a few things, but I wasn't systematic about it. I read about religious controversies of the time, and I read a lot about whaling. I did research, sometimes luckily, sometimes laboriously. Many serendipitous things happened in connection with this book. I didn't know that Maria Mitchell would be a character in the book. I hadn't heard of her. When I landed in Nantucket the first time, the cab driver started telling me about her. She is the astronomer who, from her roof walk, discovered a comet.

Another time when I went there, I was writing about the experience on the whaleboat—the small boat, not the whale ship. I couldn't quite visualize the thing. Also, I was having trouble describing the Fresnel lens. [The lens, named for its designer, Augustin Fresnel, magnifies the light in a lighthouse.] I walked into the whaling museum in Nantucket, and the first thing I saw was a sixteen-foot whaleboat. A sign on it said, "Lecture in five minutes." So I listened to the lecture—I was ecstatic, and it was very, very helpful. Then I walked around the corner and there was a Fresnel lens on display, with an explanation about that.

In some ways *Ahab's Wife* is a book about a woman finding her home. She has some homes thrust upon her, but in the end she chooses to live on the east-most end of Nantucket Island at 'Sconset. On the last day of one of my trips, a friend said, "You have to go and see the other end of the island." Our plane was leaving in just a few hours, but she insisted I do this. So I did. When I got there, the water was just booming against the edge of the island and springing up in the air, like a fountain. I was so taken by it. I said, "Una will come to live here." So some of the book,

I lived, in that sense. In terms of setting, it was extremely helpful to go to the place I was writing about. Wonderful things happened that I could not have anticipated if I hadn't physically gone there. And I had to keep going back there. I do think that in period-piece books, you have to do the careful research. *Ahab's Wife* has been pretty universally praised for its historical accuracy.

Ahab's Wife begins exactly in the middle of Una's story. Why did you do that?

I wanted to start the book with something very exciting that had a number of issues in it. So right away, the idea of the bounty hunters and the childbirth scene appeared out of my imagination as something exciting to do. I didn't know that one of the bounty hunters was going to be a dwarf. I opened the door. There were six guys standing there, all dressed in wool and fur, and one of them began to shrink. He became a dwarf. And I did not know he was coming back in the book.

He just appeared as Una did, in a way. It seems as if the book truly evolved.

It did evolve. I did have that three-pronged structure and that stayed steady with me: the three romances. But the other stuff just wove itself in and out spontaneously. The little character, Franny, on the lighthouse, appeared in just the same way. We were crossing on the ferry and I saw those goats and then I saw something else, white and small, jumping up and down and didn't know what that was. Then, suddenly, I realized she must have a little cousin and her name must be Franny and that must be her.

Did you always know that Ishmael would be the last husband?

No. It came to me as I went along.

When you came to that place in the middle, that moment when she saw him in the passage?

That was a place that I went back and wrote and inserted.

So when did you know?

I was wondering all along. I thought the muse would tell me, and at a certain point I got it. I just laughed in glee.

That first scene, was it the first scene you wrote?

Yes. I said, "I'll write this scene that's come to me, then I'll figure out what to do next." When I was finished, I realized, I can't understand this unless I go back to her childhood. I need to drop back. As that point, her father came into the picture, really as preparation for her interest in somebody like Ahab. Her father is another kind of monomaniac, to use Melville's term. At the same time, he's a passionate and fiery person.

Both of those men are towering—the absence of light. In fact, there's a lot of imagery of darkness and light throughout.

I wanted the lighthouse in there as something idyllic, because I knew there was going to be so much darkness in the figurative sense in the book. I wanted this nurturing, age twelve to sixteen, at the lighthouse. In a way, that's my bow to Virginia Woolf and my favorite novel, *To the Lighthouse*.

There were a number of bows in this book.

Yes. They're meant as sincere bows.

Una Spenser, for instance.

I didn't know her name at first. I had to wait for the name to come to me. I did think about how, in Spenser's *Faerie Queene*, Una comforted the Red Cross Knight, the dragon slayer. Ahab is a whale slayer, which was kind of a contemporary dragon. I liked the root of the word, meaning unity or oneness. The spiritual voyage in this book is about feeling at one with the universe. It seemed the perfect name, once I got it.

There's another kind of oneness, too: Una never quite gives herself away to anybody.

In some ways, this novel is an antiromantic novel. I didn't want one and only one love. The first sentence says, "Hey, this isn't that kind of book." We love many people—many of us do, anyway—in our lives.

Una's tough. She's the one who survives the cannibalism. And there's the situation with her first husband, Kit. She's able to let that go, to move on with her life. She does what she has to do to survive.

I wanted very much to present not just a female character who was equivalent to Ahab, but also I wanted a vision in place of that vision. *Moby-Dick* ends in death and destruction. My book ends in affirmation of life and creativity.

You give us that, don't you? About two-thirds of the way through the book, Una says, "And if one wrote for American men a modern epic, a quest, and it ended in death and destruction, should such a tale not have its redemptive features? Was it not possible instead for a human life to end in a sense of wholeness, of harmony with the universe? And how might a woman live such a life?" And the reader thinks, *now I know how that would be.*

Yes, I planted those lines as a "reader's guide."

Once you wrote that birthing scene and you knew you had to go back to the beginning of her life, did you write more or less chronologically?

Yes. But there were some exceptions, where my mind would jump ahead to a scene I wasn't ready for in the flow of the narrative. Anything that comes to the mind unbidden is to me the writer's gift from the muses, and I'm always receptive to it. If it comes in the middle of the night, I get up. I don't take notes. I write the thing itself until I drop. One of the scenes that came to me ahead of time was the cannibalism scene.

Were you scared to write that?

It was very hard on me to write the ordeal at sea, the cannibalism. It wasn't technically hard, it was emotionally hard. But it was one of the least revised passages in the whole novel. It just came out. But I had to—as well as I could—live that experience. I call these scenes my "grappling-hook" scenes. I've thrown the hook ahead and it lodges there, then I pull myself to it with the rest of the narrative that I've skipped over.

But you actually have written the scene. So when you get there, there it is.

Usually, the grappling-hook scene will be slightly modified, because I'll have done something in the bridging material that I couldn't have known I was going to do.

This is related to something you've done with the movement of the story. You started out in the middle, then eventually we got back to that place. But there were moments in the book where you suddenly made a huge leap ahead in time. Did that technique come to you as you worked?

I knew I wanted to jump and so I just jumped. The structure of the novel is a loop; but it doesn't just close the loop, it keeps on going. I call this book *Ahab's Wife*, but, as is the case sometimes with titles, the book walks away from its title. It's like Chekov's story "The Lady with the Toy Dog." At first, that's all the woman is to the man, but she becomes much more. Or Lawrence's "The Horse Dealer's Daughter." We have these labels for each other, but then there's a fuller humanity. So this is her label: Ahab's wife. But she walks toward being The Star-Gazer.

The glimpses into the future were jarring in a good way. They freed the novel from that feeling that long novels sometimes have: and then, and then, and then . . .

I didn't want to plod. I was very aware of that danger, so I decided I would just gather up my feet and go. But I did rework those passages quite a number of times. It was one of the technical challenges to try to keep those jumps from being too abrupt. Also, I began to be a little weary of Una's voice, myself, as her creator. That's when the letters started coming.

You use a number of devices to add variety to a long, first-person narrative: the letters; there's a section that's almost like theater dialogue; you jump point of view a couple of times.

Yes. And the chapters are very different in length. I'm using devices that I've noticed other writers use and that I think can work. It was a lot of fun for me to write those letters from a different first-person point of view.

How long did it take you to get through the first draft of Ahab's Wife?

Two years. Then it took two full years—which I thought was very fast, because the manuscript was over a thousand pages—to revise it. I revised it from beginning to end four times before I ever approached an agent with it.

Did you have to do any structural revision, or was it mainly cutting, paring, adding here and there? Tinkering?

I'd say it was mostly tinkering.

Did you do revisions after the book was sold?

About two days before I was to leave for New York to work on the novel with Paul Bresnick, my editor, he called and said, "I've sent you a letter about some things to add or change." So I got Paul's twenty-page letter. I thought, "How am I going to do this? I'm still packing."

In the Cincinnati airport, I had a layover of three hours. I had brought *Moby-Dick* with me and I was, as always, reading it for inspiration. Suddenly, I knew what I was going to do. So I went up to the guy at the counter and said, "Do you have any spare paper?" He pulled it out of the computer and handed me this wide, old-fashioned, tractor computer paper. So I sat there and wrote all the time, waiting. I wrote on the plane, wrote that night in the hotel room.

The next day, I had to read it aloud to my editor—I'd revised it, it was all crossed out. But when I finished and I turned and looked at him, he was obviously moved. He said, "It's better than I ever anticipated." I was just amazed that I'd left out something so crucial to the novel. Paul's suggestions for revision were simply wonderful.

At the beginning of our conversation, you said, "I had a novel, if I wanted to write it." Even though it's a wonderful idea with a strong image, you might not have written it. There are many ideas that all novelists have that they don't write.

That's absolutely true. Within ten minutes of having the voice and vision that launched *Ahab's Wife*, I had another idea for another completely different novel that I have not written.

Why do you think you wrote Ahab's Wife, *as opposed to other novels you might have written?*

I really was impressed by Melville's language and challenged by it. I really did feel that there was a vacancy in the concept of nineteenth-century American women. So I wrote it partly for political reasons, partly for my daughter. I wanted her to be able to quote a character who wasn't Ahab, but whose language was resonant.

Also, I did have a long-standing attraction to the sea. I think I got that from my mother, who grew up in Missouri. I remember her telling me that the first time Edna St. Vincent Millay ever saw the sea, she burst into tears. I thought, "What a strange and interesting thing." I have in my entry hall some furniture that was in the house I grew up in. There's my mother's desk. On the left, there's a sampler of a ship that she did when she was ten years old and, on the right, there's a photograph of the ocean that she cut out of a magazine and had framed. I think the fact that the ship and the ocean images were something that my mother loved was also partly behind *Ahab's Wife*.

So it's more than a good idea. There are things underneath it that resonate.

Yes. I gave up on pursuing simply good or interesting ideas long ago. This actually happened in my evolution as a writer, as a short story writer, after my daughter, Flora, was born in 1980. It changed my life as a writer, because I no longer thought it was sufficient to just write about what I *could* write about—good ideas. I really asked myself, "What do I want to write about that is very close to me, that in some way might be a help to my daughter in difficult times?" So I wrote a set of short stories—they're in *Ice Skating at the North Pole*—and the question was, "How do we survive in difficult times?" I didn't think that I could give any formula for surviving, I could just maybe catch the spirit of it. Classical music was one of the answers in that particular set of stories. And art.

From 1980 on, I required of myself that I not spend my time writing what I *could* write or what was interesting to me. It had to be closer to the bone than that. So, yes, I wouldn't have entertained the idea if it hadn't had some real resonance for me. Spiritual resonance. My writing has to be essential to who I am and how I see the world.

Is there a way you like to work, a rhythm that you find productive?

The ideal way for me to write, and the way I wrote much of *Ahab's Wife*, is to be on sabbatical and to have a steady rhythm. I strictly wrote *Sherlock in Love* this way. I decide how much I can do. With *Sherlock in Love*, I would do ten typed pages or six hours of work, whichever came first. Five days a week, never on the weekends. First thing in the morning, no interruptions. And I absolutely followed that every day until it was done. It only took about three months to get the first draft. When I could treat *Ahab's Wife* that way, I did. Except, I was older and tired-er, so instead of ten pages, I set myself the goal of six pages. Instead of six hours, I said four hours. On this new novel, when I'm not teaching or preparing to teach, I'm probably writing three hours a day.

Is it difficult to both teach and write?

It's very difficult to write a long, original novel and teach. But even when I'm not teaching, just the sheer physical strain of sitting still and focusing is so hard. I used to write in the morning and then do research in the afternoon and evening. But I can't do this research on this Birmingham book late at night. It's too horrifying. I can't sleep at night if I do. I had to discover that after a few sleepless nights. I was there, but I had no idea of the extent of the brutality.

And those times when it seems you just can't go on?

I do feel that to be myself I must write. I can have gaps in writing, and during that time I feel more and more guilty. But I use that guilt. It's like building up a head of steam. At a certain point, I'll write again, in order to be myself.

Lewis Nordan

Lewis Nordan is the author of three novels, four short story collections, and a memoir. Born in Jackson, Mississippi, in 1939, he grew up in Itta Bena, a small town in the Mississippi Delta. He earned a BA from Millsaps College, an MA from Mississippi State University, and a PhD in Shakespearean Studies from Auburn University. Before taking a job teaching creative writing at the University of Pittsburgh, Nordan worked as a fireworks salesman, soda jerk, yardman, lumberyard hand, hardware salesman, junior high teacher, orderly, night watchman, and book reviewer. His fiction, which was influenced by the DC Comics (especially *Superman*), the rhythm of nursery rhymes, and the blues, has won many honors, including two PEN Syndicated Fiction Awards, two Mississippi Institute of Arts and Letters Awards for Fiction, the Southern Book Critics Circle Award for Fiction, the New York Public Library Award for Fiction, and the Fellowship of Southern Writers Hillsdale Award for Fiction. Nordan lives in Pittsburgh, Pennsylvania with his wife.

Welcome to the Arrow-Catcher Fair, 1983 (stories); *The All-Girl Football Team*, 1986 (stories); *Music of the Swamp*, 1991 (stories); *Wolf Whistle*, 1993; *The Sharpshooter Blues*, 1995; *Sugar Among the Freaks*, 1996 (stories); *Lightning Song*, 1997

How do ideas, bits of dialogue, and events mutate and become a novel? For example, how did the Emmett Till case work its way into Wolf Whistle?

The road to *Wolf Whistle* was a circuitous one, but once I found the path, I followed it with some ease. It began with the title story of my book of short stories, *Music of the Swamp*. In that story, a couple of boys find a body—a drowned person, apparently—sunk in a lake, snagged upside-down in a pile of brush. When I conceived the story, my thought was that this was the body of Emmett Till. But when I got to the moment

257

in the story when the body is found, I knew that an infamous murder was out of place in this tale of the love of father and son. Such an incendiary detail would derail the point of my story. So I had the narrator eventually identify the body as that of an old man who had had a stroke and fallen out of his boat and drowned. These were momentary thoughts for me, quickly generated and quickly forgotten. I plunged forward with *Music of the Swamp* and made no other note of Emmett Till for the time being.

A year or so later, the book was finally published and I went on tour to promote it. On a TV show in Atlanta I was asked what I was working on now, and I heard someone answer—me, it turned out!—"I'm writing a book about the murder of Emmett Till." That was the first moment I had ever imagined that such a book would be my next project. I carried off the lie I had just blurted out by telling the audience what I remembered of the event in my childhood and escaped, finally, happy to have thought up an answer to the question and certain I had not been telling the truth.

Months and months later, I wrote and even published a story called "Get Well Soon, Glenn Gregg." A good deal of time had by now passed, and finally I got caught up on teaching duties and had time to think of writing some more short stories. I read over that recently published story and, in really a blazing moment of insight, knew that Glenn Gregg's dastardly father in that story was the murderer of Emmett Till. The falsely identified body in the river, the odd remark I'd made on that TV show, and Solon Gregg's villainy all came together there, and at that moment I knew I was writing a novel.

Solon, of course, was nothing like the real murderers, Milam and Bryant. In fact, almost nothing, suddenly, was "true" to the real story. But my course was set—a course of fiction, not docudrama or history—and that book began to pour out. I wrote 365 pages in six weeks. As I wrote *Wolf Whistle*, I listened constantly to the music of the blues—Robert Johnson, Muddy Waters—a diverse group of singers and pickers. I suspected, and it turned out to be true, that the music would wind its way into the prose.

What about Lightning Song? *How did you know it was a novel, not a short story?*

My memory of what happened with *Lightning Song* is not so vivid because there was never any question in my mind that I was writing a novel. It was one that revealed itself page by page, day by day, but a novel nevertheless. I had no plot in mind, only these characters, whom I loved before I ever really got to know them very well. They're based on a family I was close to when I lived in Alabama, and though the events are all fictional, the love I held for those real people influenced every word.

There's one odd detail about the writing of this book, probably irrelevant to this question: I was in a deep, dark clinical depression when I wrote this book. I would write each day and collapse into an almost catatonic funk. I got in bed and covered my head. I slept, I cried, I harbored dark thoughts. I got up, wrote mostly comedy for a few hours, stopped, doubted the value of my work, doubted my own value, wondered at the pointless universe, et cetera. I don't know how or even why I did this. I had no fun at all writing this book—never smiled or believed it was worthwhile—and yet I kept at it day after day. When it was finished I was worthless, a pool of protoplasm, for a long time.

Do you know the shape of a novel before you begin it?

No, never. Not even *Wolf Whistle*. Right up until the time of Bobo's death, I believed he would get away. When Hydro died in *Sharpshooter*, I was so shocked I had to take the rest of the day off. My wife had to comfort me. I came down the stairs from my office, ashen. She said, "Honey, what happened? What's the matter?" I said, "Hydro died." She said, "Oh, no. Oh God, no, Honey."

How do your characters "grow" in your mind?

I am almost always surprised by what I learn about my people. I don't mean that they come across as bizarre to me, only that their lives always turn out to be more rich and complex and filled with unexpected pain and longing and hopeful dreams, and are maybe more sweet than I originally imagined they were. This happens in large degree through the language that seems appropriate to use to describe them. The right choice of language often seems the key into their secret hearts.

How do you decide on point of view? Does one character's voice tend to drown out the others, or do you try several voices before you settle on who narrates your novels?

The novelist William Harrison once told me that the only reason to choose one point of view over another is that one makes my job easier than the other. That's advice I use with every book. There is no sense in trying to hammer a square peg into a round hole. I choose the point of view that works best, makes my job easiest. If I discover I'm in the wrong point of view, I either simply change, or I find some way to extend the function of the one I'm in.

The omniscient first person is a wondrous thing on those rare occasions when it can be pulled off. An extension of the limited third is also fine. In the chapter in *Lightning Song* where we follow Swami Don to work, to the motel room with the Indian maiden, we are actually in an extension of Leroy's so-called limited point of view. We need Swami Don's point of view and we need Leroy's imagination of it to complete our knowledge of those scenes. But in more direct answer to your question: I knew I wanted the amazing Harris to appear on the scene glittering, and I needed someone who could see and appreciate the glitter. Leroy and his point of view were invented out of the necessity for someone to love Harris without history or fear of threat. That was Leroy.

That use of first-person omniscient breaks a fundamental rule of fiction. What signals permission to do that? How do you know you can get away with it?

Usually such a thing is only possible at the climax of a story or scene—as in the first chapter of *Wolf Whistle*, where I used third-person attached rather than first person. But it is the same principle. When Alice's head explodes, she can see into the future, everywhere. The author earns such moments by creating a setting in which anything is possible if it is pushed to its emotional limits.

Could you talk about the use of magical realism? How do you know when a story needs to go beyond the boundaries of reality?

Talking about these matters is hard because we have to speak in "left-brain" language about signals that come to us from the "right brain." Or to be plainer, it's almost impossible to speak logically about the sources of intuition. Yet this is the dual construction of our lives, so it's a fair question and worthy of an attempt at an answer. Once again, the answer seems to lie in the value of the elements of a story's setting. Not entirely but largely.

Like minor characters, supernatural or magical occurrences are really only a part of the setting. Each event of this kind tells us that this is the kind of place where such a thing normally, customarily happens, where such an extravagance is really no more impossible to believe than the other events of the story. *Wolf Whistle* is, of course, my most magic-filled story. The real-life events (or pretend-like-real-life events) are more terrible than this author can quite believe, so mustn't this whole world in the story (I ask myself) be subject to similar distortions? And if so, might not some of them be benign and others sweet and still others funny, as well as horrible?

Intuition chooses those moments where the setting slides into those spaces which we call magic or whatever. But they are really only gentler representations of the distorted vision that the world presents all the time. If pressed to say when intuition guides me, or by what name, I guess I'd say it's a feel for the rhythm of the story. When the action in Red's store stops and the point of view slides up to the rafters where the pigeons are discussing what they've been watching, I was responding intuitively to something in the rhythm of the story's telling. I needed an element of point of view that only the setting could supply, somehow, and the setting provided a set of minor characters that could act as a sort of chorus and speak without influencing the action, only the rhythm of perception of the audience.

Critics often comment on the confluence of humor and pain in your novels. Do you do this purposely, or is humor just a natural outgrowth of your characters' wacky lives?

Comedy has uses, it's true—or at least we can assign useful traits to humor in a given context. But I don't think I've ever actually decided, "Here is a spot I need some humor." Once again, this is assigning left-brain rationale to right-brain decisions. And, by the same token, I'm not comfortable assigning comedy to the characters. I don't ever say, "What would a wacky guy like this do next," or even, "What wacky stuff would come naturally to such a wacky guy?"

Comedy is a result of a vision of the world. Comedy can be written by a writer with a comic vision even if that writer is depressed. I wrote the scene with the New People driving their car backward in *Lightning Song* in a black depression that lasted a year and a half. I didn't think it was funny when I wrote it; I didn't enjoy writing it. I just wrote it because that's the way I see the world. It's a comic vision, not a desire to be funny or a narrative need to lighten what is otherwise unbearable. I won't try to guess where this gift comes from, only acknowledge it as a part of who I am, for better or worse.

Do you revise as you go, or at the end of a draft?

The best way to answer this is to point out something about setting. The most valuable aspect of the physical setting of a book is its minor characters. That's what minor characters are: setting. It's not true that setting can be a character, as I've heard many a novelist proclaim. The setting can't change or grow, hate its mother, have sexual fantasies. It can't do any of the things that define a character.

A minor character, though, tells the reader, "This is the kind of place in which a person like me exists, and my uniqueness defines the uniqueness of this place." Thus, the character is essential to a definition of the setting. I tell you this to say, the first draft usually puts the major characters and the inanimate setting and the storyline into place. The second draft makes sure the minor characters enlarge and give definition to the setting, so that what the major characters do seems as truly meaningful to the reader as it is to the author. A corollary to this is that once the setting is fully realized by means of its minor characters, other matters may need to be revised, as they will appear different to the author.

You have said that Wolf Whistle *was greatly shaped by events of your boyhood, but you made a novel of those events. What made you decide to cast the autobiographical events of* Boy with Loaded Gun *as a memoir?*

Truly the modern memoir has become so debased—or liberated—as a form that there is little difference between the memoir and what used to be called the "autobiographical novel." I don't rely on that debasement or liberation as my justification of what I've written in my memoir, though. My book is influenced by the tall-tale telling that lies at the core of who I am. To use the phrase "tall tale" is to place my answer in literary terms. "Magical realism" is really just another name for the same. "Comic vision" is another.

But I didn't write the book to fulfill some literary scheme, only to tell the truth, both fat and thin, as well as I know how. The parts of the book that treat my childhood and comically recall events that were not comical when they happened reflect what those events have become in memory. The details concerning the death of my son are nearer in time and are less transformed in this way, though they too have undergone transformation. As in almost any first-person narrative, whether we know it to be memoir or fiction, there are two persons represented by the "I" of the story: the person to whom the events occurred, and the person he or she has become as a result of those events. Thus, a reader and maybe an era must decide what to call a narrative such as *Boy with Loaded Gun*.

The same is not true of *Wolf Whistle*. It is a novel and only that. The events are reminiscent of a set of events that really happened, but the similarity is really only a device (among many) of the fiction. The fact that the death of Emmett Till was central to my moral development and that it is recalled by events of my novel cannot change the fact that the historical similarity is really only a hook for the audience to hold to, a device of verisimilitude.

Do you ever lose your way as a writer? If so, how do you deal with that?

After each book and to some extent after each extended short story I imagine that I'm all written out, that I'm dry and can never be replenished. So far the passage of months has always cured the problem. Now that I have some books and stories beneath my belt, I can hold both beliefs simultaneously: that I will never write again, and that eventually I will not be able to avoid writing again.

Some novelists say that the process of writing a novel teaches them something they needed to know. Is that true for you? If so, what did each of your novels teach you?

I think I do learn from each novel, but it is a little hard to sum up that education in a comprehensible statement. Much of the lesson is—well, I guess I'd have to say spiritual. I mean, there are these technical gifts that result from an extended project like a novel. I learned in *Wolf Whistle* something about voice and point of view; in *Music of the Swamp*, something of structure. And there are psychological benefits, such as renewed confidence that I can do this big thing, solve this problem of language and structure, or work through issues with my father or whatever.

But the real issue of writing a novel is that it changes the novelist at some level of reality that can't be spoken of in merely psychological or technical terms. Writing a novel is—how shall I say this?—one thread in the amazing tapestry in which we experience the reconciliation of destiny and free will.

When I write a novel, I discover myself working toward personal, deliberate, nameable goals—telling my story—and at the same time sensing that I am not really writing this story, that it is a story concocted outside of time and channeled through me onto a page. In the writing of a novel we get at least a vivid metaphor for that paradox and a hint of the reconciliation.

I think I'd like to stop here with this answer, as it leads deep into some beliefs I hold that I have no intention of preaching. Let me just say that if we can imagine that we choose our destiny ourselves, outside of time, and that we then in life walk through those pre-life choices as if through darkness, we experience the reconciliation I'm speaking of. Writing a novel is both like this, and is a part of this. The novel comes from a willful act and also from an act that seems outside will, as we know it.

Sheri Reynolds

Sheri Reynolds is the author of four novels. Born in South Carolina, she received a BA degree from Davidson College and an MFA from Virginia Commonwealth University in Richmond. Her first two novels remaindered, her third rejected, she was living on credit cards when she learned that *The Rapture of Canaan* had been selected for Oprah's Book Club. She is an assistant professor of English at Old Dominion University. She lives in Virginia, on the eastern shore.

Bitterroot Landing, 1994; *The Rapture of Canaan*, 1995; *A Gracious Plenty*, 1997; *Firefly Cloak*, 2006

Flannery O'Connor said, "Anybody who has survived his childhood has enough information about life to last him the rest of his days." How did your childhood, your family, give you the kind of information you needed to become a writer?

I feel like I could tell stories from now until the moon turns to cheese if I wanted to. I certainly never worry about running out of stories to tell. I think O'Connor just means that everybody has stories—and plenty of them. No shortage of material. But then you have to ask yourself why the story merits telling; or, in other words, why it should mean something to somebody else. For me, this is the writer's job—to find the story within the experience, the particular slant that transcends the personal to speak to more universal themes.

As far as my "stuff" goes—Lord God, I hate to get started. There's a part of me that aches to do my writing, and there's another part of me that doesn't want to go into my "stuff." Some years I write. Some years I watch the sun set. Lately I've been preferring the sky. When I'm in this sort of place, I can't imagine why anybody would ever choose to write when they could watch the sun set. I hope I will never choose writing over making love. I hope I never miss a family vacation to work on a book. Words are not life. This is a very good thing. A story is important, but a story has its place . . .

My childhood did shape what I write, I guess. I was a terrified little kid. My parents were teenagers, living in a trailer beside my grandma's house, working very hard to make a living. My daddy was rough; my momma defended him. My daddy would shoot his gun inside our trailer, and my momma would cover the hole in the floor with a rug so nobody would know. And all I wanted to do was uncover that hole and stare at it. I wanted to tell everybody that there was a hole in the floor, and I was too scared to speak. I can't even remember why he shot the gun inside the house. As I recall, we had rats that were stealing our washrags out of the bathroom and running right down the hall with them. I think he shot his gun to kill the rats. I have a dead rat in my memory, with its mouth blocked up with a washrag, but I don't know if that's real or not.

I think one of the reasons I write is because I no longer remember whether it was real or not, whether the rat with the washrag was real, or the hole in the floor, or the rug that covered the hole. The fear was real, though, and so I need to write. And I write because I live with a guilt I can't overpower or make peace with—the fact that my daddy and momma loved me (and still love me), and I go around telling people about the gun and the hole in the floor, the rat and the washrag. There's this tension I struggle with—I was loved and I was still terrified. I was loved, and my daddy had this gun.

Where I was from, girls were made into little wives and mothers in a thousand ways; daddies buying little lacy bras and panties for sweet-faced daughters who smiled in the snapshots Mommy took. Makes me sick, this sexualization—and the complicity of the women. The dance lessons girls must take, and the sleazy costumes for the recitals. Just thinking about my cousins and niece in those costumes—the same kind I wore—that alone gives me enough fury to write. It might always be that way. If I wrote a book for every time someone grabbed my backside and felt entitled to do so, or for every time someone commented on the size of my growing breasts, or pawed them, I'd fill a library. I think that's a travesty, and I will likely be writing about it for the rest of my life.

It wasn't hard for me to find topics to write about. My head was about to blow off by the time I started writing in earnest. Writing is good for me in some ways because it turns the anger into sadness, which is, I think, the truer emotion.

Like many southerners, your work is—to quote O'Connor again—"Christ-haunted." How did growing up in the Bible Belt shape you? Was it a factor in your wanting to write?

One of my central issues has been Christianity. It continues to show up in my writing—so far in every book, even the terrible ones that I'll never publish—and I can't help it. And I'm mean to the Christians. I make fun of them over and over even though I try not to. I hope that I'll quit doing that, too, because I don't like that part of myself. I don't want to be judgmental, but I get so hotheaded that it happens in spite of what I intend.

Fundamentalist Christianity, apocalyptic Christianity, gave me a hard time when I was a girl. I thought the Rapture was going to happen and I was going to be left behind, and I lived in never-ending fear of all those plagues written about in the book of Revelations. I hardly slept for years. I kept waking up in the middle of the night, convinced that everyone had been raptured but me. I'd tiptoe to the bathroom, check the faucets to see if they ran water or blood, and when I'd see water, I could go back to bed, because I knew the Rapture hadn't happened yet. But most nights, I was too scared to turn on that faucet, because I was scared it might run blood, and I just stared at it and prayed for forgiveness.

See, I prayed to be forgiven by God, but I knew that he didn't hear me. I had prayed before when my parents were fighting, when I was scared, when Dale Meeks on my bus was grabbing between my legs and I begged to be given the power of David when he slew Goliath, and God did not come through for me. And it just didn't seem like my prayers ever made it up to God—or else they were ignored. So I didn't expect God to hear me when I prayed. I thought maybe something was wrong with me. I never felt God in church, and I never felt God when I was praying. I didn't really expect to feel God—because I worshipped false idols, and I knew it. I felt the spirit in the trees, in the stream that ran by my house, in the leaves and earth. I was so connected to the earth, but not a bit connected to God-the-Father, and so whenever I prayed, it was desperate and guilty. I just begged to be taken into heaven so I wouldn't have to go to hell.

It's only in the last year or two that I have stopped expecting the Rapture to happen. Up until then, even though I was far away from the religious background of my past, whenever bad thunderstorms would come up, I'd think, "Here it comes."

I wrote my novel *The Rapture of Canaan* to exorcise some of my bad feelings around the kind of Christianity that preaches fear. Or perhaps it would be more accurate to say that I think the book grew out of my need to deal with those issues. I wanted to tackle the hypocrisy and cruelty of this kind of Christianity—the blind acceptance of a doctrine that keeps an individual from having to think for herself or question the world she's a part of—and so I wrote this book.

How did The Rapture of Canaan *gather for you?*

No novel has ever gathered for me deliberately. If I ever try to plan a novel, or if I ever have an agenda that I want to write about, I fail. I might write the book (and usually do), but it lacks magic. It lacks soul. I don't know how else to say it. I have all these bad novels that I've written, and the only thing they have in common is that they were written because I thought I should write them for some reason. I wish I knew more about that spark—that *thing* that makes one project successful where another one will fail. I've spent much more time on books that are unpublishable than I ever did on the ones in print. The ones I've published happened like magic. Or maybe I only remember it this way. Then there are the books I slave over, revising, rethinking, reworking, and all the time I know that I'm just preparing myself, somehow, for the *real* book, the one that will suddenly be right.

Usually I get an image that involves a character. Like with *The Rapture of Canaan*—I dreamed about this baby with praying hands, except his hands weren't really praying. They were seamed together at the heart line. I woke up just enamored with these hands. For days, the image stayed with me. And I thought, "Who is this baby?" and then I thought, "Who would this baby be important to?" and then I thought, "Who is this child's momma?" and then I had the kernel of my book.

I think that a novel gathers for me when I'm really ready to tell my truth about something. This doesn't mean when I'm ready to tell my own story, or when I'm ready to tell a literal account of something that happened. It means when I'm ready to be honest, to not hide from ugliness or to not be proper or politically correct or afraid of saying the unsayable thing. Most times when I try to write, I can't be so honest. I lie because I need to protect myself, or maybe I want to protect my momma. I won't see the full truth of a situation because I can't stand to look at it. The odd thing is that when I'm actually writing a book, I think I *am* telling the truth. Then later on, I look back and say, "No wonder that one didn't work. You were hiding again."

When I look back at the books I've written that are in print, sometimes I want to hide my face, because I can't believe what I've said. At the time, I wasn't aware of all I was saying. I love and fear the way my unconscious participates in my writing. I realize that one day it might get me in real trouble, but then I figure if that happens, it'll happen because it was time.

How do you develop the plots for your novels?

Writing backwards, usually. I never start out with plot. That's just not how books come to me. I start with the image of a character. So in order to find the plot, I generally have to backtrack.

The other day, on Thanksgiving, I woke up grouchy and decided to throw my turkey off the pier. I didn't actually do this, because I felt better shortly and I wanted to cook the turkey after all. But the image stayed with me and I thought about the *character* of the woman who wants to throw the turkey off the pier. I thought, "Why would someone throw the turkey off the pier?" First answer: She's sick of cooking. She's unappreciated. She cooks for people who don't care. And I began to see a potential plot unfolding, the story backing up. What happened to her on the day *before* Thanksgiving? How'd she wind up in this unappreciated place? So plot unfolds from character.

But then I kept going with this woman, and worked another plot from the other direction, too. I thought, if you went around town and surveyed a bunch of people on why a woman would throw her turkey over the pier, they'd all suspect that she was unhappy about having to cook. *So*—let's work against the expectation. She's not unhappy about cooking. She's unhappy about cooking *turkey*. So the story opens with the woman throwing the turkey over the pier, and then she waits there for the crabs to come to eat the turkey. She has her net ready . . . and the plot extends forward from the image.

One time I wrote the beginning of a novel I've since abandoned, but it was exciting writing. I had just moved to North Carolina to become a writer in residence at Davidson College for a semester, and on my first night there, I dreamed a novel in Spanish. I woke up knowing that I had this book, a brilliant book, but I didn't speak Spanish. I had this one line in English and the rest was in Spanish, and so I began translating, one sentence at a time. Of course I wasn't actually translating Spanish, I was translating the plot from the one sentence, following the clues. Plotting is, in some ways, a combination of translation work and detective work.

The intensity of your character-driven novels is sometimes almost suffocating; your women suffer in heartbreaking ways. Would you talk about how you find your characters, how they grow and change?

My characters are all me, of course—some aspect of myself that I explode into someone new. I put my vulnerability and mean-heartedness into my characters to make it more tolerable in myself. I put my fear into my characters, and also my secret pride and hard-jawed determination. They are my best selves, my others, my shadows, my sisters. I know very little about my characters when I begin writing, and they often surprise me. They tickle me, too. They are often more brave than I am. More cocky and self-assured, although they often don't know that's what they are. Sometimes they pave the way for me. Small rebellions and large ones.

I remember when I was writing *Bitterroot Landing* and I had this character, Jael, who was like me in many ways. I was comfortable writing about her—even though my own experiences were different from hers, we had a lot in common as far as our essences were concerned—and then one day I realized that she'd gone farther than I had in her understanding of how things are. She had passed me. And I didn't know how to write her anymore. I pondered this problem for a day or two, and then I decided I'd better follow her before she got away. I kept writing—about all sorts of things I didn't know. But after I'd written them, I could map my own way better.

In my novel *A Gracious Plenty*, my character Finch is badly burned. It's one of the central, defining features of this character. When I began the book, I knew that Finch was scarred, but I didn't know she was burned. In fact, I didn't know that the scar was external or literal. But the crazy thing is that I burned her on page 3. And I was surprised. I'd been living with her spirit for a long time. This grouchy, introverted, rather difficult woman had been pestering me for a long time, but I didn't know she was burned. Then I started the book, and right away I scalded her. I remember writing that part of the book, and it was effortless, and I knew exactly how she'd been burned and what it felt like. I'd never been burned in my life—not really—but I knew it as if it was autobiographical.

I don't write from outlines, and I try to remain as open as I can be in my writing. This doesn't come from some idea of how writing *should* be done; it's just that for me, as soon as I know how the story will end, I might as well stop writing because I've already killed the spirit of the piece. So since I don't know what's going to happen next, I'm often surprised by what my characters do, or sometimes what they don't do. In *Rapture of Canaan*, I had this little boy character, James, who I thought was one of my central characters. I had planned on keeping him in the book the whole time. Then one day as I was writing, I realized I was going to have to kill him. It upset me, too, because I'd mingled a whole bunch of sweet boys that I loved into his character. He reminded me of a kid named Kenny Faulk from my elementary school who I always loved, and he also held my feelings for my cousin Paul, who I adore, and I didn't want him to die. But that same day, I wrote his death, because it was necessary to the rest of the book.

How do you choose a point of view? Is there a way that you know that a certain character has to tell this story? Do you ever change after getting into a novel?

I usually write in first person. That's just how books come to me. Most recently I've written a novel in third person, but I think I only did this to prove that I can, and I think it's a bad novel anyway. A change in the point of view is a change in the story being told, and usually when I'm tempted to switch, I am better off asking myself what it is I'm trying to avoid saying.

For me, there is no technical detail of writing that is not also associated with the psychological component of writing. I'm fascinated by this, but also frustrated by it. Sometimes it makes me want to throw my laptop [into] the woods.

In my classes, I teach about how writers make choices, and I try to get my students to examine why a story starts in one place rather than another, what the writer gains from this point of view rather than that one—why a writer may have chosen to mention Froot Loops rather than Cracklin' Oat Bran. And I know all these things are important. I know it. But when I'm writing, I am not considering these things—I was never, ever, ever even *considering* Cracklin' Oat Bran. Never. I don't know how to reconcile the part of writing that is technical and craft oriented with the part of writing that feels mystical. The technical part is what I teach, but the mystical part is what I love.

Could you talk about the often-maddening process of seeing the novel through?

I don't think of the novel as *The Novel.* It's just my work. It's just a page at a time, a sentence at a time, and it goes on for as long as it needs to in order for me to tell whatever story I'm trying to tell.

When I've been in the middle of a novel moving fast ahead, I've found it helpful to end my day's writing by just sketching out a scene. Then the next day, I go back into that scene and develop it, and by the time I'm in a place where I need to generate new material, I'm already reacquainted with my book and my characters.

Do you have any "tricks" that help you keep the patterns in the novel straight as you are writing it?

I don't really have tricks, because I don't write complex plots. Once, I printed out all the pages of a manuscript in progress and taped them to the wall in order, and I did a revision that way, scribbling on the walls. But then I took out crayons and drew all over the manuscript. I might have just been playing. I don't know that it did any good, except I think that people should periodically make a mural for their mental health.

How do you handle revision?

Badly. I either hardly do it at all or else I get stuck doing it for years and eventually can't remember what made the project I was working on so interesting in the first place. I do believe in revision theoretically, but so far, I have not mastered it.

Does teaching feed your work? What's the upside of teaching writing? What's the up side to a would-be writer of going for an MFA?

I love to teach, but frankly, I do it because I can make a steady salary while talking to people about literature. It seems almost crazy that I get paid to read poems and plays and essays and stories — and to examine them with students. That's something I feel grateful about! And also, teaching's the only marketable thing I'm trained to do. I paid for my graduate education with a teaching assistantship at Virginia Commonwealth University, where I did my MFA in creative writing, so I taught composition for three years while I was in school. Before that, I had gathered tobacco and worked for a recreation department and run the lightboard for a theatre group. None of my other training paid much. So I kept teaching. The semester system works well for me because I get time off in the summer and over the holidays to do some writing. And I like being close to a library. But besides that, my teaching and my writing don't have much to do with one another. One real benefit to teaching, though, is that I get to assign all the books I want to read.

The MFA as a degree — well, it's kind of useless in itself, but it's a good way to practice the craft of writing. I think students certainly benefit from studying with different teachers, but most of all, students who enter a writing program are assured of deadlines and a community of other writers. These things are good to have, as most writers will tell you.

I wouldn't encourage anyone to go into debt for an MFA. For me, it was perfect. I did an MFA straight out of college, when I was used to being poor and didn't mind eating macaroni every day. I lived in a one-room apartment and spent all my weekends in the computer lab at school. I got teaching experience and wrote my first novel for a class, and in the end I had an advanced degree and many good writer-friends. But I didn't have a mortgage to pay then. I would never, ever encourage anybody to go into debt for an MFA. You can teach yourself by studying every writer you read, by asking questions about the choices each writer makes.

How do you define "talent?"

I don't know a thing in the world about talent. But once, the poet Dave Smith told me something important. He said to me, "Talent is cheap, but discipline is not, and it is discipline that makes the book."

Would you talk about what happened to you—and your writing career—when The Rapture of Canaan *was selected as an "Oprah" book?*

The Oprah Experience is definitely one I'd write out in all capital letters. It was the biggest, most public thing to ever happen in my life. Obviously it was marvelous to have my book read by so many people, and I'm grateful beyond belief for all the new readers—and to Oprah for including me in a list of really incredible writers. And yes, the book sales were wonderful! I was so broke, and so deep in debt, and it felt fairy-tale-like, and a little bit like a resurrection, to be chosen for Oprah's Book Club.

Eight months before Oprah picked *The Rapture of Canaan*, my publisher at that time, Putnam, had kicked me out because my books weren't selling as well as they'd hoped. I'd been under contract for a third novel, and I'd written and submitted *A Gracious Plenty*. My editor had already told me that she liked the new book, and I thought things were settled. So one day I went to the mailbox expecting my advance check, and instead I got this severance letter. They didn't want the new book, and the old ones were headed for the bargain bins, and there was nothing I could do about it.

It was a real hard season for me. I was in a mess, holding off bankruptcy a month at a time. I had foolishly been living off of my credit cards, expecting that advance check. Anyhow, when Oprah picked *Rapture*, she didn't know Putnam had remaindered the book. So my "fairy-tale" story really was like a fairy tale in that respect.

I was singing hallelujah, too! I can't tell you what that felt like. For a while there, it had looked like my writing career might die before I turned thirty, and with the Oprah news, I had another chance. But—and this is important—I knew very well that the same book Oprah had picked had been kicked out of Putnam. I knew that the quality of the writing didn't improve just because Oprah picked it, and I knew that my value as a writer didn't change either. I might have more readers and more money, but I was the same person who'd been in trouble just months before, with no money and no readers, and no publisher, either. In hindsight, I'm glad for those uncertain months because I didn't lose my head over going on the Oprah show. It was a wonderful boost to my career, and an opportunity that I don't expect I'll ever have again. But I knew then, as I know now, that I still had my work to do. My work is not to be a best-selling author. My work is to tell the stories that need to be told.

For the most part, I'm an introvert. I didn't adjust very well, really, to being so public. My soul got a little tattered and opaque. I had another book ready to publish when I went on Oprah (because, as I said, I'd written it for Putnam), and so I sold that book, and it came out shortly afterwards. My new publisher, Harmony, sent me on a big book tour, and by the time that was over, I was just worn out. So I decided to take a break from writing and being public, and I've dedicated the last few years to other things, to taking walks and paddling my little boat around. I've written some new stuff, but I'm not ready to publish any time soon.

I shop in thrift stores again these days and don't eat anything I can't pronounce. I would handle the same experience very differently if it happened to me again. Being chosen for the Oprah book club was a huge blessing, and it came with hard lessons. I know enough to recognize that the hard lessons and the blessings are exactly the same, and that's about all I know.

S. J. Rozan

S. J. Rozan is the author of eight novels in the Bill Smith/Lydia Chin series, two stand-alone novels, and the editor of an anthology of short fiction. A former architect in a practice that focuses on police stations, firehouses, and zoos, she is a former Mystery Writers of America National Board member, a current Sisters in Crime National Board member, and ex-president of the Private Eye Writers of America. She speaks and lectures widely and for years interviewed writers at New York's 92nd Street Y in a series she originated, "Mysterious Conversations." Rozan's books have won the Edgar, Shamus, Anthony, Macavity, and Nero awards for best novels. She lives in New York City.

China Trade, 1994; *Concourse*, 1995; *Mandarin Plaid*, 1996; *No Colder Place*, 1997; *A Bitter Feast*, 1998; *Stone Quarry*, 1999; *Reflecting the Sky*, 2001; *Winter and Night*, 2002; *Absent Friends*, 2004; *In This Rain*, 2007

Let's start with the fundamental question, why mysteries?

I was always interested in the mystery and crime form. When I was a kid, I read Nancy Drew obsessively. I couldn't wait for the next ones to come out. There was also a science fiction series [about] Lucky Starr, Space Ranger—[Isaac Asimov] writing under the name of Paul French. It was about this kid named Lucky Starr, who was a young teenager who was a space ranger, but what he really did was go around solving crimes—about robots and aliens and evil scientists. That was one of the jobs he did for the Council of Science, the good guys who ran the world. He had good guys and bad guys to deal with. He had a sidekick who was weird and outrageous. It was this classic mystery series, except it was set in the future. But my all-time favorite was *Bill Bergson Lives Dangerously*, by Astrid Lindgren. It was about these three kids, Bill Bergson and his buddies.

Somebody was doing something evil in their little town and they had to thwart him. It was all very thrilling. I checked that book out from the library over and over. That was what I wanted to do—not *be* him, but write those books.

And when they finally let you into the adult section of the library?

I was a huge Agatha Christie fan, and still am. I think she gets a bad rap for being cozy and for having cardboard characters. Her characters are archetypes; she really understood human motivation and the human heart. Some of her motives are breathtaking, specifically the motive in *The Mirror Cracked*. She's also the paragon of fair play. She gives you every piece of information that her detective had, and when you don't figure it out, it's your fault. From Agatha Christie, I learned both how to deal with real human beings and how to be fair to the reader and hoodwink them at the same time.

Did you study writing in college?

I grew up thinking I was going to be a writer. Then when I got into college I got this idea that writing isn't something you can just *do*. So I went to architecture school. I was always interested in how things work—what makes a building stand up, what makes a wall bulge in that place, what's behind all that plaster. I did field work and specification writing. I had this really great job. My office was great, my bosses were great, my work was great. There was nothing about my job that wasn't your architecture dream job—and I wasn't happy. That was kind of lucky. If the job hadn't been so great, I would have thought I was unhappy because I had a lousy job. But there was nothing I could ask for that I wasn't being given. Obviously, architecture itself was the problem.

As soon as I came to that conclusion, this little voice in my head said, "Weren't we going to write a book?" And I thought, well, all right, let me try that. If that doesn't work, I can cross that off the list. I knew the book I wanted to write was a private eye novel, so I started creating these characters—and I was never so happy in my life. I went to classes, I got some writing chops. Then I started writing the book. It took me fifteen years between the time I started the first book and the time I finally quit my job. By then, I was so clearly not an architect who wrote but a writer with a day job.

Hemingway said, "Prose is architecture, not interior decoration." Does that seem right to you, based on your training as an architect?

I think it's absolutely true. Architecture is the thing itself. We used to complain in the office that the only thing the client sees is the paint job. All the work you put into a building doesn't show. Every now and then, it's not true, though—my best example of this is in Annie Proulx's *The Shipping News*. There's a scene where two characters leave town before dawn and drive east into the sunrise. She takes a paragraph to describe the sunrise, the way the light comes into the car. It's astounding. You read it and you think, she only did this because she could. She wanted to see if she had the chops to make this happen—and she did. The book didn't need it—that's the paint job. But the rest of the book is the thing itself. You don't get distracted by the prose. At the end you think, nothing really happened. This guy and his kids and his aunt moved to a new place and he got a job and he met somebody and fell in love. But you're riveted the whole time. You don't remember any particular sentence—except that paragraph about the sunrise. That's the difference between architecture and interior decoration.

Would you agree that, fundamentally, every story is a mystery, regardless of whether there's a body involved?

Yes. In every story, the reader wants to find out some answer. Why are these people behaving like this, how is it going to turn out for the person you've come to care about? If there's no question, there's no drama.

So why does the literary world discount mysteries as formulaic?

What's interesting is that the *writers* of so-called literary fiction don't tend to discount it. The readers do. There's a tremendous amount of garbage published as genre writing, and if that's all you're reading, you're right. It is a formula. Romance has this, science fiction has this—as does the literary novel. The road novel, for example. It can be Cormac McCarthy or it can be pure crapola—but it's a road book, nonetheless.

There is a need to separate high culture from low culture, especially in this country. If art—high culture, literature—is difficult to comprehend, then only the trained and sensitive and worthy can comprehend it. So the more difficult something is, the more you can congratulate yourself if you get it. Conversely, if everybody gets it and loves it, it cannot, by definition, be art. It's that kind of thinking that puts genre writing, which is beloved by a vast number of people, in the category of not-art. Every now and then, a book rises. I'm thinking of Scott Turow's *Presumed Innocent*, which is a fabulous novel, beautifully written. People said "Turow transcends the genre." Every time you get a book with a crime element that gets a tremendous amount of critical attention, they say that. They take all the cream off the top and then complain that the milk is skim. But that's hardly fair!

Your award-winning crime series that features private detectives Bill Smith and Lydia Chin is a popular one among mystery aficionados. Would you talk about how you developed it?

The original character was Bill Smith. At the time I was creating him, there seemed to be this competition going on to name characters the most outrageous thing possible. Elvis Cole, for example. Every now and then you know there's a competition that you can't win, so I thought, I'm going the other way. So he was Bill Smith. He was created to be that classic world-weary American private eye. It's a white male character—it has to be, that particular archetype. Philip Marlowe defines this best. He's been to college, but just two years, which means it didn't work for him. But he had the ability to get there. He was a cop, kicked off the force for insubordination. He had everything going for him to become a part of the power structure, but in the end he couldn't do it because the price was too high: conforming, knocking all the edges off, losing part of his soul. He narrates from that vantage point, from outside a corrupt structure he refused. His heroism is in refusing to be a part of it, but continuing to go back to it to rescue people it's sucked under.

The male private eye who refuses to be part of the corrupt power structure is the recent addition, as it were, to a heroic figure who goes back to the Greeks and comes up through the knight-errant, whose job it was to go around the countryside saving people. Heroism never really cost the knight-errant anything. He had to be very, very brave to go up against the dragon, but once he mustered up the courage he was always able to slay it. World War I created a sea change in the consciousness of what a hero was. It was the first war where the carnage on the battlefield could not be ignored. It was photographed. It was also more enormous than in other wars. The cost of heroism began to show. Now a hero was someone able to go into this evil world and rescue people, but who was changed by going there and became unredeemable himself. That's where the hard-drinking, hard-smoking, lonely private eye that first appeared in the '30s and '40s comes from. Bill Smith's character is that character.

Lydia Chin, on the other hand, is a very late-twentieth-century character. She's an Asian American woman. She might have fought her way into the power structure, but it was not her birthright, so she would never have had the chance to reject it the way Bill Smith did. Her heroism consists of rejecting everybody else's goal for her and being what she wants to be, even though half the time she doesn't know what that is. It's a different brand of heroism and the great thing about the two of them, I like to think, is that they support each other in this fight.

How, exactly, did the two of them end up together in your mind?

Having created Bill, I wanted a foil for him, a sidekick. Everybody had sidekicks in those days—a lot of them were psychotic. They're devoted to the hero, but they will kill without compunction. As far as I was concerned, the psychotic sidekick eliminated a major point in the private eye novel, which to me is about moral ambiguity and the need of the detective to make decisions when there is no good choice. I wanted Bill Smith to have to deal with the ambiguity and then have to live with the consequences. So I wanted him to have a sidekick who wouldn't shoot someone just because she knew he wanted them dead. He'd have to say, "I want you to go shoot that person." Then they'd have to talk about it, admit that they were actually doing it.

I also wanted the sidekick to be as opposite to him as possible. Obviously, it had to be a she because he was a he. She had to be small because he was big, young because he was middle-aged. And if she was someone from a completely different culture, then *everything* would be called into question. I know a lot of Chinese Americans. I've studied the culture, I've studied the art. I thought, if there's any chance I can get inside the head of someone who is not me, it would be a Chinese American woman. So that was where Lydia Chin came from. She started as a sidekick to Bill, but three chapters into that first book she's going, like, "Don't you want to know what I think?" I stopped about a third of the way through the book and wrote a short story with her in it—just Lydia, not Bill—just to see if I could handle her voice, and we got along pretty well, she and I. So when I finished his book I decided to do a book in her voice, with Bill as the sidekick. I thought I was going to write two different series, and then an editor at St. Martin's wanted them both as continuing narrative series.

How do you recognize that an idea is for one or the other?

It's always clear. The stories come out of their worlds, which are really different. His are darker and with more ambiguous endings. You find out who did it and what went on but it doesn't necessarily work out well. Hers work out better. They have the heavy Chinese content, and that comes first. I think, I'm going to do a Chinese restaurant book, now I'm going to do a book about immigrants, so how about restaurant workers? The order in which I write them is the contract. If I have a Lydia in mind and Bill's up, Lydia just has to wait.

Most aspiring mystery writers assume that you have to have the plot of a book worked out in your mind before you can begin it. Is that true?

I never have a plot. When I started *Stone Quarry*, I had an incident at the end that I could see, but I didn't know what it meant. I had the idea of unconditional love, which is usually found in families and is only interesting if the person you love that way doesn't deserve it. Otherwise it's never tested. And loyalty—which outside of family works the same way. That's what that book was about. When I started *Reflecting the Sky*, I knew I was going to set it in Hong Kong, and Hong Kong to me has always been about duality. Everything in Hong Kong is reflected in something else, big and small. The buildings are reflected in the water; Hong Kong is an island and part of the mainland. I knew that's what the book had to be about. There had to be two of everything, either thematically or in fact. That's where the brothers came from, that's where the guy having two families came from. But I didn't have a plot.

What I do is start with an idea—an emotional or thematic center for the book and a world that it's set in. *China Trade* was about the world of export porcelains and small museums because that's a fascinating world to me. *Mandarin Plaid* was about fashion, because I *so* don't get it. I read the magazines and think, why are people wearing this? What are they thinking? Then I read some really interesting books on fashion and semiotics and the meaning of display, and one of them pointed out that in the world we live in we don't need clothing at all. We could live our lives naked because we're so climate controlled. Therefore, everything we wear is to communicate to everyone around us. This stuff fascinated me. Again, I didn't have a plot.

Is there always a particular question fueling each book idea?

I'm not sure there's a specific question. There's a curiosity; clearly there's something I want to explore. I got really interested in school shootings for a while. Every time there was one, I would research it. Always skinny white boys! Columbine was what sparked *Winter and Night*. I saw one of the teachers being interviewed, saying, "How could this happen here? This is a perfect place." And I'm thinking, clearly, this is not a perfect place if this happens here. And it's *not* a perfect place, schmuck, because out of this place came *South Park*. The guy that writes it came from that school, and he said everybody knows the jocks ruled that school. Everybody knows the jocks lock the nonjocks in the lockers and beat up on them and pee on them. It's a perfect place if you're *them*. When Columbine happened, everybody blamed the parents — and they are clearly at fault. Their kids were building arsenals in the garage and they didn't know it. But the parents of the jocks have to bear half the blame because these kids would not have cracked up in the hostile way they did if they hadn't been pushed around all their lives. So *Winter and Night* was about entering that world to write the story about what really happens in it.

I tend to write books about things I don't get, like the guy in *China Trade* who shaped his whole life around a single obsession, collecting porcelain. He was based on a real person, a professor who had been stealing for years. He said he felt sorry for the porcelains because they were locked up in dark closets and museums. He was a real nut. I thought, boy, here's a character. A collector told me he thought it was a way of ordering the world. There's no order in the world, but there's order in the world where his collection is. He feels alive when he's hunting. He feels the way I feel when I'm writing a book. He has purpose.

Once you move from general curiosity to the idea of a book, how does the book evolve?

First the book is just sort of swimming around in my head. For example, the new Lydia book, *Shanghai Moon*, started with the idea that it would have to do with jewelry, something else I'm interested in. The characters started coming in and developing. But I didn't have a plot.

I knew there was a Jewish ghetto in Shanghai during World War II. The Germans were taking over Europe, trying to get rid of the Jews by expulsion. But you couldn't leave unless you could prove you had someplace to go, and nobody would let them in. Shanghai, because of a series of bizarre historical accidents, was an open port. In theory, you needed papers, you needed a visa—but in fact, it was always the British who had checked them. The Japanese had invaded China in '37 and were ruling Shanghai, and the British, as a matter of policy, stopped checking papers. They decided if they insisted on their right to do that the Japanese would say, wait a minute, you are not the boss of this anymore. We are going to do it. And then the British wouldn't be able to come and go. There was no war in Europe yet, and they were making a lot of money. So they thought, never mind. And twenty thousand Jews took advantage of that.

So I'm sitting around thinking, okay, this Lydia book—it has to do with jewelry. But that's all I know—and it's not a plot. It's not a story. But I wasn't panicking yet. And into my mind floated the Shanghai ghetto. I thought, there is an interesting situation—something that could connect jewelry and Jews, which I had sort of wanted to get into a little bit, and China, too. So I started reading memoirs. The more I looked into [it], the more astounding it got.

Eventually, I came up with a plot that was a variation of *The Maltese Falcon*, where everybody chases around for years and years after this thing they've never seen. In this case, a piece of jewelry—the Shanghai Moon. Then I got into the practical logistics. How does Lydia get involved and what does it mean?

Lydia and Bill aren't talking to each other at the end of *Winter and Night*, and she's conveniently on her own. I thought, suppose a Yiddish private eye she knows, a Jewish guy from New York, calls her up and says, "A client has come to me because there was jewelry dug up in the old Jewish ghetto in Shanghai in the excavation for a skyscraper, and [it was] stolen almost immediately." The theory is that the thief has come to New York to sell it. Where would you do that? Well, you'd do it on Forty-seventh Street, where everybody's Orthodox Jewish, and that's why the client's come to the Yiddish private eye. But the other jewelry center in New York is Canal Street, where the Chinese jewelers are. It's a newer jewelry center, but it is for real and it is big and this guy is Chinese. So maybe he would take it there even though it's all new stuff down there and they don't deal much in antiques. But what is he going to do? He may not even speak English and he certainly doesn't speak Yiddish. So the client hires this Jewish private eye and asks, does he know a Chinese private eye? That's how Lydia gets involved. I still didn't know who these people were, but it sounded like it would work.

When you felt it was time to write, how did you begin?

Rather than having what my friend Keith Snyder calls the expository info dump at the beginning, I thought, let's have the client hand these two private eyes a letter that an eighteen-year-old girl who was on her way to Shanghai from Salzburg in 1937 had written to her mother. She was traveling with her fourteen-year-old brother, carrying eight pieces of jewelry she'd smuggled out so she could sell them if they couldn't find a way of making a living before their mother came. The mother had train tickets to come in a few months, but she never got out.

Later the girl meets a young Chinese guy and they fall in love. They have this gem, the Shanghai Moon, made out of a piece of jade that's been in his family for a thousand years and diamonds from one of the pieces of jewelry she smuggled into China. She wears it on their wedding day. But it vanishes at the end of the Chinese Civil War and is never seen again. People have been hunting for it all these years. It becomes probable or possible that, though the recorded find from the skyscraper site doesn't include it, it's what's been stolen and brought to New York.

From the time the Shanghai Moon came to me, I knew it had been created to celebrate the eternalness of love, which is one of the things the war was trying to destroy. I knew at the beginning of the book where the piece of jewelry had been and why. This is one of the first books where the end was clear to me.

In *The Maltese Falcon,* the thing they're chasing after is what Hitchcock called a MacGuffin. The point was *not* to find it—and to go off chasing after it more. I knew I couldn't end that way. But I also knew that the chase was what was critical, not the thing. *Why* people wanted it, that was the issue—and who they are and what they want to do with it. The "why" is the reason for where it's been for all these years.

I toyed with the idea of it being found with the other jewelry, but that would have raised the stakes too soon. To start with, they're just looking for this stuff, but nobody has much of an emotional involvement with it. Then someone gets killed and it isn't clear why—and there are these old men who turn out to have been there.

So characters appear as a story complicates itself.

Exactly. When they come in they're often surprising. In *Concourse* I had a guy who looked like a good guy and a good guy who looked like a bad guy—and the good guy just would not cooperate. He was doing bad things, but he had really good reasons. So I thought, okay, be like that! I was talking to another writer who works in exactly the opposite way. He says he never makes a character physically, including his race, his age, until he knows what his role is in the book. I find that completely backwards. I let them come in and act. They have their voice, and eventually they take on their roles. Sometimes I say, "Okay, here's what you're going to do." And they say, "Oh, I don't think so." And then I say, "Well, somebody has to do that," and they say, "Get somebody else."

When you finish a book, do you usually have a lot of revision to do?

I revise as I go along. As I realize that "this" is actually "that," it can mean a character has to be different in the beginning. So I have to go back and change the whole thing. I've taken characters out. I could populate a whole book with the people I've taken out of the books I already have! It's a very anxiety-provoking way of working. You say, "Maybe this. Oh, God, no. All right, but if he . . . no. I can't get to an end that way." So there's not much revision in terms of story when I finish. I don't do first drafts, second drafts, third drafts. I constantly revise.

You interrupted your successful series to write a stand-alone novel, Absent Friends. *Why did you do that?*

I was set to do the next Lydia, after *Winter and Night,* and then 9/11 happened. For the first couple of months afterwards, I thought, fiction, are you kidding? In a world like this, why would anyone want to do that anymore? I was thinking on an intimate level about the smoke and bodies and the whole thing for months and months and months after everybody else was putting it out of their minds. I knew I had to write my way out of 9/11, but it was too massive, too all over the place. I was whining to every writer I knew—most of whom were also not writing. "I don't know what to do, I don't know what to write." Then a friend of mine, who was disabled by a degenerative disease, told me that he was using a cane. He said, "It's not that I can't walk, because I can. But sometimes I can't find the floor."

I told my friend Jim Grady, "That's how I feel. Emotionally. I feel like I can't find the floor." He said, "So write about someone like that. The character's right in front of you: someone who can't find the floor." I said, "Holy Toledo!" So I started with Laura, the reporter, who couldn't find the floor because her lover had just died, 9/11 had just happened—and it went from there.

The anecdote about finding the floor appears among a whole collection of seemingly random things in the epilogue of the book, called "Explanation." The titles you've given some of the anecdotes, quotations, and poems are the titles for various sections of the book—like, "How to Find the Floor." Were all these things a part of the genesis of the book?

They were. The story was the story, but the book was to me a huge metaphor for all these other things. They collected as I went along, but they were mostly there by the time the book was a third of the way done. They were all experiences that I'd had or friends had had or that I had heard about.

They weren't all directly related to 9/11. There's a story about Lincoln saving a pig and how a witness incorrectly assumes it was an altruistic act.

I love that story! Years ago, I was in a class with a woman, a poet, who'd been hospitalized for depression and self-mutilation a couple of times. I don't know what became of her, but she wrote a poem about that story. I love it because it has always seemed to me so true that no matter how altruistic you think you are, there's something in it for you—and Lincoln knew that. But most people don't.

As you said, you started writing Laura's story first. But the book ended up with three points of view in the "now": Laura, Phil, and Marian. There's also the story happening in the past. How did you manage working with four different stories?

God only knows. With the story in the present, I changed the point of view depending on whose story seemed important to tell next. The story in the past originally had only two chapters; one told a little about the boys as kids and the other told a little about the girls. But they kept expanding. I gave each kid an anecdote, and the chapters got long. So I split them up.

It took me a long time to realize that what I was writing in those chapters was the book that Jimmy had written that Harry had found. That was another "duh." Then I realized that Jimmy's book needed to be interspersed so that you could follow the story in the present and the story in the past at the same time. I was about a third of the way through the book before I really found that rhythm. But I still had to keep going back. This needs to come before that and this has to come out and so-and-so can't know this yet so I have to put it here. It was just mind-boggling.

I used index cards. I had a different color card for each of the characters, and I wrote down the scene number (not same as the chapter number), the day and time it happened (day one, early afternoon), and the central action in the scene—who finds out what, who does what, where it is . . . that kind of thing. I broke them down as small as I could. That way I could look and say, there's four whites in a row here, so something has to be done about that. I kept rearranging the order. Sometimes I'd put a scene in a different chapter.

So the book's architecture was dictated by evolution of the story.

This comes from being an architect. We don't start with, I'm going to make a four-story square building. We start with, okay, it needs to be a bank and it needs to have this many rooms in proximity to each other on this site which has this kind of sun. From that process comes the building. What the process of architecture gave me is the idea that that's okay.

At the end of Absent Friends *we're left with the knowledge of how the secrets the characters knew as adults kept them from maintaining the trust and closeness they enjoyed throughout their childhoods. It's heartbreaking when the last thing Jimmy does when he realizes he's going to die is to take the photo of Marian from his wallet and look at it, as he's done every day of his life since their breakup—especially knowing that this is something Marian will never find out.*

None of them trusted each other enough. He would rather go away and spend his life with her picture than to tell her the truth. They all did that, in a way. These people's whole lives were based on hiding a truth that they thought they were the only ones who had—and which wasn't even true. After 9/11 it seemed to me really important to talk about all the things we don't know, all the assumptions we make based on what we *think* we know.

Ultimately, the characters' lack of trust resulted in the death of Marian's son, Kevin. Did you see that one coming?

I had no idea. When I did see it coming, I tried my best to not let it happen. I tried to get out of it. But I finally thought, I can't. What Kevin represents is hope and innocence, and that's what we lost. I'd' have been cheating this book, there'd have been no point in writing it if I let that not happen.

Eventually, Laura tracks down the cop to whom Jimmy entrusted the true story he wrote about what really happened the night Jack died. But the book ends without revealing whether what the reader knows is going to come out in a news story.

I assume it isn't. What would be the point? Harry had let himself believe what Laura wanted to believe, that the truth always has to come out. But he knew that was wrong, and the fact that he had let himself believe that and screwed something up so badly as a result was too much for him. He couldn't deal. That's why he killed himself.

You said you felt you had to write the book to write yourself out of 9/11. Did that work?

Absolutely. Isak Dinesen once said, "All sorrows can be borne if you put them into a story." Writing gives you both distance and intimacy at the same time.

Would you talk a little bit about the logistics of your writing life?

I have a schedule. I worked as an architect for so many years that I found that I couldn't just wake up and roll over to my writing desk. I take a shower, I get dressed, I go buy a cup of tea. I sit by the river and watch the boats go by. I watch the birds. Then I go back and work till about two in the afternoon. That's about as long as I can do. In the afternoon, I deal with e-mail and other projects I'm working on that are not my book.

Does research qualify as writing the book?

Research qualifies until I start writing. The first couple of months, if the weather's good, I'll sit by the river and read. Or I'll go meet people. Once I start the book, the research happens in the afternoons. I read or Google or whatever. If there's something I absolutely need to know before I go on, I'll find that out. But usually there isn't. So I write four hours a day, seven days a week—except Sundays. I play basketball Sunday morning, so I don't start until eleven.

Do you set a goal in terms of how many words you write in a day?

I shoot for a thousand words. If I don't get it, I don't have a cow. But if I get fewer than five hundred, I'm very disappointed. You need a certain momentum. Seven-fifty is good, but if I'm up to, say, eight-ninety-nine, I push myself to see if I can make a thousand.

I tell people, if you can't find a way to put in an hour a day, it's not going to get done. And maybe that's okay. God knows the world is not lacking in books—and even if your book is the greatest novel never written, we'll never know we missed it. So if you can't do it except under a certain set of circumstances, move on.

I have a twenty-pound cat, the best mouser I've ever had because he has the feeling he was put on this earth to catch mice. After he got his first mouse, he went right back to the mouse hole. I said, "Look, this isn't going to happen again. You've got your face right there. What mouse is going to come out?" And he's looking at me like that cartoon—what the cat hears: *blah, blah, blah, blah, blah*. Of course the mouse came out again. That's what mice do. And he was there. That's what writing is like: you need to be there.

Jane Smiley

Jane Smiley is the author of ten novels, two volumes of novellas and stories, and three works of nonfiction. Born in Los Angeles, she grew up in St. Louis in a family where gossip and storytelling were the favorite pastimes. She was educated at Vassar College and at the University of Iowa, where she received her PhD. Her honors include the Pulitzer Prize, the National Book Critics Circle Award, the Heartland Award, the Friends of American Writers Prize, the Midland Authors Award, and three O. Henry Prizes. In 2001, she was elected a member of the American Academy of Arts and Letters. She taught creative writing at Iowa State University from 1981 to 1996. Currently, she lives in California.

Barn Blind, 1980; *At Paradise Gate*, 1981; *Duplicate Keys*, 1984; *The Age of Grief*, 1987 (novella and stories); *The Greenlanders*, 1988; *Ordinary Love and Good Will*, 1989 (novellas); *A Thousand Acres*, 1991; *Moo*, 1995; *The All-True Travels and Adventures of Lidie Newton*, 1998; *Horse Heaven*, 2003; *Good Faith*, 2003; *Ten Days in the Hills*, 2007

The variety of things you've written about over the course of your career interests me. One reviewer said about your work, "Is there anything Jane Smiley doesn't know?"

Partly that comes because I'm interested in a lot of things, so I have a pretty full body of general knowledge. My husband and I always used to sit in front of *Jeopardy*, and I didn't always beat the winner, but I often did. But anybody that's had access to a library has access to the information in my books.

Given the fact that lots of things interest you, are there ways you decide upon pursuing one idea and not another? How do you know what is "yours"?

I wouldn't say there's a way I know things are mine, but I know things aren't mine when I don't feel especially interested or intrigued by them, even though they might be objectively interesting. And I don't think of a book as a big thing anymore; I think of a book as a small thing. So I suppose I could write a book about anything.

How did you come to think of a book that way?

There was an actual moment. I had just finished xeroxing *The Greenlanders*, which was 1,100 manuscript pages. It had taken me about five years to write it, and in that time I had also gone through a lot of personal turmoil. I felt that a lot of the personal turmoil had affected the book and had come as a result of the book in some ways, and now here it was. I had it on one of those little AV dollies and I looked at it and I thought — still kind of reeling from all this stuff I had gone through — "It's just so small. A little 8 by 11 by 2 ½-inch thing. It's so small to encompass all of the last five years." That's when I realized that a book is so much smaller than the time of which the book was a product, and if *The Greenlanders* is small in my life, then everything is small.

It's interesting that you saw that as a positive thing. You could have thought, "Oh no, all that time and this is all I got from it." Instead, it seems to have been a liberating moment.

It certainly makes it easier to write more books. When you start out, when you write your dissertation, you can't believe you're going to try to write 250 pages. Then later you start thinking about your ideas in a more structured, whole way, and 250 pages seems short. You get used to having a discipline; you stop thinking it's all going to be written in one whoosh.

How do you write then? How does your research fit in? What do you know, beginning?

I'll do a certain amount of research to get started, then I'll write a little bit and do some more. Gradually, the research gets less and the writing gets more. I often make charts. With *Moo*, for example, I made a chart so I could see who hadn't appeared for a while. It came out looking sort of like a field.

So, in most cases, you know when you start out where a book is going? How many surprises are there?

A lot of little surprises, but there are no big surprises.

Do you do a lot of rewriting?

That varies from book to book. On *The Greenlanders*, I revised the first fifty pages a lot, but not after that. There are whole long, long sections—hundreds of pages long—that I didn't touch a word of.

Do you ever get stuck enough that you have to break the whole book down and come at it a completely different way?

I've never had to come at it a completely different way, but I've broken a thing down in order to understand what's going on. In *Duplicate Keys* I made little cards. There was a card for every scene that analyzed how it fit into the plot and what information was given to the reader: what was there, what I wasn't sure of, what I needed to check on. So that helped me tighten that up.

In *Moo*, I took apart the book into character threads. I had a chart as I was working through the novel, chapter by chapter, and then in the rewrite I shuffled out each character's story, read it, and decided what was missing. I rewrote those and in the third rewrite, I shuffled it all back together again and rewrote it again for continuity.

It seemed like a juggling act to me when I read it. I kept thinking, "How is she doing this?"

I consciously set up the structure to mimic an ecosystem, a kind of net-like structure. Some people did not care for that structure at all; they felt it didn't have a certain kind of gravity. But I wanted to be writing about an ecosystem. I think one of the failures or flaws of Western thought is that everything has to be about one guy, everything has to revolve about a central person, and the philosophical point of thinking about ecosystems is that no person is God, no person stands out, no person is much more significant than any other person. So part of my point was asking the reader to accept the whole, rather than to use one person as the organizational principle.

You seem to be motivated by ideas, challenged by the concept of structure.

I knew I was going to write *The Greenlanders* really early on, before I wrote *Barn Blind*, but I also knew that I had to be a fairly accomplished novelist in order to write it. So, in some ways, I was already planning for a long career, because I wasn't planning to write my big novel first crack out of the box. Often, in America, people feel that if they don't write their big novel first, they won't get another chance, so I was being, I suppose, both humble and arrogant in thinking that I would ever get to *The Greenlanders* if I started out with a little old novel about somebody's horse farm. I always assumed the best.

So, given the idea that writing novels was going to be my career, there were certain tasks, certain things I had to learn. In *Barn Blind* I had to learn how to get a bunch of characters through a period of time without losing sight of any of them or allowing any of them to take over. The chart I made for *Barn Blind* was a little different, more like a flow chart. Each person had a little design, so I would draw their design.

My task for *At Paradise Gate* was more of a structuring task. There are very few characters and it's a very short period of time. Nothing happens, and I didn't *want* anything to happen. It wasn't about things happening. But time had to pass. So I said, "All right, here's twenty-four hours and two hundred and forty pages. Every ten pages is an hour, each page is six minutes. So by page whatever, the night has to be finished and the dawn has to be here. If the time passes, then the reader will have the sense that things are moving forward."

So in some ways, coming to that novel as a reader, I think I would think, "Gee this is an interesting exercise in the novel. It's really modern in a way. Sort of Proustian. Or Virginia Woolfian." But that wasn't what I wanted to be writing. And I didn't see that as a way for me to go forward in a career of writing novels. *The Greenlanders* was going to be much more demanding than that.

So you really felt you were teaching yourself all the things you'd need to know when, eventually, you got to The Greenlanders?

Yes. And next I said, "Okay, I've got to learn to write a plot. What do I know about plots?" Well, the only thing I knew about plots were murder mysteries because I liked those. So I thought I'd try one. And it did present—well, somebody at dinner last night asked me if I'd ever had writer's block, and I said no. But actually I did once, while I was writing *Duplicate Keys*. It had completely to do with plot construction. And I can't remember exactly at what point I got stuck, or what the problem was. I think it was that I realized that the reader was possibly going to guess who did it before he would in a traditional murder mystery—at the end. That's a successful murder mystery. But I realized that, probably, my readers were going to figure it out before the end, so I had to come up with a solution for that. It was that Alice figures out who the murderer is, and when she does, the book turns away from a traditional murder mystery novel to a suspense novel. Then I realized that my model was not the classic murder mystery, but more a Hitchcockian film, like *Rear Window*, where the main character is in a new kind of danger when he has "the knowledge."

So there was a formal solution to my writer's block. So I can say that I once had writer's block, but really it was just not understanding the form and then thinking about it some more and then understanding it and being able to go on.

Writing novels seems to be a long process of trial and error for most people. Do you think it is something that can be taught? There are opportunities for people to learn how to write stories, but you rarely see a class in novel writing. Why is that?

Once in my workshop I let a student write a novel, and in another workshop a student had already started one. But it's almost impossible to have a class about the novel. The novel should be a whole thing, with one kind of energy from beginning to end, and having students critiquing other students' novels is inverse with that energy. It tempts the student who's writing the novel to go back and fix rather than to go on. I think it's really dangerous. There might be a few novelists in the world who successfully clean as they go, but I've met many more who are finally silenced by the need to make it good in the first draft. So I don't think a course in the novel would be very productive. It would be productive for people, like critics perhaps, who are wondering about the composition process, but pretty destructive for people actually writing novels.

F. Scott Fitzgerald said, "There's a peasant in every novelist." I wonder what you make of that, in terms of the kind of work a novelist does.

I have no idea what he meant. Maybe that there is someone without manners in every novelist, because, as a novelist, you have to set aside all those issues of propriety that you grew up with in the middle class. You have to eavesdrop, you have to say honest things about people that maybe they won't want to hear. You have to show an unseemly interest in money, sex, and religion. But I think the novel is quintessentially middle class. It explores middle-class life, so you're kind of torn because everything you have to set aside to look at is a big part of yourself as a middle-class person.

Interesting. I've always thought he was referring to the kind of stubbornness or stick-to-it-iveness that is required of the novelist.

I never mistake writing for work. Not real work. Real work is all day long, wholly sweating. I think writing is difficult and laborious at times, and, in certain parts of your career, calls up reserves of persistence, but let's not flatter ourselves and call it the same as plowing or pouring cement.

I have to say that I don't find inspiration for my work in the way that other writers think about their work or think about themselves as writers. I like other writers and I love reading other people's novels, but I've always felt there was a kind of grandiosity in writers' estimations of the importance of their work and, therefore, themselves. I love novels. I love to get in bed with novels and roll around with novels and revel in novels and be with novels and hang out with novels, but I don't adore or look up to novels.

To me, a novel is like a prolonged form of gossip, which both diminishes the novel and elevates gossip. I've always had a great respect for gossip. I think that what gossip does is enable people to assimilate events around them and to create an emotional and moral fabric out of their daily lives. And they do it—it's kind of a collaborative enterprise, but it's essential. I've always felt that if I run into a person who hates gossip, who doesn't gossip, they're at a disadvantage in terms of knowing how to act and what to do. They usually fall back on moral precepts.

Well, I'm really glad to hear you say that. I always feel horribly immoral because I like gossip so much.

Yes. [People who don't like gossip] usually fall back on some kind of moral righteousness and then they wonder why everybody around them is so screwed up. Really, what they haven't been able to do is take the moral precept and the particular case and find a balance between them, and gossip is what we use to find the balance between the moral precepts and the particular cases. That, to me, is what novels are for.

They used to—in the eighteenth and nineteenth centuries—criticize the novels as low. Many people criticize gossip as low. What they expected young girls and women to be reading were sermons. But sermons weren't helping them negotiate their daily lives and novels were. So that's why they were drawn to novels. I'm not saying that novels are always about particular cases. You can't live in the general all the time, or you're just lost. So anyway, that goes back to the idea of writers elevating their writer status.

The intense involvement a novelist has with her work, the constant puzzling out of problems in an alternate reality, does take its toll on real life, though. In your mind, what's the price of doing what you do? How do you work your day-to-day life around it?

In some ways the price hasn't been exacted in my case because my kids haven't read my work. I think there will be some kind of price exacted there. Maybe—probably—it'll be two edged, in that when my children read my work they'll understand me better, but they'll also feel exposed. So there's a price that will be paid, though I have no idea what it will be.

The other price is just the same as any working woman, and that is the compromises you make in order to work, which appear to your kids as things that they had to give up. They don't have the perspective to see that the compromises our mothers made in order to have us appeared to us as things we had to give up, too. If our mothers were stay-at-home moms, we felt a kind of dullness in their lives, a kind of narrowness and domesticity and sometimes a kind of neediness in them, and our fear for their fate once we, the children, were gone. All those things.

This wasn't true for me, because my mother was a newspaperwoman and did have a career, but it was true for my peers. So we perceived, or let's say we felt, a certain set of things in our mothers' lives as flaws, or we resented in our mothers' lives a certain set of things that were lacking, and we thought we could supply those things to our children's lives: a sense of the larger social and cultural life entering into the family, a sense of Mom being more intelligent and exciting, and also a sense that all of our needs didn't have to be supplied by our children the way we felt that all of our moms' needs had to be supplied by us. But, lo and behold, it works out that our children resent a whole other set of things. So it's a conundrum.

In an interview some time ago, you talked about reading biographies of famous authors with both fear and longing. How does your life as an author measure up against those lives? How is it like and not like you dreamed it would be?

If I remember that quote correctly I think I said that I realized pretty quickly that I didn't want those lives, and I guess my life has turned out much differently than the lives that I read about. I also think that [my perception of those lives] could be the fault of or simply the effect of biography as a form. I'm not sure that the depiction of those lives was accurate.

What biographies don't do is evoke what it actually felt like to be alive. In some sense that's not what biographies are for, that's what novels are for. The novels an author writes that evoke what it feels like to be alive are in a lot of ways happier and more positive and funnier than the biographies written about the various events in the author's life. I'm a person with a generally happy temperament and a positive and energetic way of moving forward, but I can see it's possible that some biographer will write some grim thing about how morally depraved and generally horrible my life was, and that wouldn't be how my life felt to me at all.

But I also think that our generation of writers hasn't had to leave the philistines the way Americans did in the '20s because the cultural world has expanded so much. We have much more ordinary lives because we decided, male and female, that we were going to go ahead and have kids and still be writers. We weren't going to be in Paris or even in New York—we were just going to be where the day-care was!

Lee Smith

Lee Smith is the author of twelve novels, a novella, and two collections of stories. Born in the coal-mining region of southwest Virginia, she has sought to honor her Appalachian heritage in many of her books. Other books have more contemporary settings, chronicling the "New South"; often, her female characters struggle with identity issues, caught between the old ways and the new. Honors include the Academy Award in Fiction from the American Academy of Arts and Letters, the Lila Wallace–Reader's Digest Award, the Robert Penn Warren Prize for Fiction, the Weatherford Award for Appalachian Literature, and the North Carolina Award for Literature. Smith likes "to cook and eat too much"; she is also an avid gardener. For many years, she taught writing and English courses at North Carolina State University. She lives in North Carolina with her husband.

The Last Day the Dogbushes Bloomed, 1968; *Something in the Wind*, 1971; *Fancy Strut*, 1973; *Black Mountain Breakdown*, 1980; *Cakewalk*, 1981 (stories); *Oral History*, 1983; *Family Linen*, 1985; *Fair and Tender Ladies*, 1988; *Me and My Baby View the Eclipse*, 1990 (stories); *The Devil's Dream*, 1992; *Saving Grace*, 1995; *The Christmas Letters*, 1996 (novella); *News of the Spirit*, 1997; *The Last Girls*, 2002; *On Agate Hill*, 2006

How did your childhood, your family, give you the information you needed to be a writer?

I can't honestly say that my childhood and my family gave me "enough information about life to last me the rest of my days," but they certainly formed my consciousness of the world. I don't really think that we have any choice about the kind of writers we are. I think it all has to do with what family we were born into and where we lived and how we first heard language—who was speaking and under what circumstances and the kind of talk they were hearing. In my own fortunate case, it was the

Appalachian speech of a half-century ago: melodic, picturesque, and very precise. I never quite attain that cadence in my own work, but it's always there in my mind, running like a stream beneath the words.

Also, I was born into a community of big talkers—both men and women. My father came from a huge family of storytelling Democrats who would sit on my grandmother's porch after Sunday dinner and bet on anything—which bird would fly first off a telephone wire, for instance. My mother had come from the eastern shore of Virginia to teach home economics and civilize them all, but it was tough going. She was a real storyteller, too; each foray out into the world yielded its little narrative. A trip to the grocery store, to the beauty shop, or to church turned into the most interesting anecdote. I remember her coming home from church one Sunday with the words, "I declare, I don't know if I ought to be mad or not! June Bevins just told me I look real good from the back!" In my mind's eye, my mother is always in her kitchen, always smoking Salem cigarettes and drinking coffee and cooking, all caught up in conversation with one of the many friends or family members who just dropped by. I had a little writing table there. They'd forget I was there; I'd just be sitting there, drawing away, and I heard all this.

Every event was turned immediately into a story. When my father came home from town, he told us the stories he'd heard in the dime store or in the courthouse or on the street. Even information was conveyed in the form of anecdote, come to think of it. You couldn't ask how to drive to so-and-so's house, for instance, without hearing a long tale about how somebody's cousin was bit by a mad dog on that very road and had to have six shots *in her stomach!*

I also spent a lot of time in the courthouse where I had my special little chair and my table in my granddaddy's office. He was the treasurer of the county for fifty-two years. There I heard a completely different kind of talk. There was a lot of talk about who burned their house down to get the money, who was getting divorced and who shot who—all this kind of stuff that I didn't hear at home. It was great. Then every Sunday and lots of other days, we would go to my grandmother's across the river from the town—just right there in the middle of town. She just kind of held court all the time and you had to go to see her every day you were in town which drove my mother to colitis at an early age. But, like on Sunday afternoon, the whole family would be there. I was really raised by older people. Lots of them. I think if I'd had playmates, I would have just run off and played.

My childhood gave me a sense of story, above all, and to me the story is always oral. If it is not literally told by a first-person narrator, it is still told to me in a human voice—not my voice, but the voice of the story itself, I guess. What I have to do is listen hard and write it down.

Out of the thousands of ideas, images, bits of conversation that you encounter in the course of a lifetime, how do you choose what becomes the basis for a novel? How does a novel gather for you?

Each novel is different, and each one gathers differently for me. I always have several novels vaguely in mind. Then, for whatever reason, one of them will become so pushy and demanding that I really have to write it. Finally, it's intense: I sometimes feel like I've got a gun trained on my head until I get it down, first draft or outline at least. For instance, I had long known that I wanted to write about religious ecstasy/obsession, but a novel didn't occur to me until I was over in eastern Kentucky interviewing a woman snake handler. We were in a McDonald's in a mall, eating Chicken McNuggets; it was hard to believe I had just seen her lifting up a double handful of copperheads. "Why do you do this?" I asked her. "It's so dangerous. You could be killed." "Well, I'll tell you," she answered with a sweet, open smile. "I do this out of an intense desire for holiness. And I'll tell you something else, too—when you've had the serpent in your hand, the whole world kind of takes on an edge for you." At that moment, I knew I had to write the novel which became *Saving Grace*.

The idea for *Family Linen* came from a real murder which took place in Raeford, North Carolina. A woman under hypnosis had remembered that as a child she saw her mother kill her father, chop him up, and stuff him down the outhouse. She turned her mother in to the FBI, and sure enough, they dug him up. I went over to dinner at Reynolds Price's house that evening, waving the clipping—and *he* was waving it, too! "I'm going to write about this," he said. "No, I am," I said. "I'll flip you for it," he said, and so we flipped a quarter, and I won. "You've got one year," Reynolds said sternly in that voice like God, and so I set right to work.

The Last Girls grew from a raft trip you took as a young woman, similar to the one in the story. What was it like to work with autobiographical material?

For thirty years, people had been saying, "When are you going to write about the raft trip? It sounds so picturesque. It sounds like something a novelist really should be writing." The problem was, it had simply been a great trip. It didn't have all this psychological stuff going on. No conflict, which is necessary for fiction. Then we all got so old. I went to my fortieth—or maybe it was my thirty-fifth—reunion, and suddenly the whole process of who we thought we were versus who we had become, and what the expectations for us were as girls then versus who we are now, became really, really interesting to me. I began to see those strands gathering into a book. I wanted to have several characters who could represent several different ways of living your life.

One is a romance writer, a comic but sad figure.

I wanted to write about this ideal of writing that we were all spoon-fed—that we'd live happily ever after. I felt a romance writer would be a good vehicle for exposing that.

Legend has it that you found a packet of letters at a garage sale for seventy-five cents and that was the genesis of Fair and Tender Ladies. *What did you think when you found the letters? Did you know you had found a treasure?*

When I found the packet of letters at a yard sale, I didn't know I had a "treasure," I just felt like I ought to go ahead and buy them. I didn't know exactly why, but I've learned to trust my intuition, so I did it. I had been thinking about a novel for a long time, a novel about the life of a mountain woman like many of the older women I'd known as I was growing up, but I'd been stumped by how to handle the passage of time in a book which would span an entire life. When I read the letters, which one woman had saved over her own real life—mostly letters written to her by her sisters—I felt that I knew all of them almost instantaneously. And they sometimes skipped years between letters . . . suddenly I could see how to do it, and I started writing *Fair and Tender Ladies* about a week later. I have a somewhat mystical belief that if you have a novel in mind, everything you see and read and hear somehow contributes to it, if you're paying attention.

Both Agate Hill *and* Fair and Tender Ladies *are frame stories based on objects from the Civil War. Did it feel as if you were writing a mirror image of* Fair and Tender Ladies *while you were working on* Agate Hill?

It didn't, but now I can see that. The main similarity was that [with each] the moment I started the book just took off. I was swept away by the story. I would just sit down and it would happen. That almost never happens, but it did with both books.

Would you talk about the research you did for the books?

My way is to try to immerse myself completely in the time and place. Lord knows, if it's Civil War and Reconstruction, you could do research for twenty years and never stop. I was a fellow for years at the Center for Documentary Studies at Duke; I'm just fascinated with documentary studies and stories that objects can tell. There were times when research almost overtook the book. It's seductive beyond belief. Writing *Agate Hill* saved my life after my son died; I think those circumstances have a lot to do with the intensity of the book. I found I was in need of a narrative that was not my own. The same thing was true of *Fair and Tender Ladies.* My mother was dying as I was writing that book.

How do you define yourself as a writer and the material that you recognize as your own?

I would have to honestly answer that I am a southern writer, especially an Appalachian writer, as my work is so oral, so formed (or informed) by human speech. Quite honestly, I think I am a storyteller rather than a real writer. I am most interested in women's lives, in the clash of expectation and reality, in the relationship of past (memory) to the present, in how we become who we are — the struggle that occurs when our biology comes in conflict with other goals that we might have.

That was true of girls in the South, traditionally. I think that perhaps it has lessened somewhat, but it's still very hard. The expectations are differ-ent, but young women now are still trying to do everything.

Your biographer, Dorothy Combs Hill, begins her work on your life with, "Literature springs from a wound." Where would you say that wound comes from?

I'm not sure it's true that literature springs from a wound. But I believe that every writer writes to *correct* something, or simply to be heard on a subject she feels passionately about. Some of us are forever trying to reach our father, or come to terms with a past trauma, or fathom the nature of love . . . we all have our obsessions. For one thing, I think I have been searching, in my own work, for what I can believe in. And sometimes I think I write fiction the way other people write in their journals: years later, when I read some story or novel [of mine], I'll think, "Oh, of course, that's what was bothering me then." When I was in my early thirties I wrote a novel named *Black Mountain Breakdown* in which a young woman ends up being literally paralyzed—hysterical paralysis—lying in bed and being fed Jell-O by the neighbors. I didn't understand till much later that that image was *me*, caught in a marriage which should have ended years before.

You have often written and spoken about the influence of religion on your life. Do you see religion as "wounding" in some way?

I don't see religion as wounding, but rather as an avenue to a kind of intensity I'm always after—in love, in my writing. I feel like we go through the world with blinders on, or earmuffs, most of the time. I want to get down to the real thing, to plug into the main socket.

Many of the characters in your novels are trying to "head home." Would you talk about this in terms of your fiction and your life?

Many of my characters are trying to get home, and of course they never can—I believe fiction by its very nature is about alienation, about being "different"; if a character feels perfectly at home in her world, then there's no conflict, so there's no possibility for fiction. Also, the writer feels alienated—at least alienated enough to stand outside the events of her life and see them as the stuff of fiction. She can be *from* but not really *of* the place of her work. She must know that place intimately, but not be totally satisfied there. Standing outside the circle is the perfect place for the artist. [It gives] that necessary "distance" which is necessary for fiction.

You have been credited with creating mythic characters and motifs. Certainly, the idea of a quest figures into a number of your novels. Is this something you have in mind as you work?

I am not really aware of mythic characters or motifs—though I taught mythology in the seventh grade for years, and I imagine some of that sunk in! I try not to think conceptually or abstractly about my work when I am doing it. It messes me up to think this way, and I lose the story. The only time I ever wrote a novel with a theme consciously in mind, the characters felt wooden to me. That was *Black Mountain Breakdown*, a cautionary tale about what happens to girls who are too passive. And of course it's nearly impossible to bring a passive character to life!

How do you work through a novel? That is, do you write through to the end, then go back and fill in the holes, or do you revise as you go along?

Each book seems to arrive with its own ideas as to how it has to get written. But in general I do a lot of prewriting. Endless scribbling on endless yellow pads about each character, where they were born and went to school and what they like to eat and watch on TV, what scares and what delights them and what they believe in, etc., until these people are literally walking around in my head, impatient for the novel to begin. Then I write a kind of outline, maybe forty pages, a rough sketch all the way through, before I start. I also have lots of diagrams and maps on posterboard. The physical place of a novel (its setting) is important to me; I have to have it clearly in my mind. And I always write the last couple of lines of the book out on a piece of paper and tape it up on the wall, so I know where I'm going as I write. Right now I can look up at my office wall and see the last line of the novel I've been working on for three years now. I've got a ways to go until I get there.

Having said that, I'm *still* surprised by what my characters "up and do," as my daddy would have put it. They're forever running off with people or breaking the law or having thoughts that surprise me—I can't really keep them inside their outline, nor do I really want to. Mostly, the outline just gives me some hope that I might finish the book. Otherwise, it's terrifying when you're in the middle and you've been writing it forever and you think you're probably crazy and there's no end in sight.

How would you define plot? How do you create it?

Somebody said there are only two plots in fiction: a) somebody takes a trip, and b) a stranger comes to town. I think that just about covers it! I'm also reminded of something Doris Betts once said: "I think about all the characters until I know what each one would be doing on any given day of their lives; then I write the story about the day when something *different* happens.

Have you ever had writer's block?

Actually, I've never had writer's block—but then, I'm not one of those writers who has to write every day. I think I probably write too damn much as it is. If I don't have anything pressing to say, I don't write. I'd rather read than anything, anyway. In fact, when I was little, the main reason I started writing in the first place was because I couldn't stand for my favorite books to end, so I'd write additional chapters onto them.

In his "Letter to a Fiction Writer," Richard Bausch said that there are thousands of reasons why people begin to write, some of them rather shabby ones, too—there usually is only one reason why they continue, and that is that the work has become necessary. What pushes you to set out on the long haul that is a novel again and again?

I agree with Dick here; the work *has* become necessary for me. I am a fiction addict. Nothing gives me the thrill, the intensity, the excitement of writing. I love that moment when everything else falls away.

What would you say to a student who asked you if he had talent? How do you define talent?

I'd never dream of telling a young writer he didn't have the talent to become a writer. I'm not even sure what talent is. I think it's a sense of language, an ear for dialogue, an interesting way of looking at the world, a feel for story . . . but who knows who's got that? Somebody who doesn't have it at twenty might have it at forty, after the world has roughed him up a little bit . . . and then whether he has the necessary drive and persistence is another matter altogether. Or maybe the world won't give him the option of being a writer; maybe he has to work at something he knows will pay the bills. Being a writer has everything to do with luck, time, and resilience as well as talent.

Theodore Weesner

Theodore Weesner is the author of six novels and one short story collection. Born in Flint, Michigan, he left high school at sixteen and enlisted in the U.S. Army. Later, he graduated from Michigan State University and the University of Iowa's Writers' Workshop. His work has been published in England, and in translation in Germany, Japan, Romania, and elsewhere, and he has received National Endowment for the Arts, Guggenheim, and Pennsylvania Council on the Arts fellowships. He has taught at the University of New Hampshire and Emerson College, where in 1994 he received the school's Distinguished Faculty Award. Writing full time since 1996, Weesner lives in Portsmouth, New Hampshire, where he walks daily by the water, sits often in downtown cafés to edit manuscripts, and has never escaped a feeling of skipping school and doing something illegal.

The Car Thief, 1972; *A German Affair*, 1976; *The True Detective*, 1987; *Winning the City*, 1990; *Children's Hearts*, 1992 (stories); *Novemberfest*, 1994; *Harbor Lights*, 2000

Many novelists describe a moment of combustion: a number of things crash in and you sense a novel forming. Harbor Lights *is a novel that has its roots in an actual news story. Would you describe how that and other novels formed for you?*

For a time I had been walking around wanting to write about possessiveness, because it seemed to visit people uninvited and do incredible damage. I was also following news stories, reading with an eye for such things — of which there are many. When the love-triangle story broke, I was taken with it at once, and felt something of a mission because the perp in the incident — a deeply damaged man, I thought — was treated without the vaguest degree of understanding or sympathy — as if he actually wanted his wife to cheat on him for thirty years, and actually wanted to kill her. "Two Die as Love Triangle Ends in Gunfire." The headline captured my interest, though the story—an open-and-shut case to most people—remained in the news but a couple days. I tucked the clippings away in a file and now and then added thoughts about characters and how I might present them in a story. Several years went by before I finally took it on as a short novel.

My basketball novel, *Winning the City*, came out of a larger consideration of writing some sports stories that dealt with losing rather than winning—the painful side of sports that is almost always overlooked, even in fiction, if sports is the subject. Ask any man or woman about experiences in losing in sports, even as fans, and you'll see a parade of broken hearts. You will also see experiences which have changed them as human beings to far more profound degrees than experiences of winning.

My young kid in this novel really is the winner of the city, because in losing he comes around to accepting who he is, where he comes from. He takes up smoking and says adios to basketball and is a better man than he ever would have been had he been on the winning team, is therefore the ultimate winner. Few readers quite got that, however—couldn't deal with the big game being lost—readers who were, I'd suggest, victims of Hollywood. A couple even had the gall to tell me they did not like the novel because the main character ended up as a loser! I hate ever to say readers didn't get it—they should be made to get it by the author—but in that novel, sports-story brainwashing proved itself so prevalent, I'm afraid, that most—not all—readers just didn't get it.

Another sports story I wrote, "Playing for Money," was about a young guy winning another kid's entire paycheck from carrying out groceries, and [then]coming to the unhappy realization that rather than win something, by winning big, he had lost, in terms of the heightened isolation he was left to endure. That, too, was an autobiographical story and an experience that, when I took a look at it, when I conceived it, presented itself in that moment of combustion you indicated.

Other times I've written from without, from research. For *The True Detective*, I researched four children who had been abducted and murdered just north of Detroit. I interviewed the parents and the siblings. I interviewed cops and rode with the cops. I couldn't make it work as a nonfiction book, however, and ended up writing it as a novel. It was a fictional experience from very much outside myself, while *Harbor Lights*, I think of as grafting. That is, it came from without and also from within. I identified with Warren, the wronged husband, and understood where he was coming from. I grafted his fundamental experience onto myself and worked from there. The inventing I did came from within me, through him as a character.

Novemberfest is a book about a middle-aged man whose life falls apart. Where did that book begin?

I always wanted to write about my army experience in Germany. It was such a satisfying, meaningful experience for me. I was seventeen when I arrived there. I was a high-school dropout and went into the army during the Korean War, and ended up the only one in my company to go to Germany. The announcements came out and they said, "Weesner, you're going to Germany. The rest of you are going to Korea." I thought, "Lucky me," and found out later that I hadn't been sent to Korea because I had yet to turn eighteen. I conceived *Novemberfest* at the time the Berlin Wall was coming down. The reunification of Germany is a crucial part of the novel. The Wall coming down was such a staggering event. It still takes people by surprise that something considered so impossible actually began to unravel and happen. It was tremendously exciting to me. I'd become a kind of Germanophile in the intervening years, so I read these stories with great relish. I knew the landscape. I'd spent a lot of time there by then; I'd made trips back with my family, and had spent a full year in Salzburg.

So in a sense it's the same, then? An event triggered the story?

I had to figure out how to incorporate the Berlin Wall, and I worked all around it. There's a background story and a present story, and the background story was my own autobiographical experience as a young kid coming of age and getting my life under control.

How did you create the separate time frames? Did you write all of one, then the other? Or did you go back and forth as you wrote?

I think I wrote them pretty much as they appear. I had the two separate narratives in mind early on, outlined and sketched. I'd go so far with the present story and think, "Okay, I can put it on hold." Then I'd work on the other narrative, going back and forth. I'm pleased to hear you say you found them both compelling. I've always felt, maybe because it was really coming from within, that the background story in Germany was more compelling and more satisfying. With the present story, I got largely into invention with the divorce. Not that I didn't know those things in various ways, but I wasn't writing autobiographically.

There is always the sense of missed connections in your novels. Things could turn out well, but they don't. Little things happen that haunt the characters forever. What Matt says to his brother about the valentine in The True Detective *is a good example. The little boy is thinking about who might have sent it to him secretly, and Matt makes fun of him, saying it was his teacher who sent it, that she'd probably sent one to everyone. It was the last thing he ever said to his brother. It breaks your heart to think of him living with that.*

I remember getting that detail from a brother of one of the little boys abducted and murdered in Michigan. I used a tape recorder and question- naires that I sent ahead of time. I talked to the brother, who was a nice kid. The mother was very poor, much like they are in the novel. The valentine thing came up, and I remember writing that over and over, endlessly try- ing to capture it. You talk about something that breaks your heart! That's exactly what I want to do. It's what I work for. I don't know if everyone does, but I have identified books I love, books that have done that to me. Those are the books I really admire and what I've always gone for in my own writing.

What are some of those books?

I always loved *A Death in the Family*. That was an important book for me. Stylistically, it had a great influence on me. I like *A Fan's Notes* a lot. It's so genuine, so heartfelt. I love "Barn Burning."

In The True Detective, *Matt, trying to help, says his brother might have run off with a rock group. When the detective asks why he would want to do that, Matt says, "Because if you were a part of that you would belong to some- thing. You would be in." That in/out motif is always present in your novels, though it comes up in different ways.*

In *The Car Thief*, Alex goes to connect with his brother and then he realizes he's not his brother. That's my personal favorite of all the scenes I've ever written. For me, it's the most powerful. He's with his brother and they're being brothers. Then he sees the mother lying there naked and it comes to him and he has to leave them. He has some kind of obligation to go where his father is, which I guess is in the same vein as these other things we've been talking about.

Even the little girl, Alice, in Novemberfest, *experiences a kind of alienation. She's not "socializing well" at preschool. Did that character grow out of your short story "Quiet Alice?"*

Yes, the story came first and I incorporated it into the novel. It was an autobiographical story about when I was living in Durham. My daughter went to nursery school at UNH when she was four years old.

Did she fail to identify the worth of the coins like the little girl in the novel did?

She failed the coin test. I was called in and told she had to stay back because of that. It was rather stupid. I ended up all those years later writing it as a story and it fit perfectly into the novel.

How much and what kind of revision do you generally do on your novels?

I'm an endless reviser. With *Harbor Lights*, I thought I was close to home when I got a first draft done. I wrote it in longhand, very small script. It came to exactly one hundred pages. Then I transcribed it onto my computer and built the story as I went along. The second draft came to exactly two hundred pages. Interesting numbers.

Then I learned I needed a sympathetic presence in the story. I thought I had one, but my agent, editor, somebody, called me on it. They didn't think there was anyone for the reader to identify with. So I picked up on the daughter and made her in to a larger figure in the novel. I had to readjust everything in the novel, but I don't mind doing that kind of rewriting. I always feel like I'm getting much deeper and doing better work.

What was the hardest book for you to revise, or the one you had the most trouble getting the way you wanted it to be?

The True Detective and *Novemberfest* were both big books, six-hundred-page manuscripts, and I had some difficulty with them. In *Novemberfest*, it was getting the two storylines to work so the reader would conclude an experience with one character in one time and then turn the page and pick up on something that had been cut off previously. I had to compose those exits in such a way that it would be satisfying and yet leave something dangling so the reader would be happy to return later.

Did you use any devices to help you figure out whether or not the alternate time frames were working?

I do a lot of outlining and making of charts, and I study them. Sometimes I go through and read openings and endings of the different points of view. This was especially helpful in *The True Detective*, where so many different characters are involved. To sustain the overall story, I had to connect moments that allowed for the development of the story and for the progression in time. Each character had to have a narrative line unfolding that was interesting on its own. I'd think about the mother, for example. What is her story and how do I make it arc in the novel? What is Matt's story? What is the detective's story? How can I interweave them so there's always progression of their individual stories as well as the overall story?

Did you isolate them, so you were looking only at one at a time?

Yes. I make a lot of note cards and notes. I sketched out the overall story from each point of view and the conflict/crisis points and would have that ready so that I could take it up and see where she was headed and what was going on in her life. And how it tied into what was going on in Matt's life.

Did you see that story as one that needed multiple points of view right from the start?

I believe I did. At the outset I was thinking of a nonfiction book, presenting different perspectives of a brutal experience. I loved Capote's *In Cold Blood*. It just blew me away, it was so good. I remember that it came in the mail one day and I read it before nightfall.

And you chose to shape the material you researched into The True Detective?

I couldn't make it work as nonfiction. I really wasn't competent to write nonfiction. I had no experience. Finally I called my editor, who'd given me a large advance, and in effect he said, "Why don't you make it into a novel?"

You hadn't considered that before then?

I'd sort of floated with it, but I was so committed to writing a nonfiction account. Then I sat down and wrote "page 1," and hardly looked back. Everything was within me.

I wrote it quickly, the first time through, at least. I was in Pittsburgh and I longed to be here, in New England. So I set the novel in Portsmouth because it was a place I could look to with some emotional pull. Then, on trips back, I'd scout the streets and walk it through and write very short chapters. I reduced it to one family, one abduction, and invented a killer. I did all that almost automatically, as a way to get out of the terrible hole I'd dug for myself.

The True Detective takes place over a few days' time. So does Harbor Lights. *Yet the other novels span years. Does the story determine how to frame it in time, based on its narrative arc, or do you try several ways of dealing with time before you find the right one?*

I like to sit back, take walks, and think about what I'm trying to capture. I often analyze, at great length, the conflict, the pain. When does it hurt most and how can I make it surface in the story? I'll take the conflict at the heart of a story and unfold it in a linear way. I taught a class called Writing the First Novel for a number of years. I would tell students, "I don't want you to come in here and think you're going to write *War and Peace*. Take any story you've written and untangle it: unfold the conflict in a linear way in your mind. When did the turn the story hinges on actually begin to occur?" For example, the story of *The True Detective* really began to happen years before, when that mother got poor. That's really the story. You can do this with anything: consider the real story and then think, when did it surface as a dramatic event in their lives?

So many student stories that I've read are compressed little novels. I've felt that if they would untangle, unpack some of these things, they would find that there's a nice novel there. That's where they should look for novels rather than trying to impose some larger consideration on their fiction, which usually screws them up. I went through that initially as a writer myself.

What do you mean by a larger consideration?

When one thinks of a novel, one usually thinks of those big books. All those pages. I took my first advance based on a couple of short stories, and it was a very exciting thing for me. I was new at the University of New Hampshire, and at that time it was three times what I earned in a year. The advance was fifteen thousand and I was paid five as an instructor. I took a year off to write the novel. I was going to write my father/son story and I started writing from the point of view of the father as a child growing up. I wrote several hundred pages. Finally, the kid was born, and I wrote some more.

Then, for the only time in my life, I was stricken with writer's block. I had taken this money, I was writing a novel, I didn't know what I was doing. It was my year off, snow was falling—and I just seized up. I was so devastated by this. I couldn't tell anyone. I was working in a little shed, and I went out there for at least a week and just sat and tried to think. Finally, one day I looked up and the snow was still falling, and I thought, put that kid in a stolen car and have him driving in a snow storm. That's what I did. My opening line approximately stayed the same from that point on.

So how would you define writer's block, then?

For me, it was just a form of anxiety. The feeling that you're failing and you don't know how to get yourself out of what you've gotten into. Not having any devices. After having that frightening experience, I don't even like to hear anyone mention it. Someone says writer's block, I just leave the room. Just quietly slip away. A week doesn't seem like a long time; people have had the experience of being blocked for years. But it was so excruciating. Seven days felt like forever.

When it went away, it just went away?

It did. I wrote my way out of it. Later I wrote a story about writer's block, and I think what I hit on in it was that you need to write one good, clean line to get out of it. One true sentence. Once you do that, things open.

What traits do you look for in the would-be novelists that you teach?

When I was teaching in Pittsburgh, a psychologist who was studying creativity thought if he could identify and recruit kids who had tremendously high SATs, they could be made into Nobel Prize winners and ultimately bring great fame to the institution. I remember saying that's not what it's about. You write out of need. You write out of hunger. It isn't your brilliance; it's the flaw in your makeup that drives you.

In terms of identifying talent in young writers, you can see the pain in their writing. You can see the desire, the hunger. It doesn't have anything to do with how well they're doing as students. At UNH, I taught English majors who were pretentious writers. They'd often write in the style of literary criticism — imitating literary criticism, trying to write what they thought a critic would be looking for. Then some kid would walk in from Engineering and just go for it, because he would have been drawn there by hunger, have a sense of the story he wanted to tell.

How do you help your students discover their best material?

My own strategy and the thing I advise students to do is to identify things that hurt, that caused pain enough to make you change how you perceive the world. When did it hurt? What made it hurt? Who were the people involved? It can be a modest hurt; it can be a big hurt. A very personal hurt, private, secret. Once you can do that, you can begin to try to create and recreate a story through characters and action.

Has the process of writing a novel changed for you over the years?

Committing to a novel occurred mindlessly when I was younger. The material was present, like a lump in the throat, and on a stroll through town I'd know what I was going to take on. Those were the days! Instinct seemed to be on the money: you did it and you scored or you failed. Now I worry over choices, and worry in retrospect that I didn't worry enough in the beginning. Writing a novel can take years: do I have the authority, will I be able to bring voice to the material? What are the practical prospects, the critical prospects for a certain novel out there in the mean world of books?

I liked the early days. As instinct processed all into single decisions, right or wrong; one day after another came up blessed with goals and with peaceful, often heated creativity. Still, looking back, it's obvious that I proceeded like an energized dope most of the time. I believe I've always possessed talent and desire, but too little awareness of professionalism and far too much ignorance of things literary and intellectual. I came from nowhere and had no examples or friends or mentors other than bad movies to follow.

Given all that, how do you think about your work in the world? What does being successful as a novelist mean?

It's one of those things that, at this point in my life, I struggle with philosophically. Certainly, any number of times, I've felt, "I got it, I did it, I pulled it off," and that's very satisfying. So success, in the end, I believe, is internal satisfaction over scenes and characters and powerful moments you feel you captured. Others may or may not feel the same, and that's how it goes. Who ever said life was fair?

Writing Exercises

The following exercises are directly based on each writer's personal observations about the writing process and specific strategies he or she described for working through a novel. They may be used in a variety of ways, depending on where you are in the process of writing your own book. Browsing is your best bet here. You probably won't know what you're looking for until — *voilà!* — you find it.

DOROTHY ALLISON

1. Consider a character you think you know well and for whom you have strong feelings, positive or negative. Write a scene with that character in it, but from the point of view of a character whose strong feelings for him/her are the opposite of yours, and see if you learn something new.

2. Defining plot, Allison said, "Something happens; something real." Generate a list of "real" things that could set a series of events in your character's life in motion. This might be as dramatic as Allison's character falling from the roof of a parking lot, or as seemingly insignificant as running into an old friend from high school at the supermarket. What matters is the power of the incident to create some kind of change in the character's life.

3. Name a trait that defines your character. For example: ambitious, anxious, easily pleased, mean spirited. Write a scene from his/her childhood that brings insight as to how that trait was formed.

4. Write a scene or monologue from the point of view of an intelligent child whose narrow life has offered few educational opportunities. Without explaining, taking care to use only words and references that such a child would know, let the reader see his/her intelligence in action.

5. Close your eyes and bring an image of your main character to your mind's eye. Consider where the character is, what the character is wearing, his/her body language and facial expression. Look for small and large details in the image that might bring insight to the character and situation. Freewrite about what the image tells you. Keep writing after you've written all you think you know, with the hope that something will float up and surprise you.

6. Identify a political issue about which you feel very strongly. Write a scene that illustrates the issue without naming the issue or providing any explanation or personal opinion.

LARRY BROWN

1. Consider all the possible points of view you might use in your novel and identify the one that seems as if it will make your job the easiest. Try that first.

2. Write your character's fantasies. What do they tell you about him/her?

3. Write a scene, real or imagined, that you really don't want to write. Write it honestly, brutally if necessary, in the simplest possible language. Like this passage from Brown's *Father and Son*, it should be as painful for the reader to read as it was for you to write: "He stopped playing around with her and just threw her on the bed. He climbed on top of her while she kicked him. She was strong for being so small but he forced her head still and smothered her mouth with his, licking her whole face and trying to unfasten his pants with the bad hand."

4. Narrate a series of events in two alternating points of view. When you're in one character's head, provide clues for what the other one is thinking and feeling through action and dialogue. For example: Tom approached his brother, his hand held out, but Brian slid his hands into his pockets and looked away.

5. Create a character who deals with boredom by inventing "mind trips" in which s/he plays out various scenarios of his/her life might have turned out if his/her family history had been different. Write a scene in which the action and outcome are affected by the main character's fantasies.

6. Larry Brown observed, "Even a person who goes around putting pistols to people's heads and executing them might have a little five-year-old niece that he is just nuts about and goes out and buys teddy bears for." Consider a person that you believe is purely evil, someone whose public actions make it easy for you to hate him or her. Then

imagine a list of small, secret, believable things he/she might do that don't excuse his/her public actions but complicate your understanding of who he/she is.

7. Load up a character with trouble, set him/her in motion in a scene, and see how he/she reacts.

PETER CAMERON

1. Create a cast of characters, related in some way, whose lives are at a turning point. Tell yourself you're writing a serial novel and make yourself write a chapter every week, tracking the characters in shifting points of view over a period of time, trusting action to guide you in creating the plot as you go.

2. Develop an idea for a novel that takes place in one weekend and that hinges on something that happened on another weekend in the main character's past.

3. Write a scene in which a character, eavesdropping, learns something that upsets him. Write another scene in which the repercussions of what he heard play out in some way.

4. Consider what a very young or very old character might bring to your novel. Better yet, just create one, place him/her in a scene . . . and see what happens.

5. Write a scene in which a large cultural event, like 9/11, figures in a small but significant way.

6. Write a monologue in the voice of a person who is both hilarious and chronically sad.

7. Write a scene in which a cherished object reveals something about the character who possesses it.

MICHAEL CHABON

1. Consider the necessity of each character in your novel. What role does he/she play? Do others play the same or a similar role? Consider what would be lost if you removed the character from the novel, and combine, delete, or adapt if appropriate.

2. Study the time structure of a novel you admire and consider what it has to teach you about the novel you are writing or want to write. For example, if the novel you want to write takes place over the course of a single summer, look at other novels with this time frame. If your novel alternates between past and present times, find a novel that accomplishes this balance.

3. "Cheat on" a novel you've been working on for a long time to start something new.

4. Consider the "why" of your characters. Look for places in your novel where there might be a disjunction between the behavior of the character as dictated by the needs of your plot and what he or she really would do.

5. Write a scene in which a famous person makes a cameo appearance.

MICHAEL CUNNINGHAM

1. Think of a real person called upon to act in some extraordinary way, one which seems at odds with his/her lifestyle and/or appearance. Create a character who looks and acts in such a way that the real person would respond, "This character is like me."

2. Brainstorm a list of "moments of being" in your character's life— crystallized moments in his/her memory that in some way define him/her.

3. Identify interesting physical and behavioral characteristics in several people you know. Play around with them until some combination combusts into a character that interests you. Put him/her in a scene, set him in motion. See if he/she comes alive on the page.

4. Let one of your characters write his/her autobiography. See what he/she tells you.

5. Make a list of the characters in your novel and consider each as a hero in his/her own novel. How do the stories differ? What do they teach you about each character's role in the novel you have chosen to write?

6. Michael Cunningham's *The Hours* grew from his admiration of the structure, style, and spirit of Virginia Woolf's *Mrs. Dalloway*. Sena Jeter Naslund's *Ahab's Wife* puts a whole new spin on *Moby-Dick*; Valerie Martin's *Mary Reilly* retells *The Strange Case of Dr. Jekyll and Mr. Hyde* from the point of view of the scullery maid. Consider how you might use a book you love as a springboard for an original novel. Write a scene from that novel.

ROBB FORMAN DEW

1. Consider the "evidence" your character has collected about his/her parents while growing up. Choose one piece of that evidence and allow the parent most at fault to tell his/her side of the story.
2. Create a character who goes back to a place he/she loved as a child. Write a scene about what happens there. Consider ways you might grow it into a novel.
3. Who holds the power in your novel? Who is powerless? Write a scene that illustrates the power structure in your work.
4. While your novel is brewing and in the heightened state of consciousness you experience throughout the process of writing it, jot down anything about the real world that seems "charged." Consider how these details or moments might be used in the novel.
5. Look through your manuscript for "freighted" details that convey information about your characters in a kind of shorthand. (For example: a Mercedes suggests a certain kind of driver, a Volkswagen Bug, another.) If you've used "freighted" details, consider where they work effectively and where you risk dating your novel by using them.
6. Read a passage of your novel aloud—better yet, have someone read it to you so you can hear and feel the cadence. Note where the rhythm of the sentences works and where it goes flat.
7. Consider what revelation about the way the world really is would surprise your character(s), either in the past or during the time frame of the novel. Write the scene in which that revelation occurs.

1. Visit the places you know will come into play in the novel you want to write. Exploring them, jot down details, take photographs. Use a handheld tape recorder to record ideas, observations, insights, lines, and bits of dialogue for the novel that float up as you go.

2. When you realize an idea that's been floating around in your head wants to be a novel, begin to collect information and details that seem to relate to it in any way. When the weight of what you know tells you it's time to begin to write, organize the information into a ring binder, making whatever divisions seem most useful to you. Feel free to put information in more than one place and to continue to gather information once you begin to write.

3. Use the time frame of a holiday to develop a novel idea, considering how traditions and expectations of that holiday may be used to heighten the effect.

4. Develop a novel idea in which the consequences of an event or events that occurred in your character's past impend upon the present time and prefigure the future.

5. Narrate a scene in first person, present tense that allows the reader to decide to what extent the character speaking is a reliable narrator.

6. Create a character based on a real person, following Grace Paley's advice to "Write what you don't know about what you know" to make the character malleable and to create new material that belongs to him/her alone.

HA JIN

1. Consider ways you might give some aspect of your experience to a character who is *not* you, maybe not even like you in any way.

2. Brainstorm a list of random facts and/or details from your own life. Experiment to create a "special order" for them, adding or deleting, to discover a story that transcends them.

3. Write a scene in your novel in a language in which you are only minimally fluent. Does it teach you anything useful about the scene's most basic function?

4. To decide which of several novel ideas to pursue, consider each in terms of the weight and power they have to sustain your interest as a writer, as well as the interest of a reader.

5. Write a scene that reflects the harshness of a political regime without making any judgment.

6. Write down the chronology of events in your novel. Write a first chapter that starts somewhere in the middle of them.

PATRICIA HENLEY

1. List the events that occur in your novel, then consider how to arrange them so that they raise and answer questions for the reader throughout the whole book. If you are revising, work with your manuscript draft in the same way.

2. Consider the emotional plot of your novel. Brainstorm a list of scenes that might reflect the characters' inner growth and turmoil. Write one of those scenes without mentioning the nature of its emotion.

3. Play out a variety of scenarios for your novel in your mind, working them through, daydreaming about them, considering how each suits your sense of how the novel should go. Stay open to scenarios that completely surprise you.

4. Experiment with using first- and third-person point of view in your novel, considering what's gained and/or lost in each.

5. Ask yourself the biggest general question you can ask of the novel you want to write. (Example: What happens to women and children in wartime?) Use that question to help you stay focused throughout the writing process.

6. Write a provocative scene involving an issue that matters to you, considering how it might spark interest in a reader unlikely to pick up a nonfiction book about the issue.

7. Write an epilogue for your novel, something that happens after the time frame in which the action of the novel occurs. Does the act of writing it deepen your understanding of the novel in any way? Now try a prologue. You don't have to include either in the finished novel—but you might.

CHARLES JOHNSON

1. Research a historical event, then write a scene from the point of view of a person outside the circle of the people involved, outside of the experiences history preserved. Consider what this person sees that the insiders can't or don't want to know about the event and/or themselves.

2. Map out a good, old-fashioned adventure story. Then consider how research and deeper characterization might complicate its effect, raising it to the level of literature.

3. Tell a story using only the structure and content available to a prescribed format for recording experience. For example: a slave narrative, a ship's log, letters, or a diary. In using these devices, be aware of their limitations and freedoms. On the one hand, they may allow the author to create a kind of private language, as well as providing the reader with information that enhances his/her understanding of how and why scenes play out as they do; on the other, such devices may lead to a story that is no more than a dry accounting of events, and/or a voice that assumes prior knowledge that a reader will need to puzzle out.

4. Create a scene in which a quiet moment reflects the oppression of a character or characters.

5. Research a famous person. Write a scene in third-person limited that reflects the reality of the person's existence without naming him/her. The reader should be able to figure out who the person is using the clues offered in the voice, tone, and use of specific detail.

6. Create a double for your character, then consider how you might insinuate him/her into the character's life.

WALLY LAMB

1. In your main character's voice, write a diary entry for a day on which something important happened in his/her life.

2. Explore myths and legends for insights into the novel you want to write and to trigger new story ideas.

3. Experiment with drawing or sketching characters, places, and events in your novel.

4. Consider the lives of people you know or used to know to discover if any of them relates in some way to the voice of a character that's begun talking in your head. If you find a match, brainstorm images of the real person to see if a story begins to form. The story may or may not include aspects of that person's life.

5. Consider how a therapist might help your character work through the issues he/she faces in the novel. Write a scene in which he/she talks to one.

6. Play out two or more possible endings for your novel, using index cards to jot down the sequence of events that would have to happen for the characters to end up at each one. Look for points where the trail goes cold and/or things seem unfeasible to help you decide which one is right. Stay open to the idea that none of them is right and watch "from the side" for an insight into some whole new possibility.

7. Create a plot in which a character's pursuit of what he/she thinks he/she wants leads him/her to the discovery of what he/she *really* wants or needs.

VALERIE MARTIN

1. Create a character who is an observer—by nature, passive and inactive. Write a scene which puts that character under a lot of pressure to stand up for what he/she passionately believes is right.

2. Put a character who is low-key, intelligent, and rational in a world that's a little bit crazy. Write a monologue in which he/she speaks about an intense experience he/she has there.

3. Write the first chapter of a novel based on a main character who feels compelled to explain "Why I did what I did."

4. Create a quiet character who is obsessed with someone else's life. Write the first chapter of a novel in which he/she begins to tell that person's story.

5. Create a deeply religious, even saintly character in whom sexual and religious ecstasy are connected in some way. Write a scene that illustrates this connection and also "corrects" the stereotype that goodness always requires self-sacrifice.

6. Create a character whose outward life cannot accommodate his secret pleasures. Write a scene in which he/she enters a world where he/she can get the pleasure he/she wants and needs.

7. To the extent that it is possible, live in your character's world. Do the things he/she would do during the normal course of a day. Experiment to discover what he/she hears, sees, and knows based on the logistics involved in various activities and tasks.

8. Sketch out a novel idea in which the main character does not change enough to resolve the issues at stake. Write an ending that throws the reader back into the story to try to figure out what the action of the novel meant and to imagine how these unresolved issues might circle through the rest of the character's life.

JILL McCORKLE

1. Considering McCorkle's quilt metaphor, write a vignette from the point of view of one of your characters. When you feel you've written all you know, shift the point of view to someone else and write a second vignette that is connected to the first in some way.

2. Choose a place that has a very strong character, then construct a character to move through it in a day, creating tension that reveals the nature of the place and its inhabitants. Consider what elements of the place's or characters' pasts will come into play as you tell the story.

3. Write a series of short pieces that reflect what you know about your characters' pasts using scene, vignette, monologue and/or dialogue—whatever seems to fit. Consider how you might use them to create a variety of kinds of flashbacks to deepen the effect of the story in present time.

4. Make a list of ten pictures in your character's photo album. They might be snapshots or formal photos, candid or posed. Choose one

and freewrite all you know from simply looking at the photo. When you've written all the image can tell you, freewrite about what might have brought your character to the moment the photo was taken and what might be happening outside the frame.

5. Consider something your character regrets and construct a scenario in which he/she is offered a second chance.

6. Write a scene in which a child is frightened by an experience. Write a scene in which the same fear is experienced by the person as an adult—and dealt with in a way that brings the child to mind. Write both scenes in the present tense, making the fear in each equally convincing and intense.

SENA JETER NASLUND

1. Consider a series of books you love and sketch out a novel that uses the series' cast of characters but also extends the idea of the series to reflect your own interests and sensibilities.

2. Explore the idea of "rewriting" a novel you love from the point of view of a different character. Feel free to use as much or little of the action of the original novel and to explore issues that the original novel ignored. Write the first chapter of the novel you imagine.

3. Look closely at the first sentence of your novel for the clues it reveals to you (and to the reader) about the novel's structure.

4. Write an action-packed first chapter of a novel that begins in the middle of the story and introduces a number of issues the novel will explore.

5. If you're stuck, write a scene in your novel that takes place beyond where the point you've reached writing chronologically. See what the scene tells you about how to proceed from the place where you stopped.

6. Consider devices you might use to add variety to a first-person narrative and/or provide information the narrator couldn't know.

7. Create a character the reader will treasure. Sketch out a novel idea that will require his/her death.

LEWIS NORDAN

1. Create a "soundtrack" for your novel, a mix of music that you think reflects the feel of the book and/or the lives of the characters in it. Play it when you're writing and/or not writing and see whether the rhythms of the music make their way into your prose.

2. Use a remembered event from your childhood, one that had implications for the whole world, to develop a novel idea that addresses how that event impinged upon ordinary people living in the time and place in which it occurred. Feel free to invent around the real event and even take a leap into fantasy if that seems appropriate.

3. Listen for the ways in which the language used by the people you know well provides a key to their secret hearts. Write a monologue in a character's voice in language that subtly reveals his/her true feelings.

4. Create a setting that will allow you to push the boundaries of reality in a believable way. Write a scene that takes place there that possesses the qualities of magical realism.

5. Create a minor character for your novel that acts as a part of the setting by conveying to the reader, "This is the kind of place in which a person like me exists, and my uniqueness defines the uniqueness of the place."

SHERI REYNOLDS

1. Create a character whose parents dressed him/her inappropriately and/or encouraged him/her to participate in inappropriate activities when he/she was a child. Write a scene from his/her childhood, then one that shows the repercussions of his/her parents' behavior in his/her adult life.

2. Write a scene in which the fears a character's religion creates for him/her come into play. Write a scene in which a character whose religion frightens him/her prays.

3. Create a character whose most defining physical feature is a scar. Sketch out the plot of a novel that hinges in some way on how

the scar affects his/her sense of self. Consider how such a character might move the plot of a novel in which he/she is a minor or secondary character. Give a character you've already developed a scar, and see how it changes the action of the novel in which you imagine him/her.

4. Start with the image of a character in action. Work backwards, imagining scenarios that might have brought him/her to this act. Work forward, imaging scenarios in which the act plays out into the future.

5. Sketch out the story of the novel you want to write, told by several different characters. Consider how the story changes from each point of view. If you already know who your point-of-view character is, consider how what you learned from this exercise might be used to deepen the story as we see it through him/her; if you don't know your point-of-view character yet, consider which of the characters you explored seems like the most interesting possibility.

6. Explore images from a dream to discover the kernel of a story.

S. J. ROZAN

1. List the novels you read again and again as a child and consider what (if anything) they have in common with the novel(s) you've written or want to write. Consider, also, how these books might help you discover material and form for original novels—whether for adults or young people.

2. Revising, look for passages that are "interior decoration" and do not contribute to the architecture of your novel. Would the novel's architecture benefit from their deletion?

3. Create a "sidekick" for your main character who is as different from him/her as he/she can be.

4. Consider a world that is both familiar and intriguing to you. Brainstorm plot ideas for a novel that is dependent upon and enriched by that setting. Write the first chapter.

5. Brainstorm a list of things that interest you—current events, past events, places, times, objects—then consider ways you might com-

bine two or more of them to create the plot of a novel. Write the first chapter.

6. Create a character who loves something you simply don't *get*. Learn all you can about whatever it is. Talk to people, read, watch movies, observe. Write a scene that shows the character engaged in the pursuit of what he/she loves that subtly and without judgment shows the reader its appeal.

7. Avoiding the temptation of an "expository information dump," brainstorm ways of beginning your novel that will grab the reader's attention, giving him/her just enough information to avoid confusion and make him/her curious enough to want to turn the page. Pick one and begin.

8. Consider an experience and/or image that haunts you — it could be from your own life or something told to you by someone else. Write a statement that describes what it feels like. (For example: Rozan observed, "I feel like I can't find the floor.") Create a character, not you, in the same emotional state. Write a scene that reflects how being in that state affects her actions, assumptions, and judgments in a difficult time.

JANE SMILEY

1. Looking at the world of the novel you want to write as a kind of ecosystem, consider the part each character plays to keep the system in balance and how the story you imagine might change if each character in it were equally significant.

2. Consider what aspect of craft you most need to learn, and sketch out a novel idea that would make you address that weakness directly. Write a beginning chapter. If you've already begun your novel, highlight what you've written so far to identify areas that reflect this weakness — and improve them.

3. Create a character who refuses to talk about others in *any* way. Write a scene in which the effect of her refusal to engage in this kind of conversation has an effect as bad or worse than gossip can have.

4. Break down the structure of your novel by making index cards for every scene. On each card, note how the scene fits into the plot and what new information it gives the reader, along with questions to consider and things that need to be checked on.

5. Make a chart or calendar that accounts for each segment of time in your novel—hours, days, weeks, months, or years. Then write on it where the scenes will be and also where you will indicate the passage of time through narrative. When you've finished, look at the rhythm in which the scenes occur, the balance of scene and narrative, the places where tension is created and/or the plot deepens. Notice whether there are significant gaps of time in which nothing happens. Use these observations to help you see ways you might adjust the flow of the novel for a better effect. The shorter the time frame, the more productive this exercise is likely to be.

LEE SMITH

1. Read a local (preferably small-town) newspaper for a week. Clip the human-interest stories, considering each in terms of the novels you might grow from it.

2. Browse a flea market or garage sale looking for objects that might play some part in your characters' past or present lives.

3. Make a list of stories you heard as a child. Write one of them in the voice of the person who told it to you. Was the story told by someone else in a completely different way? Write that story, too, and consider possibilities for tensions between them that might arise because of the difference.

4. Brainstorm a list of things your character has forgotten from his/her childhood. Consider how remembering one of them might affect the story you are telling about his/her life.

5. Look at the world your character lives in for a place where he/she doesn't belong. Write a scene in that place.

6. Consider everything you know about what your characters are likely to be doing on any given day of their lives, then write a scene or first chapter set on the day something different happens.

7. Write the last lines of your novel on a piece of paper and tape it on the wall to remind you of where you're going as you write. You're not obligated to keep these last lines in the finished novel.

THEODORE WEESNER

1. Keep a file of news stories that have resonance for you. Choose each for how it is connected to your "stuff," the issues and experiences from your own life that you gravitate to again and again. Consider ways any of the news stories might be used in or adapted for the novel you're writing, and/or how you might use one news story as a frame to which you might graft your own material.

2. Write an ending for your novel in which the main character does not get what he/she wants.

3. Create a character that's a loser. Map out a story so compelling that the reader will come to the end with an understanding of why he/she's a loser and why the story had to end unhappily for him/her.

4. Take the conflict at the heart of a short story you wrote and "unfold it" in a linear way. When did the hinge the story turns on begin to occur and how did it surface as a dramatic event in the characters' lives? Consider how you might deepen and complicate the story in a novel.

5. Explore various time frames to discover which one will allow you to tell the back story of your novel most effectively.